HEALTHusiasm

HEALTHusiasm

MAKING CUSTOMERS HEALTHY & HAPPY

LANNOO
CAMPUS

D/2019/45/444 — ISBN 978 94 014 6380 5 — NUR 802

Cover design	Peer De Maeyer
Interior design	Keppie & Keppie - www.keppie-keppie.be
Icons	www.flaticon.com
Photo back cover	Emilie Bonjé - www.emiliebonje.be

LannooCampus Publishers
Vaartkom 41 box 01.02   P.O. Box 23202
3000 Leuven   1100 DS Amsterdam
Belgium   Netherlands
www.lannoocampus.com

Table of contents

3 Health Marketing 149

Praise for *Healthusiasm*

"The journey to the future is going to be shorter, more bumpy and more exciting than companies and their leaders ever expected. We live in the best of times. Managers do not have to manage by the script, but can write their very own future. In the New Normal Future, all industry lines and value chains will melt down into one big boiling red ocean in which all companies will try to offer customers the ultimate and mass-personalised well-being. Those that want to be prepared and want to find out the why, how and what of this mega-trend, in whatever traditional industry there still ate today, need to read *Healthusiasm* to be ready for the Day After Tomorrow."

Rik Vera, co-founder of nexxworks and author of *Managers the Day After Tomorrow*

"*Healthusiasm* brings structure as well as rich insights into the complex reality of how we go about our own health. With many examples, it actually challenges pharmaceutical and other healthcare organisations to approach patients as customers or consumers, who are seeking solutions that meet their individual expectations."

Erik Janssen, VP Digital Health Solutions, UCB

"*Healthusiasm* assembles a broad range of relevant health trends and generates contextual insights for healthcare stakeholders."

Peter Geerlings, Chief Medical Information Officer, SJG Weert hospital

"As every company is bound to become a health company, this book convinces managers about the why, how and what of this evolution."

Koen Kas, Healthcare futurist and author of *Your guide to delight*

"Health marketing is evolving rapidly. This book provides a great summary of this evolution and serves as a health marketing guide for companies. It should be mandatory reading for capability building in organisations."

Nico Smets, Global Marketing & Digital Excellence Lead, Merck

---

"*Healthusiasm* provides a complete manual to a currently very hot topic: engaging people in their own health. A must read for everyone involved in healthcare today."

Carin Louis, Patient engagement expert

"The pragmatic structure, the many examples and the easy-to-use models, really broaden your scope and force you to think creatively about your own company. Upon reading this book, you surely will be inspired for many months to come."

Caroline Vervaeke, marketing expert & partner at Braintower

"Inspiring and thought-provoking, Healthusiasm will bring businesses closer to the desires of health consumers today. It's a win win!"

Natalie Bloomfield, Insights Lead, Patient & Consumer Engagement

---

"*Healthusiasm* lays down perfectly how our aim to live healthily is a fundamental customer need that touches almost any business. With well-chosen examples about this societal trend, Christophe challenges the reader to rethink current customer experiences in the pursuit for health in mind. An eye opening and transformational book by itself."

Stijn Coolbrandt, Founder Health Endeavour, BeHealth and HealthBuzz

---

"Sustainable and socially responsible entrepreneurship is high on the agenda today. Companies and brands are forced by all stakeholders to pay attention to this. In this book Christophe gives a holistic picture of how companies and brands can embrace health today, and how they can develop a strategic advantage from it. I can recommend this Healthusiasm to anyone who wants to invest in building healthy ecosystems for their customers."

Kristof De Smet, CEO, EnergyLab

Introduction

When I started writing this book, Christmas and New Year were just around the corner. That Festive period of the year when everybody socialises more than usual, eats excessively, drinks daily, sleeps irregularly, conveniently forgets to exercise, and feels particularly worse (or better) than during the rest of the year. This period of indulgence often ends with resolutions that we will do better in the year ahead. Surely, we will eat healthily, sleep more, exercise frequently, and why not... fall in love? It's been the same through the ages – a new beginning, pledging to become a better person.

> *It is thought that this tradition started 4 000 years ago when the ancient Babylonians ended a 12-day religious festival with pledges to pay their debts and return borrowed goods. Janus, the Roman god with two faces after whom the month of January was named, symbolised looking backward as well as forward. He made Romans promise to be virtuous in the New Year. Also, Christians used this new beginning to reflect on past misbehaviour and to vow to change in the year ahead.*

This enthusiasm for a fresh start is evident in the increased uptake in gym memberships, in the numbers of smokers who resolve to quit, and in the almost doubling of the matches Tinder makes on Dating Sunday (first Sunday of the new year) compared to normal. But this book is not about this type of enthusiasm because these resolutions don't last long.

> ***USA today*** *reports that 67% of gym memberships remain unused. And it takes most smokers up to 30 attempts to quit smoking, making it very unlikely that this New Year's resolution will be the successful one. In fact, more than a quarter of us have let go of our resolutions within the first week. Half don't even make it through January, according to Statistic Brain Research Institute.*

These resolutions fail because they are not rooted in a real commitment. Deep beliefs, interests and values are the drivers of real commitment and enthusiasm that could lead to lasting change. These should move someone to their very soul.

This book is not about the enthusiasm for New Year's resolutions, but about the real enthusiasm to live a healthier and happier life. As you will discover, this enthusiasm is all around us. You might even have noticed it yourself during what is perhaps the unhealthiest period of the year.

Christmas and New Year is the time of the year when we have (too) many dinners with family and friends. We look forward to it almost as much as we dread it – not because we don't want to spend time with family and friends, but because we dread the feeling of eating excessively. In the past couple of years, however, you might have noticed a change. Of course we still enjoy a good dinner. Perhaps more than ever. But we want to avoid the feeling of eating substantial meals for days on end. Since newspapers and magazines began sharing the number of calories in the average festive season dinner, we have asked ourselves – and each other – whether we really wish to go along with this. These days it is not impolite to discuss what to serve with your guests or hosts.

With the widespread popularity of specific diets – like Paleo, keto, vegan, vegetarian – and the increased consciousness of food allergies and intolerances, we now initiate discussions on what we can't or don't want to eat. And the quantity and the type of food is raised upfront. In my circle of friends, for example, it's been a couple of years since we decided to reduce the amount of food we serve at New Year's Eve. We switched to smaller portions and food sharing, so it is also easier to vary dishes according to the needs of those with specific allergies or diets. After all, it is about being together, not about stuffing ourselves. We were all very happy with that change. Maybe you have done the same.

At all those family dinners you might also have noticed the popularity of fitness trackers, though not to the extent that they are in the United States. More than half of Americans use a wearable fitness tracker daily, according to Researchscape International. But about a third of us was wearing one during the celebrations I attended. Considering that they barely existed about five years ago, a considerable number of people now 'passively' track their movement, heart rate and sleep. Some have even bought such trackers for their children aged as young as nine. In fact, fitness trackers are the most popular 'tech' gift at Christmas. They certainly are a good fit with the New Year's resolution that will be made. But that is not the main reason that fitness trackers are gifted then – they are also gifted on other celebrations, such Father's Day, Mother's Day and even Valentine's Day. This device simply generates a lot of enthusiasm because it unlocks new insights that creates consciousness and might lead to action. Even though the information gathered by these devices is limited to a couple of parameters, they offer you the possibility of learning something new about yourself.

The end of the year is also awards season, and one in particular caught my attention. If you live in Belgium or France, you might have noticed it too. After years of dominance by tech items like the digital camera, GPS, iPhone, iPad, Google Streetview, and Netflix, the readers of a renowned Belgian newspaper, *De Standaard*, voted Nutri-Score the product of the year in 2018. This five-coloured food packaging label was developed by the French Nutritional Epidemiologic Research team to guide consumers to purchase products of a higher nutritional quality. The introduction of the Nutri-Score in Belgian supermarkets clearly generated a lot of enthusiasm. But it wasn't the only healthy thing supermarkets did that year: 'Fast Fruit' or 'Junk Fruit' – fruit wrapped up like sweets – has to be my favourite here.

At every year end, Google Search Trends are in the news as well. This offers great insight into what people need, want, and intend to do. In its 2018 Search Trend report, Google noted that the year was about improving everyday life. People searched for all things good — from "how to be a good dancer" to "what makes a good role model" to "good things in life". In fact, the world searched for "good" more in 2018 than ever before and there is no sign of it decreasing. At the same time, searches became ever more personal and concrete. This is a continuation of an ongoing trend. General "health" topics having been decreasing sharply in the past decade, while more specific searches related to, for example, food, yoga, running and sleep have doubled in the same period. But for me, "self-care" is an interesting case. For the second year in a row, the search for "self-care" grew by over 30% on the previous year.

These are but few examples of how we are more than ever conscious about our health. Many more cases and examples in this book will illustrate why and how this trend manifests itself. But this book is also intended to guide health-care providers, pharmaceutical companies, consumer brands and startups through the new opportunities and lurking risks that this Healthusiasm trend brings. It covers all these different industries, and you could read the parts that are closest to your current reality (first). But the boundaries of sectors are slowly disappearing. Definitely when it comes to health and happiness. Reading the entire book will help in understanding the entire complexity of what health and happiness means to people: from lifestyle decisions to well-being, from health decisions to medical involvement. And it sure will make you understand how other sectors are approaching this trend.

There are four main chapters in this book. The **first chapter** tackles why people want to become healthy and happy. It's a broad introduction into different societal, technological and economical changes that make people want to become their best version of themselves. The actual Healthusiasm model is explained in the **second chapter**. It's a graphical representation of the different layers of health management. It also visually demonstrates how companies are expanding their own scope of impact beyond the traditional boundaries of their sector. Health Marketing, covered in the **third chapter**, helps understanding of how you as a company or brand can answer the changing needs of your customers or patients by focusing on transformation-driven marketing. The **fourth chapter** will finally provide you with the inspiration and tools to really make your customers healthy and happy.

Are you making your customers healthy & happy yet?

Wanting to be(come) healthy & happy

Technology helps us to become what we want to be

Faster, better, younger

We live in an exciting, inspiring, amazing world. There is no other way to start this book. Today, we are able to become the people we want to be – to realise our potential. We have the platforms, the tools and the audience to amplify the person we are or want to be, while in the past this was far more difficult to achieve. This chapter will sketch how these three aspects help us to do this, and how each of them has evolved. To make this tangible, each chapter contains examples from people close to me. Let me start with a vivid comparison of my father and my son that illustrates how times have changed.

> When I was born, my dad created a stop-motion movie with his Super 8 film camera. Stop-motion animation is a technique used to bring static objects to life on screen. Drawings, objects or puppets are sequentially moved and filmed frame by frame to simulate movement. Although this technique is as old as filmmaking itself, it was rather popular in the late seventies because of its use in the **Star Wars** movie A New Hope. For his film, my dad drew animals that flocked around a little baby to welcome him. Of course, this short animation was followed by some actual footage of my new born face. I reckon he must have spent several days to make the entire sequence. There was no room for error as you only had one take with a Super 8 film camera. But it turned out to be a creative and beautiful one-minute movie he could show to his circle of family and friends. Probably about 30 people must have seen it over time.
>
> Fast forward 40 years. My five-year-old son makes stop-motion movies too. By carefully moving his Lego Star Wars figurines and spaceships in appropriate locations, he creates a short story himself. The frames are captured with an app on the iPad, and I've never had

> *to explain to him how to use it. Within 15 minutes, he creates a one-minute animated movie with sounds and special effects included. As a proud father, I posted his first little animated movie on Instagram and it got 500 views within the hour.*

It's a bit unfair to my loving dad to say that my five-year-old son has made a nicer movie than he did, as my dad probably put a lot more heart into immortalising one of the most beautiful moments of his life. But my son simply has better, faster and stronger tools than my dad had. The adoption of technology has given my son the power to develop his own creativity, his reach and – even more – his personality to an extent we do not yet grasp. At this young age, he is developing skills like storytelling, picture framing, and sound and light effects that some of us have never had the chance to learn. What was amazing to us has become normal to him.

These tools also allow him to try over and over again, so he learns more, and faster. For example, playing a digital memory game, matching pairs of tiles, is three times faster than the physical one because you don't need to lay out the cards on the table, or flip the cards around to see what's on the other side. In the digital version, it is down to a push of a digital button. Of course, without a doubt the physical memory game remains crucially important for the development of fine motor skills. But alternating it with the digital version offers my son a faster, better way to develop himself at a younger age.

Digital platforms

What is true for kids and teenagers is true for all of us too. In the past two decades, technology has offered us a vast array of new ways to develop ourselves. Technology allows us to learn from others as much as it allows us to share our own knowledge. Someone you have never met, on the other side of the planet, could show you how to do something. "Technology is synonymous for connection with other people," as Sebastian Burkhard Thrun likes to put it. But he also found that technology offers a new range of possibilities. Thrun is a German educator, programmer, robotics developer and computer scientist. He founded both Google X Lab and the self-driving car team at Google. As a result, he is often considered one of the brightest minds in Artificial Intelligence. No wonder his classes at Stanford University in 2010 were among the most coveted in the world. Anybody with the slightest interest in AI dreamt of being taught by Thrun. Sadly, only the 200 Stanford students who paid the

USD52 000 annual tuition fee were allowed in. What are 200 students in a time when billions of people around the world are connected to the Internet, Thrun must have thought. So one day in 2011, he sat down in his living room and started recording and sharing his introductory classes. Over the course of a couple of months, he offered lectures, homework assignments and exams to about 160 000 people worldwide. Students were guided to forums to discuss questions among themselves. A computer graded the exams. Thrun called it a catalytic moment: suddenly he was educating more AI students than there were formally enrolled AI students in the world. This first successful Massive Open Online Course (MOOC) was soon followed by other professors and universities, making 2012 "the year of the MOOC" according the *New York Times*. Thrun then founded Udacity, an educational platform offering several massive open online courses that grew rapidly to 1.6 million users by 2014. Today, you can learn any profession or skill via similar platforms: the best basketball player will teach you how to shoot, the most renowned photographer will share his framing tricks, the best singers will teach you how to hit the high notes. Platforms like Coursera, Udemy or YouTube now allow you to share your knowledge or skill, even if you are not officially recognised as an authority in a specific area.

*One of my good friends, Frank, is a serial hobbyist. He hops from one hobby to another as soon as he has reached a certain level of skill or satisfaction. He has mastered several instruments, released multiple songs, drives a motorbike and plays Derby Skate. And I've probably forgotten half the mad skills and confusing hobbies he has acquired over the years. But I do know that he recently decided to put together a **Dax Rush Kit Car**. The Dax Rush is a lightweight two-seater sports car and is a very popular choice among Kit Car builders. Never having built a car, he relied on digital platforms to learn about mechanics and engines. For example, he picked up how to power tune the legendary 4-cylinder Ford RS2000 Escort Rally Engine from the YouTube channel greasemonkeygarage Watson. This channel has 1 300 followers who watch this guy give step-by-step instructions, from his own garage, on how to build, repair or clean several types of engine. That is impressive. In the case of this Ford RS2000 engine, there are about 15 videos of about 30 minutes each. So, after spending two years on YouTube in his garage, Frank is now racing the car he built himself over tracks, probably pondering what skill to master next.*

These types of **digital platforms** and networks have uncovered and distributed creativity and talent in an unprecedented way. In the last two decades, it truly has fostered self-development.

Digital tools

Besides platforms, there is a second aspect that has supported self-development: an extensive range of **digital tools** has become far cheaper and widely available in the past couple of decades. We all know how the computer evolved from a mainframe machine that almost filled an entire residential building, to the personal computer present in most households by the year 2000. Another well-known example is the camera. Analogue photography was limited to 36 pictures per film, so that was the exact number of pictures my dad took on our family holidays. Digital cameras launched commercially in the mid-nineties but were only just starting to find their way into the hands of serious photographers. In 1995, a Fujix Nikon Camera could shoot 1.3-megapixel photos, used a 131MB hard drive that stored 70 photos and cost about USD20 000 (the equivalent of USD35 000 today). Even the official name of this camera, the "B-2 Stealth Bomber", indicates that the market still had a lot of growing up to do. Apple was also one of the first movers in the market, launching the 640x480 pixel Quick-Take 100, built together with Kodak. To this day, the QuickTake 100 is all-time favourite gadget of Apple lovers. But neither did the QuickTake 100 pave the way for large numbers of people to devote themselves to photography.

Between 1999 and 2009, the digital camera market grew 24 times as big, because camera prices plummeted to a level that was affordable for almost everyone. With the emergence of digital photography came software tools. They were part of your Windows or Mac operating system or could easily be found online (mostly free). These allowed you to style (and often correct) your photos quickly, introducing the now widespread practice of optimising your photographic creations. More people consciously cropped their images and styled them within the available software, before carefully organising them in albums in an extension of the habit of sticking analogue photos in an album. (No wonder Facebook used the name "album" to bundle several linked photos.) Of course, we all soon realised that we were taking far too many photos to keep in our photo albums, so that soon faded out. For that period, digital photography was not only an exciting creative activity, but an expression of your style and personality.

> *The younger brother of one of my girlfriend's best friends has been a movie fan since a very young age. While other kids were playing outside, he was studying film. He carefully analysed every piece of a movie, going from the storytelling to the special effects, from the camera angles to the acting performances. Over time, he discovered several tools online that helped him in applying what he analysed. He started off by making short movie clips in his bedroom with his friends as actors. Just trying out the tools he bought or rented online. By the time he was 18-years-old, he had already launched two long-playing movies that received several local awards. Now, at the age of 25-years-old, he and his 30-year-old sister have raised several million euros to produce a theatre movie with an actual Hollywood cast. Everything he learned and realised was thanks to the availability of several tools that previously were too exclusive and expensive for kids.*

Many tools that were once the preserve of professionals are now commoditised products that are widely available. You can build a car, create a movie, build an app, or set up an e-commerce site much more quickly and cheaply than ever before. But let's stay within the field of photography for a moment and think about the impact the cameras on our smartphones have had. The quality of these cameras allows everyday users to take high-quality pictures easily, so that photography has become an indispensable (p)art of everyday life. According to estimates by InfoTrends, in 2017, 1.2 trillion digital photos were taken worldwide of which 85% were with a smartphone. That's 2.27 billion smartphone photos a day. The popularity of apps like Instagram, a social media network that made styling of photos effortless by offering 23 ready-to-use filters and editors, has extended the art of photography to tens of millions of new enthusiasts. People now have inexpensive tools at their disposal to feed the insatiable hunger for creativity and personal development. As a platform, Instagram also allows users to learn from and share with others. With over 1 billion users worldwide, it certainly shows our interest in looking at one another's photos, even when we don't know them. These digital consumers are the third lever to helping us become what we want to be.

Digital consumers

As fun as it may be to create nice things, this creativity would vanish if there weren't other people to show it to. Ask anyone repeatedly why something is important to them, and after several attempts, you will find that recognition is what it boils down to. We are all about recognition. It is what drives us to do what we do; it is what engages us. Gaining recognition is about being valued. It creates satisfaction and happiness.

The numerous social platforms like Facebook, Instagram, Tumblr, YouTube, Snapchat, Pinterest and Twitter cleverly play into our craving for recognition. Every time you receive a 'like', you receive a little dopamine hit. This reward motivates an action to become a habit. In other words, dopamine inspires us to take actions to meet our needs and desires, by anticipating how we will feel after they're met. This action could be anything from turning up the heating, to spinning a roulette wheel, to posting online. Companies like Dopamine Labs, a controversial California start-up, even promise their clients that they will significantly increase the rate at which people use any running, diet or game app by carefully tailoring the schedule of the rewards.

Today, thanks to social media platforms with hundreds of millions of users, it is perfectly feasible to find an audience that will 'like' your work, no matter how niche it may be. For example, one of my friends was really into the minimalistic design and cycling of the '50s, which is not an obvious combination. But his Tumblr blog featuring his work at the intersection of both interests gained thousands of followers and several related design jobs over time. Another friend decided to quit his job and make short movies professionally for the world's biggest brands, after his own vines went viral on social media. (Vines are six-second-long looping video clips that were popular, mostly on Twitter, for a while.)

> *I too have experienced the power of being able to reach an audience. As a teenager, I wanted to work in fashion because I liked its 'social dynamics'. People want a personal style but also to be recognised as part of a group. This eternal clash between individuality and conformity showcases who you are (or want to be) and reveals your social connections. At a macro level, fashion is therefore a reflection of a society or a group. But just as society evolves, so too does fashion. These trends were exactly what fascinated me: seeing new styles arise and fade, and identifying the creativity that erupts from them. That is why I bought myself the digital tools: a digital camera and a Photoshop licence. I created a blog overnight and immediately aligned it with my social media channels (digital platforms). After 10 months of posting my own*

photos of stylish people in the streets of Belgium, the blog had frequent visitors from over 100 countries (digital consumers). In fact, the number of monthly visitors exceeded tenfold the corporate website of the pharmaceutical company I was working for, which served millions of patients in Belgium alone. Suddenly, I featured on fashion websites across the globe and was giving trend interviews for fashion magazines from New Zealand to Russia, Germany, Los Angeles and Mexico. All I did was to use the digital tools at my disposal, and they powered it up to a level I could not have imagined. They allowed me to reach a broad range of people across the globe who 'liked' my street style pictures and trends.

Digital consumers are everywhere. If you have ever wondered how many of them are out there, here are some usage numbers collected at the end of 2018. These numbers are so staggering that it might help you to trust that you will find digital consumers who are interested in what you want to create. On the other hand, these types of numbers are so huge that it is difficult to grasp their magnitude:

- About 3.2 billion people are connected through the internet.
- Almost 1.5 billion people are considered daily Facebook users. Each day they generate a total of 3.2 billion likes and comments. That is over 2 million likes per minute.
- With over 1.8 billion monthly YouTube users, YouTube beats Gmail as Google's most popular service. 300 hours of video are uploaded to YouTube every minute and almost 5 billion videos are watched every single day.
- Since its start in May 2011, over 168 billion posts were made on Tumblr.
- The 500 million daily Instagram users post over 100 million photos and videos every day, generating up to 4.2 billion likes daily.

The term 'digital consumers' might be incorrectly understood as those you are selling something to. However, it is important to widen the interpretation to those who consume what is posted online. This might be the efforts you put into running, the rating you give to restaurants, or your feedback on newspaper articles. Let me elaborate on how 'digital consumers' also help people to become runners.

Running is surely one of the oldest sports in the world. It is also the sport with the lowest threshold because you don't need a lot of gear. Put on your running shoes and off you go. As a result, many people have taken up running but few manage to maintain their engagement because it requires a behavioural change. How then do you keep up your motivation nowadays?

While there are many different theories around installing behavioural change, one popular theory is structured around four pillars: the Me Layer, the Tracking, the Info Layer, and the We Layer. If you use running apps frequently, you will recognise the layers in the services offered by these tools. The running app provides a personalised running plan, taking into account your history, availability and ambition (=Me Layer). Each run is recorded and archived in the app (=Tracking). It provides personalised alerts about your achievements and subsequent challenges, as well as offering related articles (=Info Layer). Finally, all this is shared with your friends or fellow runners on social media or within the community of the app itself (=We Layer). Perhaps this We Layer offers people who affirm your identity. Perhaps they are fellow runners you want to compete against. Perhaps it provides a topic of conversation when you meet in real life. Whatever the case, the app functions as social pressure or recognition for achieving your goals. The people in this "We Layer" are in fact the "digital consumers" of your running activities and (also) help install and maintain your running behaviour.

Running has never been as popular as it is today. More than ever, people persist in their ambition, and running apps play a significant role in this success. These digital tools offer convenient features. After all, who doesn't want to keep track of how much they've run? Being reminded of your running programme certainly helps you to stay on track too. And the digital platform provides the opportunity to learn from the community. But running apps also link people with 'digital consumers' who might react to their activities. The digital tools, platforms and consumers of these running apps help you become a runner, if you have the ambition to become one.

Digital disruption

Waves of digital disruption

In the previous chapters, the disruptive power of the three digital sources – digital platforms, digital tools and digital consumers – was illustrated by the impact they have on who we are or want to become. The anecdotal cases described related to leisure activities, such as building cars or running, or to the creative industries such as movie making, music, design and fashion. But of course, digital disruption has an impact beyond those areas and yields successes in the business space too. In fact, digital disruption has the power to completely alter every business on the planet. I'm sure you've heard that before. But it is undeniable that thanks to the power of digital tools, we can now build products and services more rapidly. By using existing platforms, we can easily reach the right consumers. Greater access to digital tools enables more people to bring new ideas to market at a fraction of the previous cost. Digital disruption generates innovative power that is several times stronger than ever before.

> *If you are an unhappy customer with a great idea for radically improving customer satisfaction, you might have all the tools, platforms and consumers to create what you believe to be missing at present. Dissatisfaction with the price and service of transport on New Year's Eve eventually led to the disruption of the taxi business by UberCab (later called Uber). Being broke in San Francisco where hotels were often fully booked prompted the decision to start "Air Bed and Breakfast" (later called Airbnb), using one's own apartment and renting out airbeds. The frustration of not finding the right shoe in the right colour after an entire day's shopping resulted in the building of the largest online shoe retailer, Zappos.com. Finding the Weight Watchers method too cumbersome resulted in the creation of Lose It, an app that pulled 17 million users from Weight Watchers in only a couple of years.*

Most innovative digital disruptions are the result of an increased focus on unmet customer needs. In his book, *Customers the Day After Tomorrow*, Steven Van Belleghem, a thought leader on the transformation of customer relationships, explains that each new wave of digital disruption fuels fresh opportunities to better answer customer needs. He says there have been three waves of digital disruption thus far.

DIGITAL-FIRST   **MOBILE-FIRST**   **AI-FIRST**

This is a visual representation of the different waves of Digital Disruption that is inspired from the book *Customers the Day After Tomorrow* by Steven Van Belleghem. See nexxworks.com for more information.

Initially, in the Digital-First approach, companies went online to offer new sources of information to their customer. The term "information highway" probably rings a bell. This first wave also offered a degree of new services and alternative forms of communication. It was a new means of answering some unmet customer needs. But as you needed to be behind the screen at your desk to access most of these features, its impact was rather limited compared to that of the second digital wave. This wave, in which all improvements and innovations were developed from a Mobile-First mindset, offered stronger, faster and better services and experiences. The mobile phone evolved from being a communication tool to a platform with computing power that out-performs computers that were used to fly man to the moon in 1969 or IBM's 1997 supercomputer, which beat Garry Kasparov in the historic chess show-down. Smartphones became pocket search engines, making digital informa-tion available anytime, anywhere. While they weigh less than our wallets and are no bigger than a pocket, they facilitate instant personal connections that make phone conversations seem like smoke signals. A whole new range of services, solutions and experiences became available at the the customers' fingertips. That is, if they weren't victims of what soon became the mobile "apocalypse": no battery, no network or no wireless internet

> *The impact of these two waves is perhaps most visible when looking at the evolution of the items on a desk at your office or home. In the mid-eighties you might find a calendar, an address book, a typewriter, an alarm clock, an encyclopaedia, a world map, a phone, magazines and newspapers, a calculator, photos of your family, Post-it notes, to-do lists, a fax machine, your mail, customer files and perhaps even a camera on your desk. Two waves of digital disruptions later, and all these items have been replaced by only two devices: your computer and your smart-*

> *phone. (Technically speaking, they could be replaced by only one device, but we generally keep both.)*
>
> *I like to use the travel industry to demonstrate the power of the change reflected in these first two waves. This industry was a very service-orient-ed business. At first, it was thought that this type of business could not be disrupted by digital tools. People born before the eighties surely remem-ber going to a travel agency to discuss potential holiday destinations with an agent. We may have had our preferences for the type of holiday, transport or region, but that one person certainly had a great influence. For days, we pored over 150-page folders filled with destinations before returning to discuss our preferences. Their advice, based on feedback they might have had from only a couple of other clients, determined our final decision. With the Digital-First wave, the information booklet was presented on websites. It contained more pictures and later some cus-tomer reviews. Shortly after that, we were also offered the online service of independently booking flights, hotels or even entire holidays. The Mo-bile-First wave made these services faster, better, easily accessible and convenient. Then along came several additional services like tracking flight times or luggage, reading customer reviews and advice, or the flex-ibility of changing everything at the last minute. The industry that had for decades relied on providing customer service and advice was beaten on its own turf and the person behind the desk at the travel agency all but disappeared. Customers simply found digital travel services more ef-ficient and effective.*

The third wave of digital disruption is driven by putting Artificial Intelligence at the centre of a company's attention. The concept of AI is often discussed but can be rather complex to define. Essentially, it refers to computers or machines performing tasks that would ordinarily require human intelligence to be car-ried out. Compared to the first two waves of digital disruption, AI is less visible. Data analytics, sensor data, robots, machine learning and the ubiquity of wire-less internet are indeed not visible to us as such. But you might already have noticed their impact on you as a user or customer. Even though we are only at the beginning of this wave, you might feel that products, services and experi-ences are becoming more automated, faster, and even more personalised than ever before. You've surely noticed that online ads pop up for items you've re-cently scouted on some e-commerce website, that Netflix suggests other series based on what you've previously binged, or that Google maps predicts the time you should leave in the morning based on previous days' traffic. These examples of data curation and customised recommendations are the first signs of how this "AI-First" approach is improving current services and experiences. But expect more to come as we are only at the beginning of this wave. The more data that is collected, the more intelligent products and services will become. The more intelligent products and services are, the more intelligent the data assembled will be in turn. Artificial Intelligence will soon be able to automate and predict actions, even taking into account contextual variables in the moment. For example, instead of completing your query in the search engine or listing all the results by relevance, Google will give you the single answer you are looking for, even before you've typed the query. That is the power of a service fully driven by Artificial Intelligence.

> To return to the once human-service-driven travel industry, there are plenty of ways this AI-First approach will improve, or is already improving, the overall travel experience. Though digital or mobile solutions already offer more information, options and customer reviews, this does not mean that everything runs smoothly and conveniently for the customer choosing a holiday. In fact, McKinsey reports that the average purchase journey for a single hotel room lasts 36 days and hits 45 touchpoints. Even while this experience is done from the comfort of your own living room, it is an awfully lengthy experience. It also means that travel companies operate in a more competitive landscape where offers (and prices) are continuously compared. Hospitality virtual assistants that automise basic conversations with customers, like **Hijiffy** and **Utrip**, are now improving the service level to indecisive customers. But they can also increase today's all-time low conversion rates of online travel purchases. Based on a series of questions within their online tool, they offer customers personalised trip advice to make their 'impossible choice' more focused. Companies like TUI and the boutique hotel brand Personality Hotels are already deploying these customer services with success. When the customer manages his trip or when he is actually travelling, **Google Flights** predicts potential delays. After arriving at the hotel room, chatbots and AI-powered voice assistants enhance the on-property experience. These chatbots, like **Edward** from **Edwardian Hotels**, answer guest questions, carry out requests, and offer real-time recommendations. Some hotels, like **Mélia Hotels** or **Disney Resort**

> *Hotels, also offer smart bracelets that facilitate payment, or allow the wearer to skip lines or gain entrance to the different zones of the hotel. It makes the overall travel experience smoother, better and more convenient. It brings to this service-driven industry a previously unmatched level of personal services. Artificial Intelligence is effectively realising online and "offline" improved customer experiences by offering personalised information, answering customer questions, assisting hotel visitors, and supporting cashless payment systems. And certainly many more virtual assistants that are yet to be developed will further enhance the travel experience.*

Digital disruption has unleashed a broad range of innovations and improvements that are impacting the way every type of business serves customers. The first two waves of digital disruption have already altered customer experience in many ways. But Artificial Intelligence will have an even greater impact on this. In fact, customers will eradicate brands that don't live up to their expectations. And AI will have a critical role in meeting those expectations. The next chapters will outline how the Experience Economy has evolved in the past 20 years and how living up to Customer Expectations is even more key to business success.

Digital health

In the previous section, I confidently stated that digital disruption has the power to alter every business on the planet. Yet, within the healthcare industry there have not been (m)any large scale, successful innovations that have changed the face of the industry in the way that Airbnb challenged the hotel business, Amazon redefined book stores, or Napster altered the music industry. Though healthcare companies arguably invest more in innovation than any other industry, on the whole, the industry is still functioning largely as it did 15 or perhaps 30 years ago.

As it is largely publicly funded, the health industry faces multiple challenges when attempting to introduce radical innovations. Regulatory bodies make it onerous and unattractive for commercial corporations like pharmaceutical and medical device companies, or organisations like care institutions and hospitals to put in the effort required for radical change. Due to the complexity of the industry, more time and effort is required to identify opportunities and innovate. You can't "just put things online" as Zappos did in creating the popular shoe store in less than a year. After experiencing success in their own industries, non-healthcare corporations or start-ups may consider entering the medical field but are alarmed and slowed down by the regulatory complexity. Despite years of work, big tech companies are only at the very beginning of potential innovations within the healthcare business. Apple is slowly moving into the sphere of personal data and electronic health records, Amazon is manoeuvring into the hospital and pharmaceutical supply chain, and Google is venturing into medical data and devices. It may be complex, but change is on the horizon.

The healthcare system is like eating at a restaurant with your rich uncle. Even if you have selected the restaurant, the waiter will choose your food and your uncle will pay for it. To take the analogy further, the waiter might be inclined to bring you the most expensive wine, or multiple waiters might attend to your table without knowing your orders. Patients decide what healthcare institutions to go to. Physicians then decide on your treatment for you based on science and remuneration. Governments or insurance companies check and pay the bill.

What this analogy so wonderfully demonstrates is that the healthcare industry has never really been a patient-driven business. Typically, patients don't have many options compared to more consumer-driven businesses, which could end up out of business in no time if their customers chose to go elsewhere. Within healthcare, the lack of similar competition limits the motivation to disrupt the business or to create competitive advantages to the degree seen in other industries. Another limitation is that not only are healthcare providers like doctors and nurses driven by scientific methods or rigid internal processes, but their workload makes it difficult to successfully instil behavioural change.

However, disruption is becoming more and more necessary because of the financial viability of the current system. The ageing population, and the ratio of working to retired people is negatively impacting the funds available for healthcare. Healthcare institutions and medical corporations are being challenged to manage spending with innovative or cost-efficient solutions. Digital health initiatives around efficiency, accessibility and communications are being piloted in many areas of the system.

Patients are more vocal than ever. Even though overall satisfaction with the healthcare industry is high because of the outcome of care, patients now want institutions to pay attention to how that care is being delivered. As they are experiencing better services in general, they demand similar service levels when dealing with the healthcare system, and are inclined to choose between healthcare institutions based on customer reviews. Patients are also more involved in medical decisions that impact them. They are now more likely to seek a second or third opinion, and to consider their options.

Digital disruption offers people the opportunity to effect change. While the healthcare industry may have been rather slow in its uptake, it is now expected to yield a tsunami of innovations in the years to come. Look at Google ramping up its investment in healthcare by closing three times as many healthcare investment deals than it did five years ago. As usual, Google is pointing the way for other companies.

> *If you are interested in digital health disruption, check out **StartUp Health**. This group of health transformers has created a network of over 4 000 entrepreneurs, investors, industry leaders and government organisations that are working on a bold mission to improve the health and well-being of everyone in the world. Through magazines, training, videos, events, podcasts, and newsletters, this unique platform helps companies build credibility and increase their equity value over time. StartUp Health also publishes an annual report on the funding of digital health start-ups they have tracked in their comprehensive database. It contains the funding of companies that enable health, well-being and the delivery of healthcare. This report offers great insights into the growth of digital health. The 2018 report showed that funding in digital health companies has grown to almost USD15 billion per year, which is 14 times more than the investments in 2010, when they started to track digital health funding. Today, the biggest portion of investment is focused on the empowerment of the patient and health consumer, with screening and diagnostics as the subsectors that attract the most money. With the AI-first approach making its mark as the latest and potentially most impactful wave of digital disruption, we see the same evolution in the funding of digital health companies as well. Start-ups with a focus on Artificial Intelligence are consistently attracting more and more funding. In each of the past four years, investment in Artificial Intelligence has more than doubled. Therefore it can be considered the fastest growing disruptor within health*

Companies offer personal transformations
___

The evolution of the Experience Economy

The first time I heard of the Experience Economy was in the late nineties when Lidewij Edelkoort mentioned it in an article about the future of travel. Edelkoort is someone I really look up to. She is a trend forecaster, curator, publisher and educator who lives in the future. Her work has pioneered trend forecasting as a profession, providing design and lifestyle analysis for the world's leading brands. She radiates fresh ideas and an optimism about what's next, even if the pictures she paints are not all entirely positive. The article in the late nineties talked about how consumers will expect different types of travel. As this article dated to before the existence of Evernote or Pocket, I have summarised what I remember.

> *Lidewij Edelkoort explained that people previously perceived travel in terms of a destination. If you wanted to go on holiday, you simply rented a vacation house somewhere. But from the fifties, the travel industry shifted into a more service-oriented business that offered full-service holidays, like Club Med's All-In vacations. Simply renting a place to go on holiday had become so mainstream that it ended up in a price war. Adding services into the equation differentiated one player from the next, increased the perceived value of going on holiday, and allowed higher asking prices. The market dynamics of the travel industry changed radically. The same happened again in the late nineties, when service-oriented holidays no longer provided enough differentiation for customers. Edelkoort explained how the travel industry would move into more of an experience-driven industry: as people were no longer satisfied by services that had become mundane to them, they would expect experiences on holiday.*

By now, I am sure we all recognise this radical shift towards experiences. Nowadays, we feel the thrill of experiences in terms of emotions and sensations and generally cherish them more than physical objects or ordinary services. Experiences create memories. Back then, this thought was unfamiliar and unusual to me. Even as a student in business marketing and strategy, it was the first time I'd heard about the possibility of creating entire businesses around experiences. My only frame of reference for a business based on experiences was Disney World. The theme park attracts people for the experiences, while the actual products (Mickey memorabilia and the like) are props sold on the side. Even the food and parking services are paid for separately. But selling visitors these experiences, amplified – or rather exploited – the value of the Disney characters at the same time. People wanted to be around them. In that regard, Walt Disney surely was an experience pioneer.

To explain how the Experience Economy came about, let me give you the famous example from Joseph Pine, co-author of the bestselling book, *The Experience Economy*. He uses the evolution of birthday cakes to illustrate the phases that led to the Experience Economy:

> *Mothers used to make birthday cakes from scratch, mixing farm commodities (flour, sugar, butter, and eggs). Later, stores offered products that contained the premixed ingredients, making it even more convenient for mothers to bake birthday cakes. As parents became busier, they relied on the service of bakeries and simply bought the birthday cakes there. From the time-starved 2000s onwards, parents no longer bought a birthday cake. Instead, they outsourced the entire birthday party to a business that stages a memorable experience for kids, that likely included eating a birthday cake.*

How can customisation unlock new ways of value creation for your business, by serving age-old customer needs with new experiences?

While this evolution will sound very familiar and even obvious today, I'd like you to reflect on the difference between the cost of the separate ingredients of a birthday cake and the cost of outsourcing a birthday party. This is called the progression of economic value by customising your offering towards customer experiences (see graph on page 32). The more commoditised something becomes, the lower the value. The more something is differentiated or customised, the higher the price a customer is willing to pay. By customising the farm commodities into premixed products, the value of the product increased. By offering the service of a pre-baked birthday cake, bakeries were able to charge more for this service than the products that had become commoditised again. Offering a birthday experience to your child has become at least 100 times pricier than the cost of the basic ingredients of a birthday cake. But you are willing to pay because it brings you greater value.

THE PROGRESSION OF ECONOMIC VALUE

Source: B. Joseph Pine II and James H. Gilmore, The Experience Economy, 2011 Strategic Horizons LPP.

When companies are trapped in a commoditised market, they find ways to customise their offering and create value for the customer once again. The power of the different waves of digital disruption has certainly helped companies with that. A new wave of digital disruption offers a whole new range of means to better answer customer needs. It helps to customise products and services and create the consistent experiences that customers value. Digital disruption amplified the Experience Economy. It facilitates business transformation. It creates differentiation and value by staging customer experiences.

> Though **Disney World** was an early pioneer in selling experiences in their theme parks, they are using the power of digital to continue to opti-

mise customer experiences. In 2013, they launched Disney MagicBands, which were introduced as part of a major technological overhaul to the guest experience at Disney World. This plastic bracelet with RFID technology that is linked to your online Disney account is used to enter the park, unlock your hotel room, buy food and merchandise, and even facilitates a fast pass to experiences you have selected online. The bracelet helps guests to live in the moment and enjoy the experience. In fact, you don't even have to think about taking photographs as a memory of your Disney World visit. As the band pinpoints your exact location, the many cameras throughout the park take enough pictures to bundle in a photo album for you. All you do is experience it.

*These MagicBands sparked **Adidas** to present the 30 000 Boston Marathon runners with a film of the highlights of their run 24 hours later. The short movie included the runner's name and personal clips, along with their times at various points in the race. Marathon is an experience in itself. It is highly personal as each runner encounters difficulties and enjoyment at different moments. These movie clips created long-lasting memories, by enabling each runner to look back on the exhaustion, excitement and thrill of the experience.*

 Matt Bush
@mattbush71

Thanks @adidasrunning **for possibly the best swag from** the @bostonmarathon –

adidas | Here to Create Legend - Boston Marathon® 2018
30,000 Runners. 30,000 Films. Get your personalized Boston Marathon® film after the race.
🔗 heretocreatelegend.adidas.com

12:04 PM · Apr 18, 2018 · Twitter Web Client

This digital transformation of businesses has completely changed our experience as a customer. Nowadays we are accustomed to receiving online orders the next day, accessing information instantly, creating our own holidays, and having all our experiences simplified. As customers, we demand that organisations treat us as unique individuals. We expect companies to understand and empathise with us, and rate or evaluate companies and brands based on our experience with them. While we hardly ever complain, most customers claim that bad experiences makes them turn away from a brand.

Time is a scarce currency in the Experience Economy. Customers increasingly combine challenging jobs with a family and children, the desire for connection with friends, and a wide array of interests and passions. There's only so much time for all this. If customers are attracted to an experience and are willing to pay for it, it had better be worth their while. Experiences need to feel like time well spent.

Since time is a scarce currency in the Experience Economy, ask yourself which of your present offerings can really be considered time well spent by your customers.

This critical customer behaviour emphasises the importance of good customer experience for companies. By the year 2010, experiences were already considered as the predominant form of new economic output and the new source of job creation. By 2014, customer experience was considered the most important field of competition for 89% of the companies surveyed in a study by the global analyst firm Gartner. In fact, a positive and effortless customer experience can result in increased customer satisfaction, loyalty, advocacy and greater customer lifetime value. This is the competitive advantage companies want to achieve. That's why most companies have a Chief Customer Experience in place today, to safeguard this focus.

*Back in 1957, Walt Elias Disney had written the corporate vision for Disney, stating that each segment of their business would eventually serve and amplify the other. The movies would amplify the potential of books, memorabilia, restaurants, theme parks and vice versa. **Disney** is pursuing a platform storytelling strategy, which means driving collective business success, rather than optimising the returns on any one character, title or even franchise. But regardless of this visionary strategy, Disney still mostly sold content separately back then: a book, a movie, a joke, an entrance ticket...*

Now digital disruption finally offers this experience-pioneer the opportunity to truly become a full provider of experiences. Seven years ago, Disney decided to share much of their exclusive video content on Netflix, as Netflix was offering the best customer experience for watching video. With this deal ending in 2019, Disney CEO Bob Iger announced the Disney+ streaming service as the company's biggest priority for that year. It will enable the company to focus on the complete Disney offering at once. Disney+ will allow Disney to transform from a company about products, titles and characters to one that sells entertainment ecosystems. Instead of 'hiring' Disney for 90 minutes or 30 pages, customers will now be able to experience the entire Disney magic (Disney, Marvel, Lucasfilm, Pixar, and National Geographic) for a monthly fee. The online Disney account required to access the experience will in turn gather more information that will allow further customisation of the experience. Considering that the MagicBands are linked to your online account, this approach will eventually impact the experience in theme parks as well.

In a world saturated with largely undifferentiated goods and services, the greatest opportunity for value creation consists of staging experiences. The value of the experience is in the memory of any individual. In a service-driven business, customer experience has become a critical condition for success. People are no longer satisfied with the service in itself. If all services are similar, people search for the cheapest one. The experience determines whether you return or switch to other providers. Think about how your experience of the service of an insurer or a bank causes you to look elsewhere. The same is true for healthcare services such as staying in a hospital.

We have never really expected anything but a bad experience in hospital. Imagine a prolonged stay within the four walls of a tiny hospital room, which we often have to share with people we don't know. Nurses noisily bump around the room at any given time, waking you even in the middle of the night. Machines you can't control make far too much noise. With the entertainment options limited to television, it feels as if you have been catapulted back to the nineties. The food tastes the same every day, whatever it is, which takes away the joy of eating. You are never really at ease. Your physical well-being might be thoroughly attended to, but your intellectual and emotional well-being is often overlooked. That is certainly how I would describe my four-month stay in hospital with my pregnant girlfriend. How great it would have been if the hospitality had felt a tiny bit more like a hotel, rather than a battery chicken cage.

No wonder a recent Black Book survey indicated that 92% of healthcare consumers and patients saw customer experience as the top strategic priority for medical providers such as hospitals. No wonder the NHS created a document with recommendations on improving patient experience in hospitals. No wonder hospitals are increasingly collecting the views of patients to improve their experience. Improved patient experience often comes down to the integration of digital tools in the building and in processes. For example, by using a tablet, patients could control their room temperature, summon a nurse or watch a video about their diagnosis and treatment. Such innovations are being implemented almost everywhere. They will certainly help to improve service. But aren't they just the bare minimum? Are they improving the overall experience to the extent that it will prompt patients to choose one hospital over another? Customer experience is not about one touch point (like controlling room temperature) but about the entire journey. This not only demands superior understanding of patient needs across the journey, but also requires a clear organisational strategy. Within the hospital environment, I believe children's hospitals and retail clinics are currently most focused on actually selling experiences instead of digitised services.

Dayton Children's Hospital in Ohio, which serves over 300 000 children a year, has entirely optimised the patient and family experience by applying technology to facilitate "real time" communication. At any given time, parents can reach out and talk (remotely) to a healthcare professional, which completely changes the experience. After all, worried parents simply desire an immediate answer to their questions. The

Children's Hospital of Philadelphia is a great example of the use of circadian lighting to improve the overall mood of children and to instil a more positive, relaxing experience. *Doctor "U" Children's Hospital* in Kiev, Ukraine designed the most amazing contemporary facilities with trendy, minimalistic design and bold colours. The design creates an atmosphere comparable to a classroom or playground. This immediately alleviates kids' anxieties in an otherwise stressful environment.

Retail clinics are also increasingly focusing on selling experiences. Patient testimonials for *Patient's Hospital of Redding*, a small, surgical hospital, compare it to staying at a hotel "of good reputation". All patient rooms are private suites, designed as a soothing, peaceful healing environment. They are referred to by patients as an oasis in the busy hospital world. *Avreh Plastic Surgery Clinic* in Tel Aviv is specifically designed to make patients feel welcome and happy. As plastic surgery is often very personal, the clinic offers a pleasurable yet private experience by optimising every part of the interior. The mental health clinic *Saga City* in Japan provides an inviting experience for patients by creating a space that resembles an open concept library. The library serves as a common "learning" space intended for patients living with dementia and their families. It is a relaxing starting point for facing dementia. Patients and their relatives can talk and connect through learning, even with other patients. The *Parsley Health Center* in New York, Los Angeles & San Francisco is certainly created for a different healthcare experience. They have built a new operating system for primary care services that combines modern medicine and smart technology with a functional, whole body approach. The space is designed to bridge the gap between medical care and wellness, and it makes you feel calm, relaxed and empowered as soon as you walk in. Forbes described the Parsley Health experience as the exact opposite of the most depressing stereotypical experience in healthcare. For example, the duration of consultations is up to 75 minutes, compared to a maximum of 10 to 15 minutes in a typical healthcare setting.

This Parsley Health Center in New York creates an entirely different experience for people when visiting a doctor.
Source: www.parsleyhealth.com

Although experiences themselves lack tangibility, people greatly desire them because their value lies within the enjoyment of that memory. Digital disruption is offering existing companies, institutions and brands a new set of tools to facilitate experiences and create those memories. But the Experience Economy also generates a new breed of companies that is solely focused on selling Experiences.

> *Funspree is a Toronto-based start-up that sells Experiences instead of things. People can order one of four experiences that will be delivered to their home. The packages include all the essentials for group laser tag, glamping, a backyard movie night or paddle boarding. The idea behind the business is that going out to buy all the equipment for these activities could be cumbersome or overwhelming. After the package is dropped off, it is picked up again within the following 11 days.*

Just as products and services have been commoditised, so too will experiences become commoditised, making way for a new type of differentiation and value creation.

---

*What service of your business can be personalised
in such way that it will enable you to "sell"
great memories rather than good services?*

The rise of the Transformational Economy

Digital disruption is probably the greatest force of commoditisation ever. Each wave of digital disruption has had its impact on both the commoditisation of goods and services as well as the customisation of them into experiences. People buy goods and services primarily based on price. That is why companies and brands were forced to find new ways to remain relevant for their customer. Just as they created services by customising goods, they then looked into customising services. What better way to customise a service than to deliver exactly the right service? It will impress the customer in such a way that the personalised service will become a memorable event. It becomes an experience they will want to invest in, because they expect it to be worth their time and money. In customising services, companies and brands created customer experiences.

> *When offering services was no longer creating value for its customers, the fitness industry became a price driven market place. Prices plummeted to levels that made you wonder how some fitness brands were able*

> *to remain viable. However, Statistic Brain Research Institute calculated that 67% of gym members actually never go to gym and even more fail to go regularly. These "sleeping subscriptions" still make gyms financially interesting enough for some companies. Other brands started focusing on the overall experience of exercising instead, by offering customised services. Gyms now offered saunas, a chill out area, group sessions, appealing interiors and more space in between the fitness equipment, better coaching, refreshing, trendy drinks, kid-friendly spaces and even babysitting services and wellness services like massages and facials ... New brands also entered the market by primarily focusing on experiences. Founded in 2006, **SoulCycle** built on the success of spinning classes but added an experience to it. Besides riding to the beat of the music, in a SoulCycle class, you dance around your bike, use hand weights, do push-ups on the handle bars and high-five your neighbour. Instead of working around heart rate zones, SoulCycle kicks your butt and leaves you feeling totally spent. While other gyms rely on memberships to assure revenues, Soulcycle can afford to handle a pay-per-class model as the experience creates a community of "souls" who happily share their love on social media.*

However, as more and more companies and brands focus on designing experiences, danger lurks in the shadows. Experiences are being commoditised. One brand experience compared to another may not provide sufficient differentiation. But perhaps even more importantly, people could become accustomed to it. The second time you experience something is often less enjoyable than the first time. And the next few times around, the experience no longer engages you as it did before. What was once amazing has become normal. Even though experiences are supposed to be less transient than services, they will no longer create a specific joyful, positive memory. If you recognise that reaction to the experiences you've created, then your experiences have been commoditised, just as product and services were commoditised. The experiences have lost their value for your customer. The only way to escape the commoditisation trap is exactly as it was for products and services: companies and brands need to customise their current offering (again).

THE PROGRESSION OF ECONOMIC VALUE

Source: B. Joseph Pine II and James H. Gilmore, The Experience Economy, 2011 Strategic Horizons LPP.

When general experiences are no longer attractive to customers, they will not value them as before and will seek something more. They will want something more lasting than an enjoyable memory. Customers will desire something beyond what any goods, services or experiences can offer. They will want something personal.

> *Recently, you may have noticed the immense popularity of personal coaches. When experiences such as **SoulCycle** are copied and become mainstream, they need to be customised again. More and more, customers will be on the lookout for something beyond general experiences. They want something authentic and meaningful that helps them on a personal level and generates a real impact. In the world of fitness, this means feeling physically and emotionally uplifted again. Of course, personal coaches are perfectly positioned to offer exactly that personal experience. The relationship with a personal coach is based on a human connection that facilitates dialogue and co-creation. These interactions are highly personal and create a bond between the customer and the coach. Personal coaches don't just stage experiences, they offer the customer customised training that makes them feel like a*

better person. They offer their client a transformation. Sometimes this transformation can even be exclusive. **Performix House**, *for example, creates exclusive experiences by applying an invite-only policy. Once accepted, members are willing to pay 10 times the monthly subscription of an average club. But this price does not even include the cost of a celebrity personal trainer, such as former tennis-player-turned-fitness-influencer Akin Akman, which is about five times as high as the average personal trainer. Transformation clearly creates meaningful value for customers.*

What experience do you offer your customers that might (soon) be deemed no longer particularly enjoyable? What would they desire instead?

But personal coaches are not the only way to create something personal and meaningful within the fitness industry. If you design an experience that is highly appropriate for a particular person, it can't help but become life-transforming. Within the highly competitive fitness market, **The Class** *is an inspiring example that has played very well into the customer need for life-transforming experiences. Taryn Toomey, a former step aerobics and yoga teacher in New York, created what she calls a cathartic mind-body experience. Each group session is a mix of cardio exercises, body conditioning, yoga and meditation. Midway through the jumping jacks, lunges and burpees, Taryn motivates the group to release energy, vent anger or channel emotions vocally. Of course, the trend of venting anger and emotions is nothing new. Companies like* **Anger Room**, **Wrecking Club** *or* **Rage Room**, *where people can destroy stuff (like walls, TVs and computers), have seen an increased popularity in the past decade. But contrary to these rage-based businesses, The Class offers a fitness experience in a relaxing loft, featuring lit candles and succulents. It operates within a structured framework of exercise routines, while participants are permitted to express themselves individually at any time during the exercise. Taryn really wants The Class to be more than a fitness ses-*

sion where you are simply told to do exercises. It needs to be personal for each customer, even while being part of a group session. This unique approach makes those sessions transformational experiences for her customers, enabling her to create value in a market that is increasingly driven by price competition. In fact, the prices for a single 45-minute session at The Class are much higher than a one-month membership in a general fitness centre.

Taryn Toomey in her trendy, loft-like workout space illustrating the venting part of her workouts.
Source: https://taryntoomey.com

Smart businesses realise that they are selling more than a product or a service. They can be the enablers of something bigger and profound. They know that they are operating in the Transformational Economy and no longer in the Experience Economy. This is the economy in which experiences are elevated from mere enjoyment to actual personal transformation. Experiences should yield those transformations. When customising an experience to make it just right for an individual, it will transform them, and provide the thrill of growth and personal achievement.

Perhaps the most obvious industry to benefit from the Transformational Economy was indeed the fitness and well-being industry. But another industry was also very eager to switch to the transformational economy: the sports apparel business. While they are selling sports clothes and gear, these brands can certainly play into the customer ambition to becoming a better person. After all, people exercise to become better, whether it is better at their sport or healthier in general. These brands finally got a reason and the means to realise what their brand slogans were claiming. The role of these brands has shifted from inspiration to enablement: by acquiring the running app Runtastic, Adidas confirmed they were "all in" to support their customer in becoming a better person. By launching the Healthbox consisting of a wearable tracker, a scale, heart rate monitor, and several applications (Endomundo, MyFitnessPal, MapMyFitness), Under Armour empowered their customer to meet their health challenge. (The Healthbox has been replaced by a more intensified collaboration with Samsung to help enable customers to realise their ambitions.) But my personal favourite is the way Nike helps customers to "just do it" by personalising their experiences to become real transformations.

> In the Experience Economy, **Nike** had already proven its strength in generating enjoyable experiences that were hard to beat. Today, in a world where retail sales are continuously crumbling, Nike has been focusing heavily on what they call "omnichannel retail". Undifferentiated average retail will never survive, so Nike is creating stronger and more personal relationships with its customers. The **Nike Town** shops in London feature a personal shopper experience as customers can book personal stylists. It is also possible to benefit from the personal "try before you buy" service: book a shoe trial, train with the new shoes, and pick your own shoes up again at the end of the day. In Japan, Nike has created a digital waiting line so sneakerheads still experience the thrill of queuing for the newest sneaker release. In the digital age, queues have all but disappeared. But as this waiting line is a critical part of the sneakerhead experience, Nike created a virtual waiting line on Instagram. Sneakerheads were invited to visit a dedicated website to create and customise their personal avatar that would then join the queue on Instagram. Products then became available to the next in line, similar to the real-life experience. These are but some of the personal experiences local Nike affiliates are offering. Surely there are plenty more local experiences out there.

*The transformational strategy is globally driven by **Nike+**, a free loyalty programme that is meant to generate at least twice as many customer contacts. With Nike+ the company has revived the tool that allows it to remain in touch with its clients beyond the purchase moment. It was originally launched in 2008 to link the sensor in Nike shoes to the Apple Nano Pods and the iTunes store. Nike+ apps allowed customers to experience their runs and training differently by adding a technological layer. Just like other sports apparel brands, Nike supports their customers in becoming a better exerciser or a healthier person by motivating them in the same way as runner apps do (see previous chapters). In Mexico City, for example, runners could team up with one of the 11 different areas in the city and represent them by uploading their training data. A leader board ranked the areas based on the kilometres run, to add some motivational rivalry to the training. Nike similarly created the Grid run in London, where customers needed to run from one phone box to another to gain points in a competition that was mainly girls against boys.*

Meanwhile Nike was keeping the brand top of mind and was collecting the data of 140 million customers worldwide. With this data, the company is now debuting two new functionalities in the app: creating a personalised retail experience and helping customers stick to their own aspirations.

When you enter a Nike store, the store recognises you and shows you products tailored to you on the app. You can reserve products to try on, which will be held for you in a personal locker, and even check out and pay through the app (without having to wait in a queue). The Nike apps have shifted from an experiential tracking tool to a service hub that unites online and offline retail.

On top of that, based on their actual performances logged within the apps, Nike+ members now can redeem early, exclusive and personalised products or offers, are personally invited to exclusive Nike events, unlock content by Nike athletes, win sports game tickets, choose HIIT training on Apple Music, listen to meditation sessions on Headspace, or participate in fitness classes via Classpass. This loyalty programme is not based on previous transactions, like buying Nike gear. Loyalty is solely based on

> one's experience and transformation. The more work you put in towards achieving your goals, the more Nike rewards you. This is not the first time Nike has done this. In 2014, the Nike Fuelband, a fitness wearable that is no longer on the market, allowed wearers to unlock products from Nike vending machines in New York with Fuel points collected via the fitness tracker. Back then, it was about the experience supporting the quantified-self movement, but Nike is now enhancing the entire ecosystem around their transformational slogan: Just do it. It is no longer about the experience, it's about helping (and motivating) each of their customers individually to achieve their personal exercise/health ambition. The Nike+ app now holds the promise of transforming a customer's life. It's the ultimate tool for a brand to be personal at scale, to an audience that buys three times as much as the average nike.com customer.

Just as an experience was built on top of existing services, a transformation is built on top of existing experiences. But each transformation must present something more desirable than a general experience. It needs to add value for the customer. With transformations, the economic offering of a company or brand is change within the individual. The buyer of the transformation essentially says, "Change me", so that afterwards they are able to look back at a different version of themselves. This could be a single personalised experience with a big impact, or a series of experiences that transforms customers over time. While both are possible, it is expected that staging a series of personalised experiences, or transformations, will achieve a more lasting effect on the customer than an isolated transformation. But it certainly is not about mere experiences any longer.

> The most obvious examples of those transformations can again be found within the fitness and well-being industry. Taryn Toomey (from The Class mentioned earlier) organises a six-day retreat called **The Retreatment** several times a year. Her website describes this as "an immersive experience dedicated to the practice of transformation". Taryn certainly understands what people are looking for. Several yoga teachers, personal coaches, and Pilates classes present 'life changing' retreats that change you for the better. Some focus on the classes and allow you to 'design your journey' yourself. Others offer a choice of personal care treatments, chanting and other relaxing activities.

Nature retreats focus on seeking renewal in the scenic outdoors. Meditation retreats are a good way to relax the body. Spiritual and religious retreats help people find inner peace. Silent retreats have a reputation for dramatically transforming people, particularly fast-talking, go-getter extroverts, and high-powered executives. That also goes for Analogue Retreats, which bring high-profile managers together, without their smartphones or computers, and encourage them to tell stories. All these retreats, and many other alternatives such as wellness cruises, have been around for quite a while. But never have they been so popular and omnipresent as now.

If retreats sound too obvious as a demonstration of the Transformational Economy, how about a music festival that sells their experience as "relating positively to nature and contributing to the well-being of next generations". Well-being or health, represented by a leaf in the logo, is one of the five main pillars of the "love tomorrow" mission of **Tomorrowland** in Belgium. This festival unites people in a transformational event. No longer is this music festival focused only on the DJs on stage (the service), or the enjoyable event (the experience), it is about spending time in a fairy tale environment, with food prepared by star chefs, "hail cannons" to clear the skies in the morning, electronic friendship bracelets allowing easy connection on social media, a fully equipped gym area, and a campsite called Dreamville, with more luxury features than many small villages can even dream of. Every year, Tomorrowland exceeds customer expectations to leave their visitors transformed afterwards.

In the desert outside Reno, 65 000 people from all over the world attend **Burning Man** every year. It could be considered a temporary civilisation that hosts art, music, workshops in the dust. The annual event is a cultural movement based on 10 principles, such as gifting, radical inclusion, self-expression, and communal effort. There are no acts booked upfront. Everybody participates. Everybody creates. Burning Man is the sum total of the activities of its participants, and the ways to participate are as unlimited as one's imagination.

In 2015, a team of psychologists, neuroscientists and anthropologists studied the event using the BRC Census Survey. They discovered that 75% of the guests found the experience transformational. More

> *intriguing was that almost everybody claimed that "change" still persisted months after the event. They've felt differently, or perceived things and people differently ever since. And indeed, my friend and colleague, Stijn who attended the event several years ago, still has a sparkle in his eyes when asked about it. He consciously wears the bracelet every day to remind himself of that transformational experience.*

In the past, "transformations" had a time and place and were typically related to a job promotion, a salary raise, a first child, a first home or becoming an empty nester. Those defined moments of transformation allowed us to create personas with variables such as income, age, region and marital status. They were static snapshots and were easily plotted on the "family lifecycle" of customers. This theory was created in the 1960s by Wells & Gruber. As major life milestones were achieved, it changed the customer's buying habits and marketers needed to adapt their strategy.

But today, those rules no longer stand as the sole way to define customers. Not only has the authority of institutions and social conventions like marriage, education, the corporate ladder or government crumbled, but it is now possible for people to want similar things. A 25-year-old bachelor might have largely the same consumption patterns as a 40-year-old mother with teenage kids, or a 65-year-old retired grandfather. They all might have an Apple smartphone, a Facebook account, a PAX wardrobe from Ikea, similar Nike shoes, and occasionally eat at McDonalds. People are no longer living the lives determined by demographics or lifecycle marketing.

> *Motorcycle brand **Harley-Davidson** sees 10 000 women a year attending courses on how to ride and maintain a Harley. Almost half of the favourite music of people is identical, regardless of age. 23% of video gamers are older than 50 years. About half of gamers are women. 62% of Asian men disagree with the idea that "grooming products are only for women".*

Customers are freer than ever to construct the lifestyles and attitudes of their choice, thanks to unlimited access to information and the abundance of options. They consume the products, services and experience that fit their lifestyle. But more importantly, they seek the evolutions that make them feel like a better person. Customers are in fluid but constant evolution, so it is necessary to understand the beliefs and transformations that drive them. They look to brands to learn life skills, outsource daily tasks, or realise personal life goals. For these transformational customers, digital disruption is no longer just about serving pragmatic functionalities (as in The Experience Economy), but more about enhancing lifestyle and pursuing beliefs. When a company or a brand manages to do so, it will generate the most powerful bond between the company and the customer.

Instead of serving only a pragmatic functionality, how can you use the power of Digital Disruption to help your customers in pursuing a personal lifestyle or belief?

Customers want personal fulfilment

From loyalty to relevance

The March 2018 edition of the *Harvard Business Review* carried a lead article stating that marketers need to stop focusing on loyalty. Written by Accenture, the article referred to recent consumer research from Kantar Retail, indicating that 71% of consumers claim that incentive-driven loyalty programmes don't make them loyal at all. After years of mass production in the 1960s, market research segmentation in the 1980s, and the Channel innovation strategy in the 1990s, companies have been focusing on customer retention with incentive-driven loyalty programmes. Loyalty has had its share of success and certainly remains important today. However, the improvements and innovations that were realised by the different waves of digital disruption see people buying increasingly because of a brand's relevance to their needs in the moment.

Previous sections discussed how the Experience Economy personalised products and services, and how the Transformational Economy upgraded general experiences into personal transformations. By increasingly focusing on the personalisation of goods, services and even experiences, businesses are ensuring that they are meeting the needs of their customers. This will make loyalty programmes less relevant for marketing purposes, unless they are created in the light of this Transformational Economy.

> *In its updated Nike+ strategy (see previous section), **Nike** has indeed accomplished a free loyalty programme that not only rewards (transformational) behaviour, but also rewards customers with personally relevant (transformational) services and experiences. A similarly personalised loyalty programme is offered by the ExtraCare programme by **CVS Pharmacy**, a subsidiary of the American retail and healthcare company CVS Health. Based on 16 years of data, the 77 million ExtraCare customers receive personal recommendations of relevant products and offerings, as if a personal shopper is assisting them. They also receive relevant information about products and services, tailored to geographical factors such as regional allergy alerts, weather conditions, or spreading flu symptoms.*

Even if loyalty programmes struggle to achieve the same degree of customer retention as a decade ago, customers might still be attracted by it if – and only if – it truly answers the customer's relevant needs in the moment. Nowadays, having their needs understood is significantly more important to the customer than receiving offers or discounts. No longer will customers be retained by simply offering financial incentives. Customers will have to be attracted (again) through personalised experiences, based on their relevant needs.

---

*Can you design loyalty programmes that help
your customers fulfil their own aspirations?*

Self-Actualisation drives consumerism

Today, brands and companies have every reason to serve a customer's most relevant needs in the moment. Their job is to create personal ties with their customer in ways that recognise and understand those needs. A good starting point is Abraham Maslow's "Hierarchy of needs". The American psychologist created a model of human needs that is often represented by a pyramid. The earliest version contains five hierarchies of needs, while later versions of the model were extended to eight. But for our purposes, it suffices to explain its impact in terms of three overarching needs: Basic (Functional) needs, Social (Emotional) needs, and Self-Actualisation (Aspirational) needs.

HIERARCHY OF NEEDS

Aspirational — SELF-ACTUALISATION NEEDS

Emotional — SOCIAL NEEDS

Functional — BASIC NEEDS

Simplified version of Maslow's Pyramid: The hierarchy of needs

Basic (Functional) Needs are the things humans need for immediate survival and safety. It encompasses both biological and physical needs (air, food, water, shelter, clothing and sleep...) as well as protection (order, law, stability, family...). People are preoccupied with these Basic Needs until they are met. That's why basic needs have long been the biggest market. Even today they still make up a vast part of the economy.

Social (Emotional) Needs take up the middle of the pyramid. They include things like connectedness, love, respect, intimacy, attention and ego. This has long been the second biggest market. The success of social media platforms like Facebook, Instagram or LinkedIn can certainly be explained by the human need to belong to a group, as well as the need for recognition and self-esteem.

Self-Actualisation (Aspirational) needs, at the top of the pyramid, have so far been the smallest market. They include the desire to live up to one's potential, to seek personal growth and peak experiences, to be happy, to find meaning... People typically don't worry about these needs as long as their basic and social needs aren't partially met. It's not that they are not important, but they are less urgent.

However, for many people, most basic and social needs are increasingly being met. This isn't to say that problems of poverty, food security and resource access aren't still very much present in too many parts of the world. But the overall shift to basic and social needs being met is undeniable. For example, according to the US Department of Labour, the amount of money Americans have spent on food annually as a percentage of family income has significantly and consistently dropped over the past 100 years. This indicates that people have money freed up to fulfil other needs. As more and more people have the time, space and stability in their lives to simply focus on themselves, they will pursue Self-Actualisation. What once was the smallest market has now become one of the biggest growth opportunities to provide products, services and experiences. Offering customers ways to fulfil these aspirational needs has become important for any type of business. In 2013, the Huffington Post called Self-Actualisation the next big consumer market. Shortly after, Trendwatching.com even stated that Self-Actualisation is the future of consumerism. Simply observing the people around us reveals that they are increasingly focusing on personal growth, finding meaning in life and achieving their greatest potential.

> *Retirement used to be the moment in life when people finally got to achieve their dreams, travel the world or turn a hobby into something worth living for. After all, retirement could be thought of as the moment when all other needs in Maslow's Hierarchy had been met. Nowadays, however, people don't want to wait until that moment. Halfway through their careers they might take a sabbatical to travel the world. Some might even switch careers and turn a hobby into a business, if they didn't do so at the start. Perspectives on life have changed, reflecting the view that you shouldn't wait until retirement to focus on yourself.*

> *Another very obvious example of Self-Actualisation is related to running. Earlier, we discussed how running apps help people to start and persevere with running. They help people in their pursuit to become sportier, healthier or in better shape. According to 2017 numbers from Statista, staying healthy or staying in shape is the primary motivation of over 70% of runners. For more than half the runners, it is also about achieving a goal or meeting a personal challenge: being able to run five or 10 kilometres, or perhaps even a half or full marathon. These aspirational needs have made running increasingly popular. In fact, Running-*

USA calculated that, between the years 1976 and 2016, the number of people who completed a marathon in the US grew from 25 000 to 507 000. But its popularity is also visible in other regions like Europe, Africa, South America and certainly Asia. For example, the Chinese rising middle class increasingly aspires to a healthier lifestyle, just like their Western counterparts. Within only five years, the number of running events in China grew tenfold, attracting almost three million people. Clearly, aspirational needs are often sought out and answered in running. When running a marathon is no longer sufficiently aspirational, some people switch to ultra-running. Races in this discipline are (considerably) longer than the traditional marathon length of 42.195 kilometres. Some even go up to 100 miles or 48 hours of running. In the past 12 years, the popularity of ultra-races is manifested in their 1125% growth from 160 to 1 800 races worldwide. Extreme runners, like Nick Butter, even run 196 marathons in 196 different countries in less than 550 days. Talk about aspirational needs!

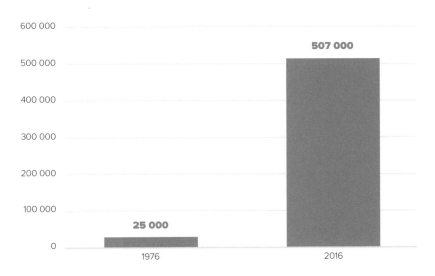

MARATHONS COMPLETED IN THE US

Number of marathons completed in the US, as measured by Running USA together with Athlinks

People have always wanted what was rare or elusive. In the 18th century, it was oranges, in the '60s it was All-in holidays, and not too long ago it was once-in-a-lifetime experiences. But recently, people increasingly look for personal growth and Self-Actualisation. Even as everything else has become easier to acquire or experience, personal growth still requires more effort, time, money and desire.

Could you take a part of your business and turn it into something that helps your customers in achieving personal growth?

As these aspirational needs continue to spread across customers, we will see more companies and brands offering increasingly meaningful products, services and experiences. However, Self-Actualisation remains the most difficult need to appeal to, because a single product or service does not comprise a person's entire identity. After all, it does not seem possible to achieve Self-Actualisation by owning a shoe or by going on holiday. However, brands can cleverly play into these aspirational needs by leveraging their mission statements, values, and even optimised processes.

> *Clothing is a good way to explain how products and services answer the various human needs as presented in Maslow's Hierarchy. First of all, clothing answers the basic functional need of keeping us warm and safe. But it also helps us to identify with a group by dressing accordingly: the grey bankers' suit with a red or blue tie, the bikers' leather jacket with stitched back patch, the shiny red-lacquered soles of Louboutin stilettos... Clothing answers our Social (emotional) needs by creating a sense of connection with others as well as by feeding our need for self-esteem and recognition. The '80s were all about materialism. Brand-names were important and on display. Recognition was sought in wearing fashion brands (RayBan, Ralph Lauren, Swatch, Esprit, Lacoste ...) as a sign of prosperity, wealth and taste. In the 2000s, luxury brands became more accessible by launching capsule collections on the side (for example, H&M collaborations with Karl Lagerfeld, Moschino, Versace...) or by making slightly cheaper accessories and one-off pieces in which the branding was highly visible. Since 2010, the number of followers or likes on*

social media then brought — for some — the sought-after esteem and recognition of one's fashion style. These social influencers were seen as "worthy" of receiving the first or exclusive pieces of a new collection by the brands themselves. But at the same time, fashion had also become even more of a personal statement: both in the sense of having a personal style that was no longer dictated by brands or trends, as well as a social statement against fashion's throwaway culture. People now ask how the design, process and consumption of a product is impacting the world around them. After oil, the fashion industry is the second largest polluter. For example, every year, fabric dyeing uses five trillion litres of water or the equivalent of two million Olympic-sized swimming pools! People object to this. And this expression of Self-Actualisation is altering the way customers buy fashion brands. By focusing on sustainability and ecology, fashion brands now try to feed these aspirational needs. In the '80s, **Guess** was an example of a brand that attracted customers with its name. Nowadays, this Californian company has an important eco-collection, offering jeans that are produced with less CO_2 emissions, with sustainable water and energy consumption, and lined with recycled plastic bottles. **Adidas** has launched a shoe with an upper made entirely from threads and filaments produced using plastic "saved" from the ocean. At first, only 50 pairs were auctioned to those who pledged on Instagram that they would reduce their consumption of single-use plastic, but several million were sold the following year. Adidas has committed to using only recycled plastic from 2024. There are many other examples of established brands making an eco-conscious shift of some sort. But it has become essential for them to do so, as a whole new breed of fashion brands that choose only eco-friendly fabrics, avoid chemicals, and use recycled materials are entering the market and attracting aspirational customers. For these start-ups, it is not about changing anything. It is just the normal thing to do today. So even if the purchase of a jacket in itself does not achieve Self-Actualisation, the conscious choice of an ecological brand enables a customer to feel that they have become a better person. **Patagonia** is perhaps the best example of a clothing brand that actively promotes Self-Actualisation in the store window. Instead of focusing on selling clothing, Patagonia authentically markets passion and responsibility for the environment. The case of Patagonia will be further elaborated upon in the transformation-driven marketing section.

The travel industry is another excellent example of an industry that is leveraging the need for Self-Actualisation. Earlier, we saw how the travel industry has already moved into an experience business. Travellers want more than a simple visit to a new destination or days spent relaxing on a beach in an All-in resort. Instead, the travel they seek is an experience. But this experience now needs to be more than an enjoyable memory. As the largest industry intelligence platform of the travel industry, Skift has identified that travel focused on "personal fulfilment" was one of the Megatrends in 2018. A survey conducted by Skift found that 54% of the respondents rated the importance of "personal fulfilment" at least seven out of 10. Although travel is already a source of once-in-a-lifetime experiences, customers now feel the need to broaden their perspective. The most desirable experiences are those that provide them with unique skills or new knowledge. They should be enabled to express their creativity or do good for others. People don't just want to travel to Cuba. They want to interact with the locals and learn what it is like to live there. They want to travel to Everest Base Camp in Nepal and return as a more tolerant and empathetic person. They go to Rwanda to see the gorillas firsthand and are humbled by nature forever. This need for personal fulfilment is changing the entire industry.

**ON A SCALE OF 1-10, HOW MUCH IMPORTANCE DO YOU PLACE
ON TRANSFORMATIVE TRAVEL EXPERIENCES?**

(10 = MOST IMPORTANT)

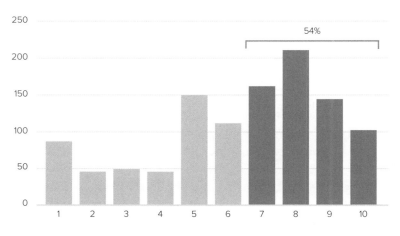

The rise of transformative travel, Skift survey 2017

Airbnb *wants to make you feel at home wherever you go. Not only can you stay with a local at their own home, but they provide enriching "experiences" in an authentic encounter with the location.* ***AccorHotels*** *in Dubai are offering full moon yoga sessions on the beach. And airports are becoming wellness destinations in their own right. For example, Singapore's* ***Jewel Changi Airport*** *not only has many gardens and trails within the airport, but also the world's largest indoor waterfall. Airports even offer fitness services to frequent travellers. Brands like* ***Roam Fitness*** *provide workout facilities behind airport security. The* ***Sanctifly*** *members' club allows travellers to book airport hotel gyms and other wellness facilities. These types of wellness services present Self-Actualisation opportunities for the entire travel industry, including hotel chains, big travel organisations, and home-sharing players like Airbnb. How great would it be to easily benefit from a local wellness or fitness service while away from home?*

The rain vortex indoor waterfall at Singapore's Jewel Changi Airport. Photo by Rids on Unsplash.

Relevant transformations for Self-Actualisation

Under the pressure of commoditisation, the economy has evolved from products and services into personal experiences focused on transformations. Today, brands and organisations are guiding customers to realise their life goals and to pursue their beliefs. In a world where basic and social needs are progressively being met, customers are seeking to achieve their full potential, to be happy and to find meaning.

To a great extent, companies are positioning their products and services not just as objects or even enablers of general experiences, but as essential elements in the creation of an improved self. Customers choose products and services according to how closely they match their preferences and interests, but also according to their ability to enable them to transform themselves (medical, health, well-being and lifestyle), their lives (relationships, work and society) and/or their environment (nature, animals and the planet). These are the three main pillars of transformation. Rising concern over negative impacts on health, society and planet will be one of the most powerful forces reshaping traditional consumption patterns for decades to come. These transformations will require urgency and not-to-be-underestimated commitment by brands and companies, as they will shortly evolve from minimising negative impact to actively generating positive impact.

---

*Transforming their world, their environment, or their life
is not only something your customers want to do,
but something they expect you to help them with.
How is your company making an impact for them?*

Companies and brands should be taking these three pillars into account when bringing products, services or experiences to the market. Which one of these fits best with your company's mission and vision? What transformation pillar(s) find customers most relevant to your business? Are some of the pillars more naturally linked to your business? Or is the reputation of your business the worst on one or more of these pillars? In an age where relevance has become more important than loyalty, these three transformations are indeed the relevancy people are seeking in today's brands. If existing companies fail to fulfil this need, a large selection of "guilt-free" new players that are typically more focused on customer relevancy is available to fill this void. As Guy Kawasaki likes to put it, "Great companies start because the founders want to change the world... not to make a fast buck." That is the competition exisiting companies are up against today.

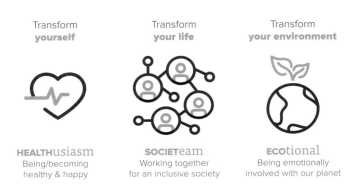

Transform **yourself**	Transform **your life**	Transform **your environment**
HEALTHusiasm	**SOCIET**eam	**ECO**tional
Being/becoming healthy & happy	Working together for an inclusive society	Being emotionally involved with our planet

Transforming their environment (the Ecotional Trend) is relevant to people who are looking for emotional involvement with the world. These people are marching the streets in protest against the environmental policies of their governments. Surely they require companies and brands to similarly focus on sustainability and durability. Choosing brands that make them feel actively engaged with their ecological beliefs seems only right to them. This Ecotional trend is steadily becoming a very important factor in customers' choice of one brand over another. They are receptive to authentic efforts by brands that care about the environment. Of course, it is understood that this transformation is a long-term shift. They will want the sense that the brands and experiences they engage with are moving in the right direction. Many brands already understand this and are riding the waves of sustainability and anti-waste movements by authentically incorporating this into their company culture. Failing to take purposeful action focused on transforming the environment carries the risk of becoming irrelevant to their customer.

> *Besides planning to produce cars with 25% recycled materials, **Volvo** has also set up initiatives like a two-day ocean waste clean-up in Chile. **The Pakistani port city of Karachi** has announced plans for a range of new buses that will run on bio-methane made of manure from Kara-*

> chi's water buffaloes. Funded partially through sales of a special-edition whisky, **Glenmorangie** will restore the oyster population and reefs in Scotland's Dornoch Firth, making this the first restoration of an entire reef in Europe. As water is the basic ingredient of whisky, it is a natural fit for the brand.

People who aspire to a fully inclusive culture are looking for those values in the brands and companies they buy from. In their search for Self-Actualisation, these customers expect brands to back them in transforming their lives (the Societeam Trend). They want to work with brands on improving societal issues like inclusion, equality and diversity. Companies and brands have always tried to create value for their customer by being relevant, but have overlooked the needs of marginalised groups for too long. And it is no longer simply a tactic or a strategy – it's not enough for brands to highlight issues on billboards. Brands and companies need to proudly embed it in products, services and experiences. A corporate mission and company culture has the potential to have an impact on society.

> **Bancolombia**, one of Colombia's big banks, portrayed a gay couple as its customers in a recent advertisement for same sex insurance. In a region where homosexuality is not yet accepted, it led to heated public debate. By boldly answering the debate with "Inclusion should be seen as normal", Bancolombia not only took a strong stand in the debate, but also made an effort to change public opinion. The **NBA**'s flagship store in New York reopened as the first sensory-inclusive retail location in the world. It makes the store accessible for shoppers with special sensory needs, such as those with autism, PTSD or dementia. This was followed in July 2018 by UK supermarket chain **Morrisons** who rolled out a "Quieter Hour" across its 439 stores nationwide. The aim is to make visits easier on autistic shoppers who struggle with the noise associated with retail environments. With this approach, the NBA and Morrisons emphasise the importance of including minorities. But large groups, like Muslim women, are also often less well served today. So **Nike** created the Pro Hijab to help Muslim women to excel in sport while being able to maintain their core belief in covering skin and hair. Joining the likes of Nike, **Net-a-Porter** hosts a dedicated webpage for modest wear, **Dolce & Gabbana** launched a ready-to-wear line with female Muslim fashion and **H&M** introduced a modest fashion line with clothes that cover more

*of the skin. On the battlefront of gender equality, the **Financial Times** has released a bot, called She Said He Said, to alert its journalists to feature more female experts in articles if a gender discrepancy is identified in the article's sources.*

Are your Ecotional or Societeam efforts part of your PR or are they a core part of what you bring to the market?

Finally, customers certainly prefer brands and companies that help them in transforming themselves (the Healthusiasm Trend). They are not only conscious, but even enthusiastic, about managing their health and happiness. They realise that reaching their full potential through Self-Actualisation starts with becoming the best version of themselves, physically and emotionally. That's why their favourite brands and organisations are the ones with products, services and experiences that actually deliver on this. Brands need to – at minimum – show they care about their customers' health. And the brands that provide ways for their customers to transform themselves will remain relevant in the long run.

How has your industry traditionally failed to care about the health of your customers?

Feeling in control of your health and happiness has become a basic customer expectation. As a result, the Healthusiasm Trend is greatly influencing customers buying from health insurers, retailers, food brands, hospitality, sport brands, and healthcare organisations. These organisations have an obvious connection to one's health. But just as any brand or company can find customer relevancy in the Ecotional and Societeam trends, Healthusiasm also offers a new range of opportunities to attract or even maintain customers. Companies selling plastic 10 years from now risk becoming insignificant to their customers. Brands known for a lack of diversity will soon become inappropriate to buy from. Companies that don't offer healthy products, services or experiences also risk becoming irrelevant.

The three trends should not be seen separately. It is important to note that there is in fact some overlap between these three desired transformations. Because environmental actions can also impact our health and happiness, the Ecotional Trend does overlap with the Healthusiasm Trend. Think about the use of plastic bottles and the effect of oestrogen on our bodies. The negative effects of herbicides and pesticides have stimulated the organic industry. Recent legal verdicts against the use of those dangerous products were taken with both the planet and our health in mind. People are also starting to see how climate change is affecting our health. The World Health Organisation calculated that pollution has contributed to 4.2 million deaths worldwide. In China alone, air pollution results in over a million premature deaths per year. On the other side of the spectrum, the Healthusiasm Trend also overlaps with the Societeam Trend. When people feel included or when diversity is accepted, it positively impacts mental health and happiness. Healthy, happy people can be both the driver and the result of parts of the Ecotional and Societeam trends.

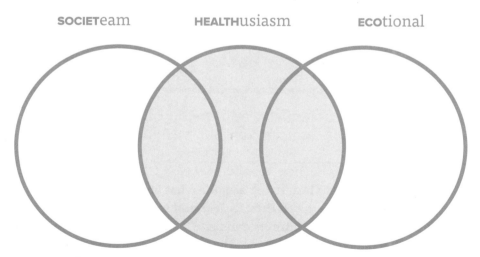

SOCIETeam　　　HEALTHusiasm　　　ECOtional

The Healthusiasm trend overlaps both with the Societeam and the Ecotional Trends.

66

This chapter explained *why* people want to be(come) healthy & happy. It summarised how the different waves of digital disruption amplified the Experience Economy into a Transformational Economy. It illustrated how digital disruption has helped in meeting the basic and social needs of people and how they now strive to become the best version of themselves. People now want to transform themselves, their lives and the world around them. Self-improvement has become such a strong need for customers that they demand Healthusiastic efforts from every type of brand and company. But before diving into how companies and brands can answer this need, it is critical to disclose the Healthusiasm Model. In the next chapter we will demonstrate *how* people want to be(come) healthy & happy. It will disclose the different layers of this Healthusiasm trend in which customers orient themselves, and companies profile themselves. Let's dig deeper into the dynamics of this Healthusiasm trend in the next chapter.

Healthusiasm

The Healthusiastic person

People want to transform themselves to become as healthy and happy as possible. The personal drivers have been discussed extensively in previous chapters, and an explanation given of how Healthusiasm results in the preference for brands and companies that facilitate transformation. But who are these Healthusiastic people? Are they patients or consumers? Are they Millennials, Gen Xers, Baby Boomers or perhaps even part of the Silent Generation? Should companies take into account the expectations of women rather than men? This chapter will explain the different – or perhaps similar – behaviours in these categories in the light of the Healthusiasm trend.

Generational likeness

Generational differences have always existed. But in recent years, the assumption is that the differences have grown because of the rise of technology and variation in uptake from one generation to another. As younger generations have been raised with these new technologies, they are perhaps more likely to have adopted them. But is that really the case? And do these differences also apply to the Healthusiasm trend for which technology is often used? I beg to differ. Starting with the youngest generation, I will summarise the main characteristics of each generation in relation to attitudes towards health and happiness.

Centennials

The youngest generation was born between 2000 and 2015. This means that very few of them have reached adulthood. So should we pay any attention to these kids when analysing Healthusiastic people? They are not likely to have many health issues, and are probably not interested in instilling healthy behaviour yet, are they? That may well be true, but there are other reasons to conclude that this generation does in fact carry some weight.

In 2019, this generation, which is also called Gen Z, represented almost a third of world's 7.7 billion people. For certain brands, Centennials are therefore one of the largest and most influential audiences to reach. On top of that, the behaviours of Centennials is an early indicator of what is to come in the next decade, which helps brands and organisations to prepare for the future. Another reason to pay attention to Centennials is the influence they have on their parents (see below), whose parenting style is characterised by recognition and appreciation of their children's opinions. As Gen Xers (see page 68) were the first children with both parents working outside the home, they decided to approach their own children differently and offer them a lot of influence in family decisions. As a result, the lifestyles of Centennials are already relevant today when describing the Healthusiasm trend.

The top priority for Centennials is the pursuit of fulfilment. Self-expression and improving the world are their 'status' symbols. However, Centennials don't just want to connect with brands that define a certain lifestyle, but with those that support them in achieving their goals. It's about transformation and self-actualisation. The study "Getting to know Generation Z" by Barklay and Futurecast (2017) explains very well that Centennials are more likely to purchase branded products that make them happy. They share these ideals with millennials but approach them from a more pragmatic – and less idealistic – point of view. Living in a mobile reality during their formative years, this generation has never known anything but pragmatism and convenience, so they won't settle for anything less. If what they are searching for does not provide instant gratification, they are gone. Brands and companies should be loyal to them, not the other way around.

How can your company be loyal to your customers?

Instead of enjoying the present, Centennials are more concerned about their future than other generations. Their perception of reality leads them to think ahead and prepare. Stability and safety are more important to them because of the slow-moving economy since the 2008 financial crisis. Centennials are therefore more risk-averse and mature. They display responsible behaviour and are very interested in their own health and well-being. This generation smokes, drinks and parties less than other generations at that age, often claiming that self-care is a much bigger deal for them. After all, the risks and downsides of those activities have been drummed into them at school, at home and in the media from an early age. But they also firmly believe they have other, more important things to do than going out. An entrepreneurial focus is evident in their drive to learn new things. However, they opt to learn something themselves or through a more efficient, non-traditional route than schools.

This generation wants to live life to the fullest, while approaching it in the most *pragmatic* way possible. They realise that they have to make choices to attain this, but they will always prefer *stability* and safety over freedom. As you will discover in the next paragraphs, Centennials can therefore be considered as "Millennials on steroids" with a hint of the values that baby boomers approve of.

Millennials

Millennials are just as interested in health and wellness as the Centennials are. This generation, born between 1980 and the late 1990s, grew up when obesity was at an all-time high. During that period, technology enabled greater access to health and wellness information and put personal health monitoring into the palms of their hands. Health is a daily, active pursuit for Millennials. It's part of their persona and general interest.

With the presence of social media in their lives, healthy living, and radiating joy and beauty as a result, even gives social status. No wonder Millennials are eating more healthily and exercising more frequently than older generations. They also smoke less and drink alcohol less regularly. It's a lifestyle choice that is intrinsically interwoven with other activities. Together with the Centennials, Millennials are therefore often labelled "the most health-conscious generation ever". But it is important to note that this is not particularly due to the fact that they have more time available as they are unlikely to be married or have children yet – rather, it's an intrinsic part of their life.

For Millennials, working out is not about leisure or the chore of staying slim and getting fit. This is the generation that grew up with 'exergames' like Dance Dance Revolution, the Wii Fit console and, later, Zombies Run and Pokemon Go. For Millennials, exercise is a social, fun experience. Think about community-based workouts that are quick, yet effective, like SoulCycle, Crossfit and High Intensity Interval Training. With these innovative classes, fashionable activewear and social platforms, exercise is about the lifestyle attached to it. That explains why they are spending relatively more of their income than older generations on health and fitness, even while they are earning less.

One quick look at Millennial social media feeds showcases that healthy eating is as much part of their lifestyle. Instagram soon tells you that Millennials are a food-loving generation that embrace the eating-in, dining-out and takeout food trends. Compared to other generations, they have a "fewer meals and more snacks" approach to eating and are interested in a diverse range of flavours from various ethnic and cultural backgrounds. Millennials crave the convenient, healthy, and unique taste experience. They are increasingly reading food package labels and are avoiding food additives. However, Millennials are less concerned with scientific claims, and instead seek out locally produced, organic, non-packaged, unprocessed food. They want to know more about how food is grown and prefer their food to be sustainably farmed or produced. In their search for healthy foods, Millennials can be influenced by advertising, reputation, and experiences in which they recognise the personal lifestyle they aspire to. But these 'digital natives' are likely to seek confirmation from online information, reviews, and recommendations from their own online social networks.

Millennials behave similarly when looking for medical information or healthcare providers. As with exercising and healthy eating, they pursue unique experiences and the convenience to connect (with physicians) via technology. As health is part of their persona and general interest, they want to build a personal and individual relationship with their healthcare professional. This type of participative relationship makes Millennials very loyal to their healthcare network. However, one negative experience might quickly cause them to make a change.

Generation X

While *individuality and lifestyle* is the predominant currency that matches with Millennials, *time and energy* can be perceived as the greatest need for Generation X. Born between the mid 1960s and the late 1970s, this generation grew up when the divorce rate tripled, and mums went to work en masse. Gen Xers were brought up to stand up for themselves and became independent at a very young age. Most Gen Xers are now at the peak of their career. At this stage in life, people generally focus on leading more fulfilling lives. But at the same time, they are managing their time and energy to be able to meet the expectations of their husbands, wives, children, colleagues and friends. No wonder Gen Xers are increasingly making healthy choices to gain or maintain energy.

As Gen Xers have a tendency to be knowledgeable and make informed choices, people from this generation are considered the first true health consumers. They typically shop for healthcare the same way they shop for retail goods and services and use more information sources than other generations when making decisions. With their limited time in mind, this group tends to select activities that are done when convenient for them. There is less interest in team or individual sports that require a lot of time and planning. For example, having a home gym simply means increased efficiency for them in saving valuable time. For that reason, many go out running or biking by themselves, equipped with wearables to track their progress. The added value of having a personal coach, on the other hand, is gaining popularity in this generation, particularly because of the increased impact of both training and nutritional education.

As with working out, Gen Xers seek convenient food that requires less preparation time. Although they also like international foods, they are convinced that food is about more than just taste. Food is about maintaining or gaining energy. As they want to make conscious food decisions, they actively seek information online, including ratings and review sites. A particular focus of their search may be on the reputation and public perception of a brand, but they mostly read labels and nutritional information. After all, they are looking for healthy foods that boost their energy. Many Gen Xers therefore rather prefer all-natural products, and are even willing to pay more for them.

Regarding their medical situation, Gen Xers choose to visit a physician based on their reputation and experience. It should come as no surprise that this generation will have done significant research prior to an appointment with a healthcare professional. This may include information about potential diagnoses and treatment options found on the internet. Because of their limited time, Gen Xers are seeking direct communication with their doctors and pharmacists. They have short-term expectations and won't hesitate to switch healthcare providers based on their experience.

Baby Boomers

Compared to Millennials, for whom health is part of their lifestyle and persona, Gen Xers are increasingly consciously making healthy choices to gain more energy. Baby Boomers, on the other hand, are increasingly health conscious because they are dealing with more chronic illnesses as they grow older. This generation, born before 1965, rode a roller coaster of change during their youth, witnessing the Vietnam War and the moon landing from their living room television set. They grew up in an environment of rapidly developing diagnostic technologies and surgical therapies and they were the first generation to have access to immunisation and antibiotics.

But Baby Boomers were also brought up to create an impactful change and set out to do so. Think about how they pushed against the status quo, raised their voices by protesting against the war and advocated for women's rights. *Impact* typifies this generation. And as they grow older, this generation is increasingly preoccupied with disease prevention. They want to impact their own health by focusing on overall wellness and healthier lifestyles.

One of the most obvious signs of Baby Boomers living more healthily is the current popularity of fitness within that generation. With a growth in memberships of 500% in the past decade, Baby Boomers are the fitness industry's main customer at present. But this generation is not new to fitness. They saw the advent of aerobics, the rise of bodybuilding, and the popularity of jogging in the eighties. But while fitness eventually became an expression of pop culture (think lycra, leotards and leg warmers), the early pressure on boomers to exercise didn't have feel-good roots. It was caused by angst over decreasing fitness levels, and the surge in heart disease and cancer rates. Typically in this generation, their ambition was to have an impact on their own life, as well as on the lives of others. Baby Boomers changed the world with ground-breaking AIDS bike rides and breast cancer walks raising millions for worthy causes. They led an unprecedented fitness revolution towards a golden era of health. And now, they are doing it over again with the aim of living and ageing more healthily.

Baby Boomers have the highest BMI of all generations. Healthy eating, first in terms of portion size, is very important for this generation. But health concerns play an even more important role in their choice of food. Because of the prevalence of chronic diseases (such as high cholesterol, high blood pressure, diabetes and osteoporosis) in this generation, their choice of food is strongly influenced by the sugar, salt and fat content of products. As this generation did not grow up with takeaway meals or fast food, avoiding these was already a natural reflex. But that does not mean Baby Boomers are not interested in the nutrient, fibre and probiotic breakdown of foods. In fact, the majority of this generation checks the ingredient list on product packaging. This confirms that Baby Boomers are looking for ways to *impact* their own health.

While Baby Boomers grew up without the prevalence of technology, they cannot be considered technologically ignorant. In fact, most have embraced technology and are active internet and social media users. This generation engages more with technology than is often assumed and seeks health information online as often as other generations. But when addressing their health concerns, many of their searches tend to be more focused on treatments, medications, side effects, and risks. This does not mean they won't ask their healthcare providers many questions. But they want to be sufficinetly informed to be able to ask the right questions to impact their health. Following their doctor's visit, they are sure to research the doctor's recommendations as well as additional health information online.

Although the pursuit of healthy living is clearly not unique to Baby Boomers, the decision to impact their lives with a health and wellness focus has driven permanent changes in today's society. After all, in addition to making decisions about their own health and wellness, Baby Boomers are also likely to act as caregivers for their parents (Silent Generation) and as advisers for their children (Gen Xers or Millennials). Because they influence other generations to such a great extent, the increased enthusiasm among Baby Boomers for living an active healthy life is often considered one of the most *impactful* changes in today's world.

Silent Generation

One of the biggest influences of Baby Boomers is clearly seen on the Silent Generation. Of course, this generation is not considered the most trend forward group. With only about half of those aged 75+ using the internet regularly, this is the lowest penetration of all generations. However, the Silent Generation is very much engaged with their health and happiness, although in more traditional, mainstream ways. They also have a broader definition of health and wellness than younger generations. It goes beyond physical health and good looks. More than other generations, it encompasses relaxation and feeling positive about oneself.

Enjoying time with loved ones is the most important driver of health for the Silent Generation. It's about aspiring to well-being and health, even if one's physical condition is not what it used to be. To achieve this, they still rely on their doctors to manage their personal healthcare and seek health information directly from them. Compared to other generations, they have not changed their views on health management that much, but they are more conscious of their actions. The Silent Generation doesn't easily buy into contemporary health and wellness views but sticks to traditional health advice (avoiding fat, salt, excess sugar, processed meats, and full fat dairy). But taking vitamins and minerals in supplement form perfectly complements their traditional thinking on health and wellness. More than ever, those aged 75+ are consciously engaged with their health, as this Silent Generation still wants to *enjoy* life as much as possible.

Conclusion

When briefly analysing the different generations, it becomes clear that people today are enthusiastic about managing their health and happiness. The majority in each generation claim to be eating healthier than the year before, and even more report planning to eat more healthily in the future than they do today. Regardless of our age, we are indeed interested by and occupied with our health. *Individuality and Lifestyle* might be the most important driver for Millennials, while *Energy and Time* is seemingly driving the choices of Generation X. Baby Boomers want to *Impact* their own health and happiness as well as that of others. The Silent Generation just want to *enjoy* as much as possible. Whatever the driver, compared to the same age group a couple of decades ago, people are more consciously managing their health. After all, isn't that why we say that 40 is the new 20, or that 60 is the new 40?

But while this chapter highlights some obvious generational differences that are mostly related to the education and environment of their specific time, it is important to note that in our society demographic models based on age, for example, no longer stand as the sole truth. Even if there seems to be a common driver within one generation, it remains important to realise that today's reality often and easily allows for non-traditional behaviours. Thanks to the opportunities offered by the waves of digital disruption, people of all ages are creating their own lifestyles and identities. Old conventions no longer stand. People from different generations are not necessarily behaving as they "should".

Let's face it: we all move in a world of shared information, ideas, and culture. Everyone has access to a universal offering that does not differ according to age. Society no longer dictates lifestyles by your age, gender, sexual preference or other demographic characteristics. This "Post-Demographic Truth" means that it is increasingly possible for us to express our own individuality and be who we want to be, rather than according to our demographics. In a world where self-actualisation has become the most relevant need for people, it makes perfect sense that we will take up the behaviour that best fits our aspiration to health and happiness.

Could you let go of solely focusing on the demographics of your customers, and rather focus on who or what they want to be(come)?

What does this mean for brands and organisations? It is important to take into account where people are coming from demographically, but more so, where they are going or who they want to become. The message of this chapter is that regardless of the different backgrounds of each of the generations, all generations are focused on improving their health. All generations want to become the best version of themselves.

Swedish retailer **Åhléns** *has understood this trend very well. The store is known for its wellness concept, Sports and Balance, which aims to provide customers with the clothing, equipment and even books to live an active and healthy lifestyle. Keeping in mind that the trend of focusing on improving health is common to all generations, the store promotes its wellness concept across them all. Daniel Karlsson, store manager at Åhléns City Stockholm, explained that their customers want an active lifestyle throughout life, regardless of their age. Training is an increasingly important part of their customer's life, with health and happiness being a more important driver than appearance and body image. Knowing that the Baby Boomers are the biggest customers of the fitness industry, they used Barbro Bobäck as the face of their campaign in 2015. Bobäck wanted to live a more active* *life so she took up running. It is important to mention that she was 68 when she did so. Three years later, she won gold at the Veteran World Championships, becoming the world's fastest 71-year-old. In using Bobäck as the face of their Sports and Balance campaign, Åhléns confirmed to the fastest growing fitness generation that it's never too late to get active. However, as the trendy activewear could just as well be worn by Millennials, it also indirectly promoted a healthy and active lifestyle that speaks to all generations. If she can do it, so can you.*

What generation of your customer base or patient population could be more interested in your offering than you currently assume? Or what generations could amplify what you stand for?

The world's fasted 71-year-old for Ahlens. Campaign made by Forsman & Bodenfors (https://forsman.co/). Picture made by Eric Josjö at Söderberg Agentur (www.soderbergagentur.com).

The similarities between sexes

It certainly is interesting to look at the sex of the Healthusiastic person. Are there any differences between men and women in their health behaviour? Is one sex or the other more inclined to embrace this Healthusiasm trend? I beg to differ (again). Of course, the health of men and women is not the same. For example, life expectancy of women is currently higher; men tend to have more life-threatening chronic conditions like coronary heart disease at a younger age; and as women live longer, they are more likely to develop debilitating diseases like arthritis. To some degree, the gender gap in health is related to the different genes, chromosomes, hormones and metabolism between the sexes.

But a significant part of this gap has always been induced by social and behavioural differences. Throughout their lives, women and men adopted behaviours that were strongly influenced by their social context. People have always followed their stereotypical gender roles. Men were more exposed to stress and hostility because of their focus on work. Women had a much larger and more reliable social network. Men took more risks and are more often exposed to aggression or violence. Women generally took responsibility for the household meals and ate far more healthily than men. On the other hand, women exercised far less often. Do these social and behavioural differences explain the difference in life expectancy? Can it still be concluded that women live healthier lives and are more susceptible to the Healthusiasm trend? The Medibank Health Index Score answers these questions.

This initiative by **Medibank** *in Australia aimed to measure and track national health by observing changes across seven aspects of health (nutrition, fitness, BMI, medical health, mental health, smoking and alcohol). The Health Index was started in 2007, at a base of 100. On behalf of Medibank, Roy Morgan Research talked to approximately 1000 Australians each week, to gather hundreds of details about their health, from the food they eat, to the exercise they do, and the bad habits that might be holding them back. The latest results published in 2016 indicated that the overall health of men and women had grown by about 2% in the past 10 years. However, counter to the expectation that women live more healthily, the Medibank Health Index Score also showed a higher score for men than for women. We all simply want to live more healthily, regardless of our gender.*

Are you working with stereotypical gender beliefs that might be worth rethinking?

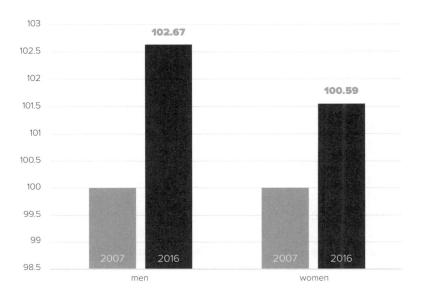

Medibank Health Index (2016). For more info visit www.healthbrief.com.au
Research conducted by Roy Morgan Research from July 2014 – June 2015.

Conventional perceptions of differences between the sexes are no longer to be taken for granted. As explained in the generational differences, men and women are creating their own lifestyles and identities. They do not necessarily conform to the usual social roles, nor are they behaving as previously considered normal. More and more women are riding Harley Davidson motorbikes. Powerlifting and cycling have become some of the most popular sports for women. Men take up yoga more often than women do, and are more open to grooming than before. Men are also more often responsible for cooking the meals at home. What's more, there is now no social taboo governing these lifestyle or hobby choices. There is more freedom, more choice and more social acceptance.

Conventional social behaviour no longer holds. It is difficult to predict the impact this might have on the health of men and women. But it certainly will have an impact of some sort, at some point. One clear example is this: historically, men were more likely to drink alcohol, and in amounts that could damage their health. In fact, men were three times as likely to develop alcohol-related problems. A recent study published in the *British Medical Journal* (2016) reported that women now drink as much as men. While the researchers did not investigate the exact reason for this trend, the authors assume that the changes in women's roles could be an important explanation. No wonder more businesses are moving away from the stereotypes for men and women.

***HIMS** understood very well that it was time to throw out old thinking on who is likely to engage with health and wellness products, services and experiences. This New York start-up is a lifestyle and wellness brand for men, whether they're 18 or 70 years old. HIMS is a one-stop shop for advice, medical care and products, covering anything from hair, skin and nutritional products to erectile dysfunction solutions. It's stylish and trendy, and it's for men only.*

Hims. Handsome. Healthy you. Source: www.forhims.com

Is there a part of your product offering tailored
to one sex that might speak to customers or patients
of the opposite sex, if appropriately targeted?

*Several companies have grasped the opportunity of the growing number of men doing yoga. **Moon & Son** offers stylish apparel for men who practise hot yoga while **Lululemon**, the established yoga apparel brand, partnered with Vancouver's **Stanley Park Brewing** to produce a lager. It reinforces their image and helps attract the attention of their new male customer. But as the differences between sexes have diminished, the Lululemon craft beer also speaks to women.*

Do you know what part of your business could (have)
become more unisex than before?

*To reinforce the shift from stereotypical gender behaviour, the Belgian translation agency **ElaN Languages** has included an "unbias" button in their translation software. They strongly believe that languages all over the world contain gender biases. According to a long line of linguistic research, these words actively influence behaviour, actions and perceptions. Now, their software offers unbiased translation of gender biased words, such as firefighter (fireman), mail carrier (mailman), police officer (policeman) and birth assistant (midwife). With their software, ElaN Languages helps to create a gender balanced world for mankind... Sorry, humankind. It reinforces the freedom to take up any personality, identity and behaviour one desires.*

This does not necessarily mean that men and women currently behave in exactly the same way, health-wise. For example, according to PEW Research Centre (2019), women are more likely to express a strong interest in health and medical topics, and men, in science and technology. But most of the studies I researched for this book found only slight differences between the sexes. One sex does not generally behave in the opposite way to the other. It is important to understand that the differences are merely nuances.

Health perception

Let's start to highlight these small differences by looking at how men and women perceive health in itself. Today, both sexes understand the connection between diet, exercise and health very well. Lifestyles are indeed changing, with a new emphasis on healthier diets and regular exercise. However, women tend to consider health more as a "difficult and complex project" associated with maintaining an appropriate body shape. Women are more worried about their body. This focus on appearance is also why they tend to rate themselves less healthy – and more health conscious – than men. Men rather connect health with being fit and with the ability to do physical activities. They are also less likely than women to perceive themselves as being at risk from illness, injury, or any other health problem, despite historically having more chronic diseases and dying at a younger age.

Sport and exercise

Some small differences are also present in the approach of men and women to sport and exercise. As can be assumed, sport has always been a big part of the lives of most men. Since boyhood, exercise was a fun, competitive pursuit that allowed them to spend time with friends. You will indeed encounter more boys in sport clubs than girls. But while there is a bigger difference between boys and girls, the gender gap narrows significantly with age. When older, men practise only slightly more sport than women, and do similar amounts of physical activity, such as walking, biking and gardening.

One of the most visible habits in society today is that many men and women are engaged in exercise. A study conducted by Ipsos (2017) confirmed this very strongly as no less than 89% reported exercising once a week. But even more important is that the popularity of exercise has grown significantly in the past couple of years. According to the US Bureau of Labor Statistics, 19.5% of the population aged 15 and older participated in some form of exercise on an average day in 2015, while participation was 15.9% in 2003. This relative increase of about 22% over 15 years really showcases how both men and women are increasingly managing their health with exercise.

What recent evolutions might have been under the radar but could actually be a sign of a radical shift that will impact your industry?

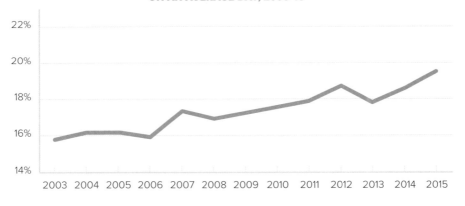

PERCENTAGE OF POPULATION ENGAGED IN SPORTS AND EXERCISE
ON AN AVERAGE DAY, 2003-15

US Bureau of Labor Statistics (2016)

Food

There are both similarities and differences related to food as well. Both men and women believe that you are what you eat, but they do have somewhat different eating habits. Women tend to eat more fruit and vegetables, yoghurt and diet drinks. They have a greater interest in healthy diets and often consume food that is lower in energy value than men. This might be explained in part by the fact that women are more concerned about appearances than men are. Women are also generally more aware about eating-related issues and are more often motivated to adopt a better diet. In restaurants, women are more likely to order the healthiest options on the menu, such as sushi, salads, and vegetarian dishes, while men are more likely to order meat or poultry. In fact, men generally eat more meat and bread than women. They also typically consume more sugar-sweetened beverages, wine, beer, and high-protein foods.

Regardless of these nuances, both men and women take responsibility for their health and food plays an increasingly important role in managing it. Nielsen's 2015 Global Health & Wellness Survey, which polled over 30 000 individuals online, found that the mindset of men and women on healthy foods has shifted substantially in recent years. Most are willing to pay more for products that boost their health and help with weight loss. James Russo, SVP Global Consumer Insights at Nielsen, explains that while economic concerns remain important for consumers, health and wellness concerns are at the forefront of their purchase decisions. Russo also mentioned that consumers progressively understand a food's nutritional value or the overall health risk associated with it. The majority in both genders actively make dietary choices to help prevent certain conditions, such as obesity, diabetes, high cholesterol and hypertension. About 75% of both men and women indeed often read labels carefully for nutritional content. The fact that men and women want to know more about the foods they consume also explains why companies now mention health benefits more often on their packaging and labels.

SmartWithFood supports those who try to interpret incomprehensible packaging labels to strive for balanced nutrition. It offers them customised and automated advice while shopping. As a start-up within the Belgian retailer Colruyt Group, it has a clear goal: consumers need to have easy access to food products that meet their personal requirements and lifestyle. Taking into account intolerances, allergies and preferences, SmartWithFood supports the customer in finding suitable products. Moreover, SmartWithFood also focuses on families in which everyone has their own preferences and nutritional needs. Using the app, you scan the barcodes of food products to check whether the ingredients match the preferences of the various user profiles. For example, if a product contains potential allergens, such as lactose, that negatively match the active profiles, the app shows alternative products that are safe to consume. SmartWithFood draws its data from product information from different databases, and is also assisted by a team of experts, such as dietitians, retail experts and IT specialists, who complete the data in the scan results.

Healthcare

If asked about their health, both men and women generally report very good to excellent health. However, women seek medical care more often than men. They tend to visit a general practitioner more frequently. Even when health problems do show up, men are less likely to immediately consult a healthcare professional. Stereotypical social behaviours may still play a role here as men used to be taught to deny and ignore pain. However, when men do decide to seek healthcare, they prefer to seek hospital care while women see a primary care doctor first.

Conclusion

When brands or organisations are looking to bring health products, services or experiences to their customers, they shouldn't automatically assume they will fit one sex only. However, it might be worthwhile to reflect on behavioural nuances in order to communicate effectively to each sex. Don't oversimplify by assuming that the sexes behave in opposite ways. Behaviour is no longer dictated by gender stereotypes. Both sexes want to impact their own health and happiness.

The patient revolution

While a large part of the book discusses people in general, the question of whether or not a patient is Healthusiastic can also be raised. In the past, patients have always been seen as passive regarding their health. The doctor was the most important person in town, and patients simply followed their recommendations. The only thing patients needed to do was remember to take their medication on time. But the patient is evolving into an active participant in their own health. This chapter will explain how I see the patient advancing through the different stages of engagement.

The Informed patient

The behaviour of patients has radically changed in the past two decades. The first wave of digital disruption brought search engines that offered multiple sources of information. Patients were then able to search online through vast amounts of health information, even before being diagnosed. Early in this first wave of digital disruption, more than 80% of the population regularly looked up health information on Google. It was (and still is) the most popular activity online, topped only by sending emails. The reason for this popularity is obvious. Patients often lack the information they so sorely need. That's why patients in particular soon became active. However, informing themselves about symptoms and diseases was generally not beneficial. While looking up common symptoms, they tended to come across information about severe diseases. Doctors confirm that the early days of Dr Google were characterised by self-diagnosed patients anxiously entering their rooms. One of the main reasons was that very little of the medical information online was of sufficient quality. Some may argue that this situation still stands. But the difference is that the healthcare industry was barely present online 15 to 20 years ago. Most information came from sources that could rarely be traced to a medical or healthcare professional, and nor was it medically validated. This led to self-diagnoses that were not often based on medically sound information or reflection. A second reason is related to the novelty of this information source. Online publishers were not fully aware of the impact their information might have on the average user, nor did the patient know how to navigate the abundance of health information. People tried to be "informed" but often became misinformed.

Your customer certainly lacks some information or is somewhat confused by the information available. What obvious expertise, residing in your organisation, can make them more knowledgeable?

The empowered patient

Even today, an astonishing 1% of all Google searches are symptom-related. Without a doubt, there are still cases of self-diagnosed patients anxiously storming into their doctor's office armed with the results of Google searches. But it is no longer as dramatic as in the early days. People now find their way to more reliable health information, specifically tailored to patients. Most patients nowadays also realise that not all information necessarily applies to them, even if it may seem so at first. But while Rock Health (2016) reports that 56% of patients still search symptomatic information prior to consulting their doctor, patients now go online more actively after their visit to the doctor. This allows them to look up information they might not have understood very well during the consultation. One's reaction to a diagnosis can be so emotional that it blocks the ability to remember what was said. Also, receiving lots of medical or technical information may be too much to digest immediately. Patients can now go online to find more in-depth information and so better understand the brief conversation with their healthcare provider. It allows them to find more information on causes and effects of their condition as well as ways to deal with it. Often, the doctor has referred them to appropriate online sources. With this information, patients become knowledgeable and "empowered" about their own health.

*There are a couple of well-known websites that focus heavily on empowering patients. **WebMD** is an American network of websites, known primarily for news and information on medical, health and well-being. With about 140 million unique visitors per month, it is one of the top healthcare websites worldwide. The content published includes symptom checklists, pharmacy information, drug information, supportive communities and doctors' blogs on specific topics. It has more visitors than any other leading private or government healthcare website, even though it's often criticised for sharing sponsored information. Only **Healthline** generates similar traffic, longer visit duration, and more page views than WebMD. But that is likely because it mostly focuses on non-medical, non-drug related health topics. They talk to larger crowds of people and stay away from potential pro-pharmaceutical campaigning. Healthline aims to be the most trusted reference in one's pursuit of health and well-being. But while both of these sites generate approximately 50% of their visitors from outside the US, language-specific health websites are of course also very popular within their respective countries. **Doctissimo** is the leading online health source in France and is also globally one of the most popular health websites. The same is true of **Alodockter** in Indonesia, **Tuasaude** in Brazil and many others around the globe. They have become such a go-to reference that they don't even have to advertise. Patients either already know about the website or discover their content when searching for specific health topics. These websites empower patients by answering health questions that possibly weren't handled by their doctors. But they also know how to address patients and health consumers, often cautioning them to talk to a doctor first. They don't just educate about health and well-being, but also about how to deal with this type of information.*

*For what specific health or well-being topic
could you easily become the reference for,
without requiring online advertisement?*

With the second wave of digital disruption, the mobile-first approach made information become available any time and anywhere. It was also the instigator of the success of social networks that were mostly accessed via mobile phones. Social networks made it faster and easier to access information. People only needed to register, connect with friends, post on their profile and comment on topics. Within about 10 years, these networks generated a total of 3.484 billion users worldwide, according to Hootsuite and We Are Social (2019).

Because they really simplify connection and communication, social networks allow you to get into contact with almost anyone you want to – like-minded people, celebrities or even fellow patients. They have given people a voice that can reach anyone potentially interested in their message. And as messages are typically shared as bite-sized chunks of information, they are also easier to digest.

Social networks are having a major impact on the way we inform ourselves, including on health topics. The downside of this two-way communication may be that not all health information is as valuable. Health information shared by non-experts may be confusing or incorrect. As with the first health websites, patients need to learn how to deal with this new type of information, and mostly with its source. However, it does offer opportunities to rapidly increase awareness or to connect with fellow patients. Social networks are really empowering patients.

> The **ALS Ice Bucket Challenge** in 2014 was probably one of the most successful fundraising and awareness campaigns for ALS, a disease that causes the rapid death of the neurons that control our muscles. The challenge shared on social networks encouraged people to dump a bucket of ice and water over their own or someone else's head as a symbol of the impact of receiving a diagnosis of ALS. Within just a couple of weeks, ALS

*associations received over USD100 million in donations. The social media success of **Movember**, an annual event that involves growing a moustache during November, increased awareness and annually raises similar amounts of donations to men's health issues such as prostate cancer. Social networks can indeed be very successful in reaching millions. Early in 2019, a simple picture of an egg proved the point. The egg was liked 53 million times on Instagram (the most ever) in a mere couple of days. It turned out to be a mental health awareness campaign.*

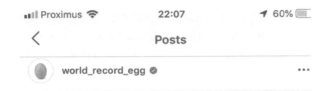

The most liked picture on Instagram was actually a campaign for mental health.

Because awareness empowers patients, their relatives and their environment, what is a good cause close to your business that you could be more vocal and social about?

*Social media also empowers patients by helping them to find their peers. Patients really want to share their own experiences. They also are keen to learn from others. The US social network **PatientsLikeMe** was inspired by one family's experience when their brother was diagnosed with ALS. They realised that ALS patients around the world have similar questions about treatment options and what to expect. PatientsLikeMe now connects over 600 000 patients with others who know first-hand what they are going through. Today the website covers more than 2 700 health conditions, with new members joining daily from the US and other countries. By sharing advice, treatments and resources, patients can learn from the aggregated data of others with the same disease. By communicating with others, they receive support that empowers them in their management and control of the diseases. **Carenity** is similarly empowering 150 000 patients across Europe by putting forward patient networks for 900 different diseases. Empowering patients is about bringing relevant information to them. This does not always have to be scientific information. Patients can also be empowered by experiences and even opinions that are practical and re-latable, and that acknowledge their emotions.*

In a system largely driven by science and rigid processes, can you make the overall patient experience more humane, by enriching them with relevant, bite-sized, non-scientific insights?

The Active Patient

With the invention of app stores, smartphones started offering tools and platforms to "actively manage" their health. They allowed patients to capture and gather data themselves; they gathered contextual information like activity, steps and sleep in the background; and they also reminded patients when necessary. But at first, the tools in the app stores generated the same difficulties for patients as the internet did in the early years. While there were already 100 000 health apps within the first couple of years, their quality and usefulness was doubtful. It took some time to find the good ones, and for the inferior ones to become better or disappear. But even today, there are still about 320 000 mobile applications that are health-related (spread over two major app stores). Each day more than 200 new applications are added. It remains difficult to find the valuable ones. Clinical grading takes a while and is not yet fully adapted to agile technological product development. That leaves the numbers of users as well as the user reviews often as the only quality indicator for patients. This is very limiting in a sense. But on the bright side, with all these tools and platforms at hand, patients are slowly becoming more and more enabled to impact their own health by "actively managing" it.

> Diabetes is a chronic disease that requires daily management. If you have diabetes, it is likely that your healthcare provider has recommended that you keep your blood sugar level as close as possible to that of someone who doesn't have diabetes, to eat more healthily and to exercise regularly. These patients used to keep track with booklets, notes, and paper diaries, if at all, which was so onerous that they welcomed convenient tools to manage their disease. Many start-ups jumped on this huge need, but very few offered the right quality and experience. Today, the Austrian MySugr app is probably the most popular among them. Founded in 2012 by diabetic patients who knew first-hand what was needed, it now helps over 1 million patients in 35 different countries to actively manage their diabetes. This FDA approved and CE marked application offers tools to log and track blood sugar, medications, and exercise. Gradually building on these basic needs with gamification, any type of diabetes patient can now gain points by completing challenges. The MySugr app not only helps patients to manage the disease, but to move away from the "Diabetes Monster". It generates a more positive attitude in patients as it enables them to control a disease that has long been considered practically impossible to manage properly. Little won-

der that pharmaceutical giant Roche, an early investor in the app, became an exclusive shareholder of MySugr app in 2017.

What resources or tools can help your customers or patients to take control of something that feels totally out of their reach?

*Adhering to medication also requires everyday management. Many patients with chronic illnesses really struggle to adhere to their recommended medication regimen. People either never take their medication, stop prematurely, or don't manage to take it as prescribed. In fact, about 50% of people on prescription medication don't adhere to their treatment. As medication doesn't work in patients that don't take it, non-adherence is also sometimes called "the silent killer". Statistics show that death from non-adherence to one's own medication happens about 10 times more frequently than from homicide (and is about 30 times greater in those over 50). People find it difficult to adhere to their medication, often because they aren't fully aware of the importance of doing so. During the Digital-First wave, I already created a first medication adherence tool as a web-based information source that sent email reminders. Of course, its impact was limited because people needed to be behind the screen of their desktop. The second wave of digital disruption offered mobile notifications on the smartphones in the pockets of patients. With over five million registered users in 135 different countries, **Medisafe** is the most popular adherence application even though it is not yet medically certified by the FDA or EMEA. Starting as a visual representation of a vintage pill box, it virtually presents the different medications that need to be taken during the day. Notifications prompt patients to take action. The data gathered by Medisafe helps them to better understand patient behaviour and to adapt their application accordingly. By facilitating the right trigger at the right time, Medisafe allowed patients to make an impact on the management of their health. It has made a seemingly impossible "obligation" more convenient and easier to achieve.*

*As managing one's health always comes
with some hardship, what obvious or hidden obligations
could you alleviate by facilitating convenience?*

The second wave of digital disruption is also characterised by the rise of wearables. Wearable technology became popular with the Bluetooth headset back in 2002. Between 2006 and 2013, devices like Nike+ and Fitbit were released to track steps. While their initial designs were clip-on devices, their bracelets really became popular in 2014. With the introduction of the Apple Watch at the same time, 2014 is often considered the year of wearable technology. Other wearable devices, such as those that measure blood pressure, track seizures or warn about sunlight exposure, continue expanding the industry. The Medisafe app now also connects to the cap of physical pill bottles via Bluetooth, recording medication intake without needing user responses to notifications like "Have you taken your meds today?" Each of these devices accomplishes passive measurement of vitals, biometrics and actions. And as manual inputting of measurements is seldom (if ever) required, health tracking has become easier or even "ambient". With these wearables now connected to our smartphones, they are starting to generate a dashboard of our health.

If you've attended one of my keynotes over the past few years, you might remember me comparing health management to the way we manage our cars. Just a couple of decades ago, our cars weren't equipped with sensors providing direct feedback about their status on a dashboard. Back then, we were supposed to do an annual check-up that obliged you to leave your car at the garage for a couple of days. On returning the car, the mechanic couldn't really give you any guarantees about its functioning, even in the near future. But according to him, everything "looked" good. If your car suddenly didn't start, it was difficult to know what was wrong. A mechanic would need several days to figure out the cause of the problem.

Nowadays, our cars have several dozens of sensors that connect to the dashboard to give us its status immediately. Is there enough petrol? Is the battery still charged? Are our rear lights still working? Even before our tyres run flat, our car will warn us. Some cars even have services that track their status remotely so that the driver is called and assisted if necessary.

Today our health still largely depends on those annual check-ups. Just as our car did several decades ago. Once a year, you have your blood checked at your primary healthcare provider. It takes several days before you receive the results and the doctor can't give you much of a guarantee about the near future. But everything "looks" good. If something suddenly goes wrong, it's difficult to know what exactly has caused it. A doctor might need several days or weeks to figure out the true cause.

Wearables are slowly making a change to this situation. For example, the Apple Watch now measures your heartbeat every few minutes. Compared to your doctor who listens for 30 seconds a year during the annual check-up, this watch now feeds a lot more information on the heart into a dash-board on your smartphone. It builds up information about the status of our health, to a much greater extent than before. Similar to the dashboard in our car, notifications can even warn us if our heart rate exceeds a certain pre-defined limit or when irregular rhythms are identified. While it cannot predict a stroke or a heart attack at present, it's only a matter of time be-fore wearables will be able to feed our dashboard with this predictive infor-mation. With about 50 million people walking around with Apple Watches, more people, whether in good health or otherwise, have the tools and dashboard to actively monitor their heart and health. Several other devic-es and companies are following the same path towards the creation of an active health dashboard.

Is there any type of information or insights your customer would benefit from, if unlocked and displayed to them?

The Connected Patient

Patients grabbed the opportunity of being "informed" and "empowered" during the first wave of digital disruption. With the second wave of digital disruption, patients are collecting data and "actively managing" their health with mobile solutions and wearables. This marked the first three phases of the patient revolution. As the AI-first approach is gaining ground, it will now be important to unlock and "connect" all this data. You have to measure to know, but you have to share to interpret and understand. What's the value of information and data if not shared with and evaluated by other doctors, caregivers, or smart algorithms?

---

*What data will really create value or accountability,
if shared between patients, healthcare professionals
and smart algorithms?*

Currently, relevant medical information is stored in Electronic Health Records. Every patient has his own digital record which includes demographics, medical history, allergies, and laboratory test results. But even if the information would be properly coded (which at present is rarely the case), it is seldom shared with other healthcare professionals beyond a single discipline, hospital, region, country, or, most certainly, continent. The risk of not sharing data is that other healthcare providers don't dispose of the medical history of the patient. But it also makes it difficult to instil accountability across multiple stakeholders or towards the patient.

Within the healthcare system, we are starting to see some slow initiatives to connect different healthcare providers and allow them to share data. However, these health records are information documented during single visits, which is stored away from patients within the healthcare system. These records don't structurally capture the patient's reality between visits. How did symptoms evolve day by day? What was the opinion of the physiotherapist? Did the osteopath learn anything new? Did the patient eat/sleep/feel well? What did the patient do when he suddenly felt worse? There is little information from other stakeholders, like osteopaths, personal trainers, or dieticians, that is shared with or used by that physician (or vice versa). Over and above that, health records generally don't include patient-generated information (like activity, sleep, food intake, emotions), that are gathered via mobile tools or via wearables. With about 50% of people using their health and fitness apps more than once a week (Flurry 2018), this store of information cannot be underestimated. It can be very valuable, for instance, in lifestyle diseases. But while this general data is still left largely untapped, other valuable data from fairly new health services (such as DNA analysis, microbiome tests) is simply ignored. Different types of data are being generated everywhere, but current systems don't allow these to be easily connected. We are not yet fully in the fourth phase of the patient revolution. Even if patients are increasingly interested in actively managing their own health by capturing data (phase three of the patient revolution), this data isn't yet used by health professionals. It is never analysed, nor connected with other relevant information. Even if patients are looking for ways to have their health managed holistically within a multi-disciplinary team, doctors and other healthcare providers are not connected, nor trained to include this in the patient's anamnesis.

> *Early in 2019, **Apple** announced a beta version of its health app that will allow iPhone users to store and share their medical records from a range of healthcare systems in the US. This is an important step in solving the interoperability issues that plague the electronic health record data systems. In the future, the app could indeed evolve into allowing patients to add real-time data, such as exercise and sleep patterns, to their medical records. That would give care providers a much fuller picture of the patient's health, and help manage chronic illness, promote preventative medicine, and improve overall quality of care. It would also, to some degree, make it possible for patients to take the ownership of their health data back into their own hands. About a decade ago, both Google (**Google Health**) and Microsoft (**HealthVault**) launched a similar initiative that aimed to return ownership of health data to patients and hand them the power to share it between healthcare professionals. But Google stopped supporting the service when they introduced Google Fit. Microsoft announced that it would shut down all activities related to HealthVault by the end of 2019. It remains a very difficult setting to operate in. But with the growth in the quantity as well as the quality of health-related data outside the healthcare system, connecting all this data will be a natural evolution in health management.*

In a digital world in which all sorts of data can be captured, what data that currently is not being used would help patients in managing their disease as well as their life?

Connecting and interpreting all types of data might be a bridge too far today. But there are certainly some initiatives that are a step towards better connection with patients and that take more information into account than is gathered during sporadic visits to the doctor. This is extremely important as receiving healthcare as an individual is fundamentally a human process. That's why the importance of efficiently and effectively connecting with patients should not be underestimated. In an era of escalation in administration and relative decline in the number of healthcare professionals, time pressure is putting the personal interaction under stress. Telemedicine is one of the initiatives in early bloom that has the potential to make healthcare personal once more. While it has been present on the market for about 40 years, only now has it been able to gain some traction. Telemedicine is the delivery of remote clinical services using technology like online video conferencing and messaging. It is used mostly for intermediate consultations, diagnosis follow up, patient monitoring, and medical education for patients. It improves the availability of care as patients can connect with doctors anywhere and anytime.

> *A premium version of the previously mentioned **MySugr app** now also connects patients with diabetes educators via messaging and video conversations. This service provides great intermediate support between medical appointments and creates a more personal relationship between the physician and the patient. It improves the experience and the overall impact of diabetic care. **MediSafe** is also improving the user experience with support between medical appointments. By integrating with Health Records by Apple, it eases the import of medications directly into Medisafe – automatically and instantly – from institutions supporting Health Records on iPhone. Patients no longer have to manually add medications, which ensures correct warning in case of drug interactions. They also receive*

*relevant push notifications related to medication intake. By being integrated in the Health app, physicians gather information that previously wasn't tracked between visits. **BeterDichtbij** has launched a similar service in The Netherlands to simplify connections between any type of patient and healthcare provider. As patients leave the hospital while still recovering, BeterDichtbij assures patients that care is always nearby. People can reach out via the app to ask any relevant medical question, read lab results, or order a refill. Each conversation is also automatically filed in the Electronic Health Record of the respective patient, to assist doctors in capturing all relevant data. All of the above examples technically accomplish more and better connections between patients and caregivers. But most of all, they bring information to patients in their time of need, while facilitating impactful methods to coach patients in place of time-poor healthcare professionals. The connection actually establishes a deeper partnership.*

What two-way connections could you establish with your patients to partner with them in a very personal way?

*A perfect example of connecting is the **All4cure** knowledge sharing platform, founded by Anthony Blau, a medical scientist and professor of haematology who diagnosed himself with myeloma in April 2015. To improve the prospects of cancer patients, Blau decided to set up a web portal for them. As the name suggests, All4cure features three interlocking communities – patients, myeloma experts and researchers – that collaborate to find a cure for now and for the future. It offers connections between all the parties. Patients can learn from one another as well as get in touch with experts for specific questions. Researchers can easily connect with caregivers as well as recruit patients for clinical trials with new experimental drugs. This knowledge platform is unique in that each patient has his tumour genetically sequenced. That information is shared online and used within the community to study the relationship between the impact of the medication and the specificities of the tumour. All will then decide on the best treatment for the individual case. This multi-way connection between* *all parties not only brings relevant stakeholders together, it also leverages the power of collaboration around data sharing.*

> *What existing (or future) tools and technologies can you exploit to set up collaborations between different stakeholders and truly help them to benefit from the involvement of all parties?*

The Engaged Patient

While these examples show early initiatives of growing connections between diverse stakeholders and even different types of information, the reality today is that stakeholders are not easily reached, and information is prevented from being shared. Patients are looking for ways to have a bigger impact on their health, but they often lack the connections to bring data and information to gain more meaningful insights. The fourth phase of the patient revolution is only at the beginning of its venture.

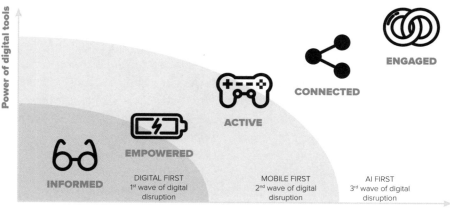

PATIENT ENGAGEMENT = level of knowledge X power of digital tools

Patient engagement is the result of the level of knowledge multiplied by the power of digital tools. When a patient is sufficiently "informed" ahead to start a discussion with his caregiver, when a patient is "empowered" to reach out and find additional, more in-depth information about his condition, when a patient is leveraging mobile solutions and wearable devices to "actively manage" his health, when a patient is *"connected"* with all the different stakeholders to leverage all sources of data and information, *then* a patient has become truly "engaged" with his own health. While the fourth phase of this patient revolution is showing the very first signs of blooming, patients are currently in the midst of discovering the third phase of this patient revolution: they are increasingly active in managing their own health. Before we look at what portion of the patient population is sufficiently Healthusiastic to be empowered and activated now, let's ask ourselves:

What (1) knowledge are you unlocking and what (2) tools are you making available to service patients in their search for better engagement?

(Pro)active segments of the population

In previous chapters, we showed that both sexes in each generation are increasingly occupied with their health. Patients are also more active than ever before. Does this mean that literally everyone is following this Healthusiasm trend? Not exactly. Although there are signs that even the least health-conscious people are somewhat more aware of their actions than a couple of decades ago, they can hardly be seen as actively managing their health. This chapter will summarise the conclusions from segmentation studies that actually quantify the current Healthusiasm trend.

Patients managing diseases

In their Rising Consumerism report (2015), Deloitte did an interesting analysis. The objective of the segmentation was to help companies to address consumerism in the healthcare and health insurance industries. This consumerism is typified by patients who increasingly change doctors, request a second opinion more often, are looking for alternative treatment options and are paying for health solutions out of their own pocket. As these patients take on more responsibility, they also become more demanding towards healthcare providers. These changing expectations require healthcare organisations to become more customer- or patient-centric. Organisations need to better understand the consumer's attitudes and behaviours in order to address their expectations as best they can. This becomes even more important because new entrants are flooding the health industry with customer-focused technological innovations, convenient solutions, and even scientific discoveries.

While the Deloitte report primarily focused on consumerism in the healthcare and health insurance industry, it does contain some valuable insights that help to assess the size of the segments of people that are actively managing their health or illness. Deloitte has identified two categories – passive and active – and six unique consumer health segments that navigate the healthcare system in very different ways. A discussion of each of the segments identified is beyond the scope of this book, but the active-passive distinction is worth mentioning. Around half of the population falls into the passive category, either simply following the recommendations of healthcare providers without many questions or are not engaged with their health at all. The other half of the population actively manages their health by looking for alternatives, more information, and additional expertise and opinions. From this description, this "active" category could be considered the most receptive to the Healthusiasm trend. However, the limitation of this Deloitte report is that it was focused mainly on patients in relation to their healthcare provider or health insurance company. A second segmentation study will further elaborate on behaviour towards personal health management in general.

Patients managing personal health

In 2011, InSites Consulting conducted a global health behaviour segmentation study with Across Health, a Belgian omnichannel customer engagement consultancy firm. The online survey was conducted among 6 000 patients from 14 different countries. It investigated their attitudes and (online) behaviour, going beyond the relationship with an illness or a caregiver to their personal health management in its entirety. Deloitte had found that the active and passive categories were similar in size and this study confirmed it.

About half of the population is actively managing their health. This active category leads a healthy lifestyle, believes in prevention, and is focused on combining healthy food with exercising. When they are ill, they are highly involved in their health management, asking their healthcare providers about it, as well as actively collecting information themselves. Though this study focused on a broader aspect of personal health management, it reached the same conclusion: half of the patient population is receptive to the Healthusiasm trend. Whether this conclusion also goes for health consumers in general will be demonstrated by the next study.

People managing a healthy lifestyle

A third interesting segmentation study was recently conducted by c2bSolutions, a company started by two former marketing managers at P&G's healthcare division. With their extensive expertise on consumer perceptions and behaviours with regard to health and wellness, their mission is to help organisations and brands to develop products and services based on the needs, motivations and attitudes of health consumers. Their psychographic segmentation research (2017) reports that two consumer segments that take up almost half of the population are the most proactive towards their own health and wellness. A third segment was even proactive towards the health management of others. But the study also showed that even less (pro)active segments are taking action to impact their health to some degree. For example, the research revealed that a staggering 70% of all respondents were actively taking steps to prevent illnesses. In fact, only about 17% of the population admitted to having a rather unhealthy lifestyle and had no intention of changing it.

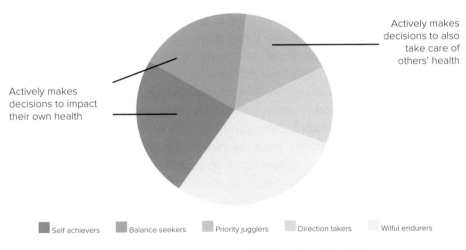

Psychographic segmentation research (2017) by c2b Solutions (2017)

Health conscious people

Regardless of whether the segmentation study was about patients managing diseases, patients managing their own health, or people managing a healthy lifestyle, each study showed that about half of each of these populations are most inclined to fit the behaviours strongly linked to the Healthusiasm trend. But while this is already a considerable proportion, it became obvious that even the other half is more health conscious than before.

Are you offering half of your customers the possibility to take health-impacting decisions?

The Healthusiastic decision

"You are what you eat" is not a new concept. And we know that in essence it is true. If you eat well, you are much more likely to be healthy. If you prefer junk food over fresh vegetables, then you are less likely to be healthy. It is as simple as that. It's just a matter of making the right food choices. Researchers at Cornell University estimated that we make on average 226.7 micro-decisions each day on food alone. Of course, personal food choices are not the only Healthusiastic decisions we make. Our decisions influence our health far beyond the scope of food choices. In fact, it's estimated that the average person makes about 35 000 micro-decisions each day. Of course, many of those decisions aren't conscious. But becoming healthy and happy starts with a multitude of smaller daily decisions: what to eat, how much to sleep, how much exercise to get, and so on. In combination, these micro-decisions can have a very significant impact on our health indeed. Who you are today is a result of your decisions. It starts with us. No matter how we feel in a certain moment, health and happiness are simply byproducts of good decisions.

In making decisions that impact their health and happiness, people are either eagerly anticipating an improvement or anxious to eliminate a negative element of their lives. Customers are generally excited about their decisions. They look forward to receiving something. About 85% of the time, people make decisions as consumers or as customers. But in 15% of the situations, people make decisions as patients, and generally made in an anxious state, when they are looking for immediate relief. This chapter takes a look at the different decisions people make as a patient or as a customer. It also explains what types of new decisions people make as customers or patients in the light of the Healthusiasm trend.

When customers make decisions

Because the words customer and consumer are used interchangeably, it's important to understand the difference as well as the dynamic between both actors. But it will help to understand why the word "customer" is generally used within this book. Theoretically speaking, customers refers to persons who buy goods and pay for them. Consumers are the ones who consume or use the goods. Both words are commonly confused with one another. Depending on the specificities of their business, brands and organisations could be focusing on the customer and the consumer, as both might have an impact on their business.

> *A retailer buying milk to resell it is a customer, a person buying milk is a customer, a person drinking milk is a consumer. Of course, the person who is buying might also be drinking the milk himself, making the customer the consumer at the same time. Milk brands might communicate the health benefits of drinking milk daily to convince the mother (the customer) concerned about the health and well-being of her child (the consumer). But milk brands might be branding the milk in such a way that the child influences his/her mum, as cereal brands do. The mother is the customer who looks at the return she might receive for a certain amount of money. Her decision is generally made either at the time of the purchase or "investigated online" prior to going to the store.*

CUSTOMER   **CONSUMER**

The customer is often also the consumer

The consumer influences the customer

Influenced by value creation
in the Transformational Economy

Seeking Self-Actualisation and personal growth

Customers are the king of the decisions. Typically, they have the freedom to choose from a generally broad range of options that each have a clear cost attached. With plenty of information at hand, they make their decision based on a cost-benefit evaluation. In case of a repurchase, this evaluation can be based on their own experience or that of the consumer. But in the Experience and Transformational Economy, experiences are becoming so personal that the customers will be the consumers of the transformation themselves. The customer will make the purchase with the (personal) transformational experience in mind.

> *The motivating experience of SoulCycle training allowed the company to offer a pay-per-class system. This system in itself builds no loyalty to SoulCycle. There is even the risk of the loss of the customer after each session. But offering the consumer such a relevant experience establishes a more genuine loyalty. It also allows SoulCycle to offer the customer the experience of flexibility. SoulCycle does not need any membership. After each session, the relevant "consumer" experience ensures the purchasing decision by the customer (who is generally the same person).*

Customers also have the freedom to decide not to purchase anything at all. But if they do decide to add a product, a service or an experience to their life, they expect it to come with excitement and an immediate benefit. In case they are not satisfied, there is an after sales service to help them. These are the specifics of customer decisions.

For the purposes of this book I tend to go along with the semantic, intuitive interpretation of both words. A **consumer** typically "consumes" the product. A **customer** is someone you might want to build a personal relationship or share an experience with, or someone to whom you could offer a transformation.

Is it still valuable to distinguish between your customers and consumers? Or does the experience or transformation you are offering make it redundant because each person purchases and consumes?

For these simple reasons, I prefer to refer to customers rather than consumers when discussing Healthusiasm. The customer is the one who will make the decision (to become healthy and happy). He or she is also more of a real person with whom you can personally connect, which is critical in the context of self-actualisation. But the customer is also the consumer of the experience in today's experience and transformational economy. That's why the word "customer" is chosen for the subtitle of this book: Making customers healthy & happy. Customers in this book refers to shoppers, drivers, guests, visitors, travelers, patients and anybody else who takes decisions. The fact that the word consumer is often debated within the healthcare industry (as healthcare is not 'consumed') is also a good reason to stick to the word customer. In the next section will be explained how archetypical patient decisions are indeed entirely different than traditional customer decisions. But we will highlight how even patients have more freedom of choice to impact their health nowadays.

The archetypical patient decisions

One of the most notable changes in the current healthcare landscape revolves around the growing involvement of patients in their health management and care. They have become so engaged and informed that the industry is beginning to refer to them as consumers. Many will argue that the two aren't synonyms, and that the labels aren't interchangeable. Even when patients are more informed and engaged, they don't make the decisions in the same way as a consumer or even a customer.

But patients do also make decisions, of course. At the very least, they should be involved in the decision making by their healthcare providers – even though those decisions may be difficult. But patient choices are typically limited and related information (such as cost) is often lacking. The result of their decision might also be unclear because it remains hard to objectively characterise care as good or bad. However, patients could find themselves in situations where they have no option but to make a decision, because they want "to get rid of something". Obviously, these decisions bring a lot of anxiety, and they don't really come with "customer service" to sort out any issues afterwards.

	Situations in which a person is a	
	CUSTOMER	**PATIENT**
Archetypical decision	Lifestyle decision	Medical decision
Pressure	Freedom of choice	Must decide
Dominant feeling	Excitement	Anxiety
Number of options	Broad range	Few (if any)
Available information	Real time & transparent	Very little
Outcome	Immediate benefit	Unclear
After 'sales' service	Helpful	Limited to none

The above description can be considered typical for a patient who has to make a medical decision. The situation is entirely different when customers make lifestyle decisions (see table). As a result, many argue that patients should not be considered to be customers or consumers. That is still largely true for the typical "medical" decisions in which patients are involved. But patients do also have the option of making other decisions that impact their health. After all, looking after your general health becomes even more important when you have been diagnosed with a long-term disease. That's when people are most motivated to make an impact on their own body and mind. Maintaining overall health could help them to continue to do the things they enjoy, as well as the things they need to do. Those patients will indeed make decisions to actively impact their health. And for these decisions, patients will have more options, more information, more freedom and better service.

Diabetes has long been considered a 'lifestyle' disease that benefits from decisions like dietary change and regular exercise. But can't this be said of all chronic diseases? Patients with cancer, Crohn's disease, chronic pain, and osteoporosis could all benefit from these types of decisions, couldn't they? So too, Alzheimer's and arthritis patients, or any others with chronic conditions. Even patients with acute conditions are increasingly looking for ways to actively influence the consequences of their illness or the illness itself. These choices help patients to actively impact their health and happiness.

While many of these diseases aren't treated as lifestyle diseases by the healthcare system, and as several of those choices are not (supposed to be) offered by the healthcare institutions, patients turn to other types of brands and companies for help in making these types of impactful, Healthusiastic decisions.

The types of Healthusiastic decisions

Regardless of whether we find ourselves in a situation as a patient or a customer, we can make different Healthusiastic decisions ranging from very targeted medical decisions in which we are involved, to broad lifestyle-related options from which we can choose. Let's go through each of the four types of decisions.

Medical decisions

When thinking about Healthusiastic decisions, medical decisions might be the first type that comes to mind. When we are "managing a disease", or when we are starting to deal with one, we are making medical decisions – or, at least we should be, if our healthcare provider involves us. These decisions are typically options that are part of the healthcare system and require endorsement by a doctor. For the most part, they include medication intake and surgical procedures related to a specific (future) disease. Generally speaking, they are taken by a small proportion of the population.

Health decisions

Health decisions focus on disease prevention, so they are made more frequently than medical decisions. But health decisions also involve our physical and mental health. They are also made on the basis of some (publicly known) scientific facts. But instead of disease management, the objective here is to "prevent our physical and emotional health worsening". Most of these health decisions don't require the support of a doctor, but doctors are now recommending them more often than in the past. Actors in the healthcare industry often refer to this as the increased focus on wellness by healthcare providers.

Health decisions is about the active approach of cultivating awareness and taking decisions that prevent our health from declining. Smoking cessation, for example, is a typical health decision. It is publicly known that smoking damages health and that quitting can prevent your health from worsening. Smokers generally make this decision themselves, although a doctor might strongly recommend it. Other examples of health decisions are when an obese person decides to lose weight, or when someone starts running to keep their heart fit.

Well-being decisions

A person's well-being is often described as their current state of health and happiness. Well-being decisions are taken to "maintain that state". The impact of these decisions goes beyond physical or mental health. Instead, it's about feeling good. They might be based on (some form of) scientific fact, but they are often rooted mostly in beliefs. It's about achieving a quality of life that encompasses happiness, health, social connection and life purpose.

Well-being is an outcome that appeals to almost the entire population. These decisions are therefore common: people go to a sauna to feel better. Work-life balance prevents burnout. Going to bed early will make you feel less exhausted the next day. A recent study by the mindful drinking movement called Club Soda for example showed that 52% of people cut down on alcohol to improve health. A well-being decision doesn't necessarily require a recommendation from a healthcare professional. Even without a recommendation to exercise, people do so for their own quality of life and well-being. It makes them feel happy and healthy, and offers purpose (run that marathon, win the championship), and social interaction with friends.

Lifestyle decisions

The most common decisions are the ones we make every day about the way we want to live. Lifestyle decisions are about the things we usually do or choose to do. They typify our individual attitudes, interests, values, or our views on politics, religion, health, intimacy, and more. Lifestyle decisions differ from well-being decisions in that they don't focus first on feeling good mentally and physically. Lifestyle decisions are about "the style of living we desire". They are about our status, our thoughts, and our related actions. It's much more about how these decisions make up our own identity than how they impact our body or mind. We decide on the work we want to do, the type of travel we prefer, the speed at which we adopt technology, the type of relationship we want to have with friends and family, and "the clothes that make the man". Activewear is a good example of establishing a sporty and healthy lifestyle or identity.

Lifestyle is the most visible manifestation of our social difference. A large part of it is directly built by conspicuous consumption of the elements that fit the social position we decide to adopt and the recognition we desire. For example, we can buy legumes at the exclusive organic store, we can buy a salad at the retailer focused on discounts, or we can grow the vegetables ourselves. Each of these customer decisions can create or affirm our desired lifestyle. But another important part of our lifestyle is indirectly determined by our education, our income and the environment in which we are born, grow, live, work and age. These social determinants play an important role in the everyday Healthusiastic decisions that people (can) take. Therefore, lifestyle decisions are mainly a combination of who we want to be and what we are able to do. But these decisions certainly impact our health.

THE DIFFERENT HEALTHUSIASTIC DECISIONS AND THEIR DESIRED OUTCOME

DECISIONS	OBJECTIVE	DECISION BASED ON	DESIRED OUTCOME	POPULATION	EXAMPLE
Medical decisions	Manage illness	Clinical studies & HCP decisions	Impact on the medical condition	Small & targeted	*Medication*
Health decisions	Prevent health from becoming worse	(Publically known) scientific facts	Good mental & physical health	Half of the population	*Smoking cessation*
Well-being decisions	Maintain health & happiness	Beliefs & assumptions	Great feeling of mind and body	Majority of the population	*Sauna*
Lifestyle decisions	Establish identity	Desired identity & social determinants	Style of living	The entire population	*Activewear*

People make many Healthusiastic decisions in any given day. As a customer, they traditionally make lifestyle decisions that determine their way of life and establish their identity. As a patient, they are typically involved in medical decisions that determine the impact of their disease. As explained above, the decisions that are taken in these two stereotypical situations couldn't be further from one another. But from the descriptions of the different Healthusiastic decisions, it should be obvious that people take several decisions that impact their health, regardless of whether they are in the situation of patient or customer.

MEASURES PEOPLE TAKE TO MAINTAIN THEIR PHYSICAL HEALTH

Enough sleep	**Healthy food**	**Exercise**
66%	59%	57%

Source: Survey among more than 28 000 consumers in 23 countries.
Which of these activities do you do regularly to maintain your physical health?

A study conducted by GfK in 23 countries (2015), showed no surprises when people were asked about the activities they engaged in to actively manage their health: getting enough sleep is the most frequently answered activity, followed by healthy eating and exercising. Each of these activities was mentioned by the majority of the respondents, confirming once again that over half of the population is actively taking care of their own health. However, it's important to understand that these activities can be the result of any type of Healthusiastic decision. Some healthy foods can be a lifestyle decision that establishes a certain identity. Others can make you feel good or bring proven benefits to your physical health. Clinical studies are even reporting that food affects our genes, so food choices now become part of a medical decision as well. Eating healthy food certainly is a Healthusiastic decision. So too, getting enough sleep and exercising. But they are Healthusiastic decisions that can be made with different objectives. It's important to set and answer the appropriate expectations for your customers. For example, even though organic food was launched mainly for environmental reasons, customers more often buy it with their own health in mind. But even then, these reasons can be driven by a desire to confirm their image of health-consciousness with products that are considered healthy, to feel great physically because they are organic, or to prevent their health from worsening because they know that pesticides will impact their health.

If your brand is bringing a health product, service or experience to your customer, what type of outcome(s) are they really expecting?

Establishing a health-conscious identity

Owning the most expensive or the latest goods has taken a back seat to looking good and healthy. Living healthily has become the status that customers desire more than material goods, which is why people are making more and more lifestyle decisions to live healthily. In a time that is dominated by cataloguing our lives on social media, looking good and healthy are the new luxuries that consumers want to enjoy and flaunt.

Open your Instagram feed to discover the 1.2 million pretentiously well-framed #avocadotoast pictures and you'll know what I'm talking about. These pictures are supposedly shot in one of the many new-places-to-be that serve only avocados. But the photos could just as well be taken in a hipster coffee bar, carefully curated at home or proudly made at work. Avocados may have been around for about 10 000 years. Today they are sold more often than oranges, even though they cost four times as much. As they are seen as very healthy (although most customers don't really know exactly why), people are willing to pay the price.

This willingness to pay is high for many "healthy" products, for example, for organic food. Research from data company IRI found that sales of no-antibiotics-ever meat grew 45% between 2016 and 2017, even though a typical food basket that includes organic or antibiotic-free meat is 40% more expensive than its non-organic alternative. This preference for natural products is also manifest in the decision on skincare products and deodorants. People decide to buy these and many other "healthy" products to create or confirm their image as a health-conscious person, which is greatly desired today.

How can your products, service or experience rightfully strengthen the health-conscious image of customers?

Even when suffering from a life-altering disease, patients want to live life as normally as possible. Going to work, continuing studies, meeting with friends, performing household tasks or travelling the world might all be things a chronic patient does not want to abandon. After all, staying active is very important for your own identity and personality. Patients take an enormous number of "lifestyle decisions" to optimise living with their disease or to maintain their identity and personality. They can do more shopping online, sit down to do the ironing or bulk cook items on a good day. They may plan ahead more often, to avoid sudden stress, decide to ask family and friends to lend a hand in the house, employ a gardener or a cleaner, or have the groceries delivered. If some desirable trendy products no longer fit their 'adapted' life, they might look for other ways to establish their identity. Each of these many Healthusiastic decisions will define their way of living with the disease, maintain their identity, and indirectly impact their health or happiness.

Feeling great in mind and body

Well-being is all about feeling good in body and mind. People now are looking for ways that help them feel good. Even though certain healthy lifestyle decisions may upgrade your health-conscious image, they do not make you feel intrinsically good. Feeling good in body and mind is not about your identity or the things you own. It's rather a state of health and happiness that you want to maintain.

One of the greatest threats to maintaining this state is stress. While stress was necessary for survival, modern security and luxuries have often rendered these fight-or-flight responses obsolete. We now experience stress as unnecessary or detrimental to our health and happiness, certainly when it persists after the external trigger has passed. That's why many well-being decisions have the objective of stress management. Work-life balance is a very good example of how people take well-being decisions to feel better. As our lives are characterised by 24/7 connection, a lack of work-life boundaries, and living in urban nature-deprived areas, people are looking for ways to feel good mentally and physically. They focus on time management techniques, decide to work from home or organise their day differently. People even expect their employers to recognise these needs by implementing corporate well-being programmes that facilitate this.

The increased importance of well-being decisions is also visible in the immense popularity of meditation, which could justifiably be labelled as the most popular health trend. Meditation is now as beloved as yoga, reaching about 15% of the population, but is growing much faster. A recent study from the Centres for Disease Control and Prevention (CDC) in the US, reported that meditation grew 250% between the years 2012 and 2017, while yoga "only" grew 50%.

> *The sleep, meditation and relaxation app Calm is a good example of that popularity. With about 40 million downloads in only a couple of years, it became the app of 2017 and remains the top grossing health app in app stores today. Calm is also the first mental health company ever to reach the status of unicorn (a company valued at one billion dollars). The popularity of running, sleep and food apps falls under the same category of*

tools that help people to feel good. The abundant availability of tracking, information and management tools helps people make conscious decisions about exercising, sleeping and eating, which they believe will impact the way they feel.

Patients also just want to 'feel' good in body and mind. We know that life does not have a fixed path. Significant events or changes will inevitably occur and bring uncertainty. Patients are even more aware of this reality. Sudden events and uncertainties are part of the progression of disease and patients are often confronted with a range of emotions related to the impact of the (new) symptoms on themselves, their family and their future. Patients typically suffer from a great deal of stress. Talking about their emotions can therefore be a very important well-being decision for them. Even at work, patients might have to discuss their career path or decide on the time they need to optimise their work situation to their reality. These "well-being decisions" are some typical Healthusiastic decisions that help patients feel better.

Preventing health from declining

Some decisions go beyond feeling good. These decisions are taken to achieve a clear impact on physical or mental health. People generally make health decisions because they don't want their health to worsen. Often, they even expect these decisions to have a positive impact on their health, just as smoking cessation prevents a decline in health or shortness of breath. But there are plenty of other health choices that confirm that people are interested in impacting their physical or mental health. With the increased knowledge and conviction of the impact food has on health, we certainly see more people making health decisions about what they eat.

When shopping or eating out with friends, you must surely have noticed how "gluten-free" has invaded our lives in the past 10 years. Gluten is a type of protein found in grains including wheat, barley, spelt and rye. Although diagnosis is rather complex, it is assumed that about 1% of the population is suffering from a gluten allergy (Coeliac disease), according to the Beyond Celiac organisation. It is a physical condition that irritates your gut. Next to gluten allergy, it's estimated that 6% of the population suffers from gluten intolerances and sensitivities that might cause similar symptoms, like diarrhoea, constipation or fatigue. This awareness has resulted in many self-diagnosing gluten intolerances and therefore buying gluten-free prod-

ucts. Today, Nielsen found that 11% of households buy gluten-free products, while roughly 30% of the public would like to cut back on the amount of gluten they are eating, according to market research by the NPD Group. The market for gluten-free products has grown by 50% in the past three years. People are consciously making decisions to impact their health even though there is no medical diagnosis to back up this decision. But the scientific facts about how gluten could impact health are enough for many to decide to live by that diet, even if other scientific facts claim that there is no need, or that they should proceed with caution.

PERCENTAGE OF THE POPULATION INTERESTED IN GLUTEN-FREE

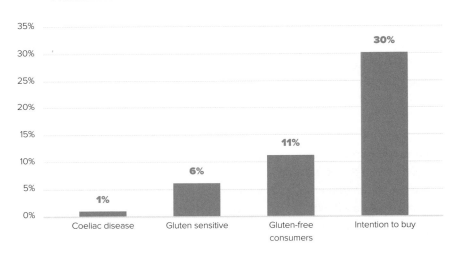

Although brands should carefully consider moving into a largely science-based field, which of your products or services can be optimised in the light of new (scientific and behavioural) insights?

Healthcare professionals might certainly recommend that patients eat healthily. Together with avoiding alcohol, smoking cessation, and regular exercises, these recommendations are probably the most common. But they remain a conscious decision by the patient. If they are focused on safeguarding their physical and mental health, they should be motivated to follow up on these recommendations. These Health decisions lower the chances of acquiring co-morbidities and can also reduce the impact of some specific symptoms, such as pain and fatigue. And people are actively looking for that. The search for alternative treatments is also considered to be a measure to prevent their health from declining.

The popularity of Health decisions is obvious when strolling around in supermarkets. Claims like low cholesterol, gluten-free, high-protein, or fat-free are widespread – on any type of food. These claims vary with some focusing on the impact on health or body, and some on the nutrient content. This is in an attempt to "scale up" products from being subjective choices to Lifestyle decisions that reinforce the identity of the customer, to Health decisions that actually claim a health benefit. This guides customers in their purchases. Studies show that health claims on food packages can be convincing enough for customers to skip the nutrition facts (ingredient labels). Some products don't put claims on the packaging but create an (often false) image of healthfulness instead. Drinking 'vitamin water' may feel like a Health decision (based on the image it radiates) but is misleading to the customer if it contains high quantities of sugar.

This type of health promotion is called Healthwashing. The term describes the practice of presenting and advertising products and services as healthy when, in reality, the customer is being misled. The prevalence of healthwashing has prompted the FDA and EMEA to regulate health claims on food. But meanwhile even products like mattresses, shoes or air-conditioners are increasingly promoted with health claims. Today, it's not uncommon to see lawsuits filed against companies that make false health claims in promoting their products. Some companies go to great lengths to appeal to customers with health claims, which just goes to show that Health decisions are becoming increasingly important for customers.

Managing a (future) illness

On diagnosis, treatment of the condition is required to prevent the disease from progressing too fast. Reimbursement criteria, the cost of the medication, clinical evidence and experience of the available treatments are factors that influence the treatment options the healthcare professional suggests. As a chronic disease has a profound impact on the patient, in most cases, doctors discuss the options directly with them, to discover their preferences. How does the patient live and work? What type of medication administration might best fit their personality? What are the most common symptoms? In this way, doctors directly involve their patients in these medical decisions. With acute illnesses, treatment decisions are also more often than not discussed between the doctor and the patient. This involvement is really what patients require. Because patients want to feel like tmey themselves have an impact on their own health.

For customers, Medical decisions is about "managing" future medical conditions. People are not yet considered patients and there is generally no medical professional involved in the decisions. These decisions are powered by rather new technology and science that, for example, allows you to monitor your health via frequent blood analyses or even to predict future conditions via genome sequencing. Monthly blood analysis, ordered without medical prescription, helps customers understand the evolution of their health in key areas by tracking dozens of health markers. Through medical feedback, people then learn the status of their kidneys, liver, thyroid gland, and cardiovascular system among others. DNA sequencing of genes (often called DNA tests) or analysis of the bacteria from the gut, nose, mouth, skin or genitals (often called microbiome tests) are increasingly popular medical decisions. What once cost a million euros and took 13 years to get results, now costs EUR 100 and takes about an hour. But commercially speaking, we are at the beginning of this mega revolution. Both "tests" have the potential to provide customers with very valuable information on their health in the very near future.

*At the end of 2018, the personal genetic service **23andMe** became the FDA approved direct-to-consumer DNA test for detecting genetic variants that may be associated with medication metabolism. In order words, this test helps understand what role, if any, genetics plays in a person's reaction to drugs (pharmacogenetics). The approval of this pharmacogenetics test is a step forward in making information about genetic variants available directly to consumers. It will improve discussions with healthcare providers about what medication to take and how much. Early in 2019, 23andMe also received approval to offer customers a test for two genetic variants of hereditary colorectal cancer syndromes. It's the second test associated with cancer risk for which 23andMe has received FDA clearance, after receiving approval for three genetic variants associated with* *increased risk of breast cancer. Although both screenings rule out only a minority of the breast and colorectal cancers, it does offer a clear sign of where this is heading. And customers are eager to conduct these tests. At the start of 2019, nine million people had already conducted a DNA test with 23andMe, according to MIT Technology Review (2019). It displayed a growth of no less than 300% compared to the previous year. None of the other market dominant DNA tests, which offer only ancestry analysis, show similar growth.*

Most tests will be sold as a view on the potential 'risk' for multiple diseases, influenced by either genes, microbes and/or daily habits like food intake. They help people to better understand their own body. What are my risks for certain diseases? What vitamins or minerals are either elevated or reduced in my body? How does my body react to alcohol, gluten or lactose, for example? What is my risk for sports-related injuries? What is my pain sensitivity? Will I go grey early? What food should I be eating to optimise the functioning of my body? These are all questions people would like answers to. The latter, often called Food as Medicine, is rapidly becoming popular. It's the science of the influence of food on how our genes behave (nutrigenomics) and of the different ways our genes 'use' certain foods (nutrigenetics).

*One of the world's largest food companies, which brought us Nesquik, Nestea and Smarties, is now poised to bring us personalised nutrition. In reaction to the popularity of health decisions that came with a lower demand for sugary treats, by 2018 it had already sold off its US candy unit and spent billions to acquire the dietary supplement maker **Atrium Innovations** and **Novartis Medical Nutrition**. **Nestlé** is on a mission to address health problems that are associated with food and nutrition. The Nestlé Institute of Health Sciences has invested a lot in medical research to develop tools to analyse and measure people's nutrient levels. In Japan, Nestlé has now rolled out a programme in which 100 000 people collect their DNA at home to receive recommendations on dietary changes. The recommended specialised supplements can be sprinkled on or mixed into a variety of food products, including teas. **Campbell Soup Co**. bought San Francisco-based start-up Habit, which uses DNA to make diet recommendations, offer nutritional coaching and recommend tailored meal-kits. As people are increasingly interested in making medical decisions, it's expected that all food companies will follow suit. In fact, Mintel (2019)*

119

> *reported that already today, 42% of British consumers are interested in a personalised diet based on their genes/DNA.*

Customers make the medical decision to learn about their body even when they are not sick. They want to know what type of food to eat, sports to participate in, or beauty products to use to impact their health. Customers seem to have an appetite for these types of insights, even while the tests are only at the initial phase of their journey and based only minimally on science. But in future, these types of medical decisions taken by customers will be the norm.

> *It's not only the food industry that will benefit from the affordability and accessibility of genome sequencing. British skincare brand **Geneu** offers customers at Selfridges a same-day DNA testing service as part of its Personalised Serums package. But in today's day and age, you don't need to go to London, of course. There are many more e-commerce sites run by dermatologists that sell similar DNA-based skincare products. Even **L'Oreal** is jumping onto the DNA-personalised skincare band wagon. Athletes and sporty people can also benefit from DNA-personalised training. **38 Degrees North** holds fitness boot camps in Ibiza, based on a DNA test people need to send three weeks prior to the training. The five-day training and dietary schedule is then personalised to your DNA to achieve maximum impact. Perhaps you are a wine lover? Then **Vinome** can create wines that are perfectly suited to your DNA-personal palate. From 2020, sushi fans can book a table at **The Sushi Singularity Tokyo** restaurant. After having booked a table, the restaurant will then mail a health kit that asks for a DNA sample, urinalysis and enterobacterial flora examination. With the results, the customer will be served enhanced meals based on your DNA Health ID.*

People make plenty of decisions every day. Whether we find ourselves in the situation of patient or customer, more and more people are making Healthusiastic decisions. Patients make Health decisions and even Lifestyle decisions. Customers make Well-being decisions and even Medical decisions. About half of the population, regardless of age and gender, is making decisions to actively impact their health in some way. This is a trend that is becoming visible everywhere around us. The following chapters explain how you should understand and react to this trend.

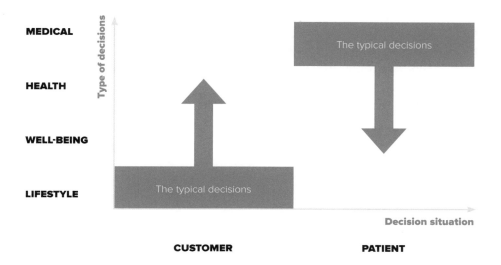

The Healthusiasm Trend

About 150 years ago, men wore tailored suits with a bow tie, pocket watch and handkerchief. Going out, men topped this off with a waistcoat, hat, and gloves. Women wore skirts, dresses and gowns that had many layers of fabric. These could be silk or satin but were mostly very uncomfortable. A corset was worn underneath to maintain a narrow waistline. These clothes were not pleasant to wear, but people went to great lengths *not to look poor*.

Ever since, clothes have become much more comfortable and casual. Bit by bit, even sports clothing took up room in wardrobes. Bruce Lee was one of the first to bring the classic tracksuit into mainstream '70s fashion, even for activities that were not remotely active. Run DMC made the classic Adidas shoe trendy in the '80s. Nike Air Max was identified with a specific subculture in the '90s. And of course there are many more examples of how specific sport clothes have suddenly been appropriated for everyday use.

But in the past three years, activewear has become everyday wear. In a time where people want to actively manage their health and happiness, activewear demonstrates how health and well-being are truly ingrained in our daily routines. You'll see women walking the streets in yoga wear, middle-aged men wearing jogging pants, or grandmothers rocking Nikes. Being the healthiest and happiest version of yourself also means not becoming inactive as you grow older. What better way to prove that 60 is the new 40, or 40 is the new 20 than to wear sports clothing? In contrast to 150 years ago, you can say that people go to great lengths today *not to look old*.

1870
I hope I don't look **POOR**

2019
I hope I don't look **OLD**

Trends and S-curves

There was a time when whitening teeth, smoothing cellulite and battling ageing with health treatments was kept secret. Today, the pursuit of health is the new status symbol much as it was the Céline bag five years ago. There was a time when taking a photo at the gym was considered inappropriate, but now Instagram feeds contain plenty of selfies of people working out. Our Instagram is in fact the digital proof of our healthy identity. Today, it's basically the only acceptable lifestyle brag. No longer is bragging about a car or the money you make the thing to do. The recognisable sweater from the personal training centre, the geometrical designs on activewear or the green smoothie in hand might be the most desirable look today. It is a display of self-care, discipline, and responsibility. For some, healthy living might even give a sense of moral superiority.

The S-curve

But don't make the faulty assumption that Healthusiasm is only about the afore-mentioned desirable 'image' of healthy living, or that this fashionable profiling is the sole driving force behind Healthusiasm. That would imply that it will disappear as quickly as the desire for a Céline bag, waist-high trousers or colour-block combinations. That is not the case. Healthusiasm is a Macro trend that has been around for several years and is bound to be here in the long term. It's important to understand that Macro trends are global trends that gradually permeate our world. Initially they are rather imperceptible. Their slow growth means that we are influenced unconsciously, until we consider them normal. It's often only after a couple of years that we realise that the values and aspirations of society have changed. That's also why Macro trends always get a lukewarm reception.

The impact of Macro trends is often overlooked at first. Many miss these critical changes in society. Peter Hinssen, one of the most sought-after thought leaders on radical innovation, leadership and the impact of all things digital, carefully explains this in his first book, *The New Normal*, by illustrating it with the dynamic of S-curves. As you might have learned from Hinssen, an S-curve has a turning point (see below). At this point in the curve, change is accelerating at its fastest pace and becomes normal. For example, Hinssen explained that as from this turning point onward, digital became the new normal in our society. It was a Macro trend that was largely ignored in the past, that "suddenly" had become unavoidable and indispensable.

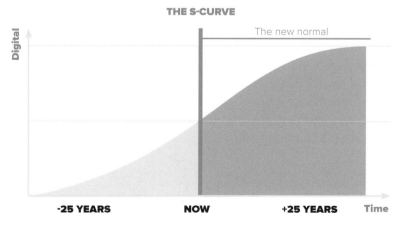

The digital S-curve by Peter Hinssen showing that Digital is the New Normal.
Visit www.nexxworks.com to learn how this company inspires organisations to act on the Day After Tomorrow.

Healthusiasm is at a similar turning point on its own S-curve. But I believe that the Healthusiasm S-curve has a slightly atypical form because it starts from the very basic, ever-present need of being in good health. People have always been preoccupied with their health. Ancient Greeks brought offers to Apollo and Asclepius, while in medieval times people prayed to Christian saints. Though the desire to be healthy and happy has always been very present, impacting one's health was then merely based on belief. People lacked the knowledge and solutions to feel empowered.

In the 1960s, medical revolutions gave people a feeling of being less at the mercy of the Gods (or luck): mass-produced penicillin saved millions of lives from World War II onwards, the birth control pill enabled women to prevent pregnancy, the tranquiliser chlorpromazine revolutionised psychiatry, and organ transplants became a medical technique for survival. From that point in time, it felt as if we *could* effectively do something about our health if necessary – though that feeling was somewhat diminished in the early 1980s with the onset of the deadly AIDS epidemic. At the time, the ageing population also suddenly faced the rising incidence of the memory-robbing Alzheimer's disease, which attracted considerable media attention. But the increase in heart diseases and cancer was what probably prompted people to take responsibility for their own health.

This coincided with an all-time high in alcohol consumption and the increased popularity of fast-food restaurants. Even after years of advancement, people found that medical science couldn't solve everything. So they started taking care of themselves. The fitness craze in the 1980s was probably the first strong indication that people *wanted* to influence their health. But it was also visible in other trends. According to Gallup (2018), more people stopped smoking in the 1980s and alcohol consumption never ever again hit the peak it did in the 1970s. This was perhaps the first time people were actively preventing their health from becoming worse. It was also the period when governments launched their initial small-scale preventive measures.

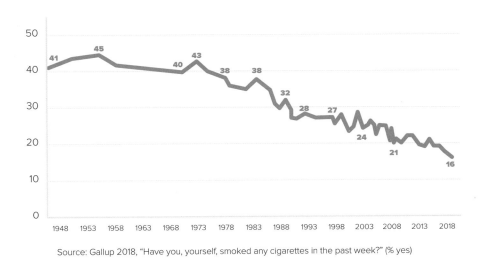

PEOPLE WHO SMOKED CIGARETTES IN THE PAST WEEK

Source: Gallup 2018, "Have you, yourself, smoked any cigarettes in the past week?" (% yes)

In the following decade, the widespread success of pharmaceutical blockbuster products continued to illustrate the general willingness to better one's health. But real personal influence on one's own health was still limited. It wasn't until Dr Google came along in the early 2000s that people really started feeling more empowered. With all the valuable information and tools that followed, we felt more capable of actively measuring and impacting our health. The term Quantified Self was coined to describe the widespread practice of logging personal metrics. These measurements allowed us to build knowledge about our own health. Our prayers were finally answered – we could now influence our health – and we became really Healthusiastic.

But we are only scratching the surface of its potential. As the impact of digital disruption lagged in the health and medical scene, it is likely that we will now see rapid introduction of the Healthusiastic advantages of technological innovation. This empowerment is highly anticipated, because its positive impact in other industries has already been experienced. The expectation is that it will increasingly empower us to answer the basic human need that has prevailed for millennia: to be healthy and happy.

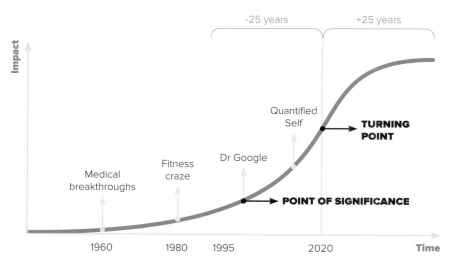

The Healthusiasm S-Curve: We are now at the turning point where actively managing
your health and happiness has become the new normal.

The Macro, Mini and Micro trends

The Healthusiasm trend to actively impact one's health and happiness is a Macro trend that has already been around for a number of years. With about 50% of the population now actively managing their health, it has grown past its turning point into the new normal. Its impact on our society means it has become indispensable and unavoidable. Healthusiasm will not disappear in the way a particular fashion item could lose its appeal. This "risk" of rapid disappearance is the case only for Mini and Micro trends, which are derivatives of the Macro Healthusiasm trend.

The relationship between those different trends can be compared to a tree. It all starts with a seed from which a slim trunk with a few twigs and leaves develops. As the years pass, the trunk grows thicker, more branches appear and with every season more and more new leaves grow that are only slightly different from the previous ones. A Macro trend is the basis and, just like the trunk of a tree, it can live a long life, perhaps even beyond 50 years. Mini trends are the branches that originate from the trunk. These can easily last for 15 years. Micro trends are like the leaves that change a little every season.

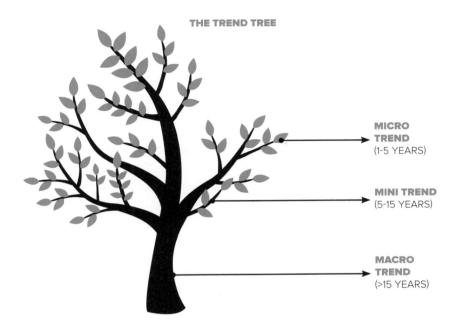

Although Mini trends grow from Macro trends and last for many years, they don't intrinsically change our values and aspirations that much. However, they are more visible than Macro trends and are therefore more frequently covered in the media. Think about how the trend to connect and share, among others, has been widely debated in discussions about social media. Or the trend towards less desire to own material things, reflected in articles about carsharing. Of course, some Mini trends that are currently in the media might originate from the Healthusiasm trend: for example, think of how the fashionable, healthy image of celebrities became the perfect soil for a new Mini trend that originated from the aspiration to become as healthy and happy as possible. For as long as time, people have been attracted to the lifestyle of the famous, who always look so amazingly beautiful. If only we could become as healthy and beautiful as them.

Well, in a world where everyone can become who they want to be, celebrities are now helping others to live healthily too. They share their work-out routines, food choices, sleeping habits, and reading materials. These allow anyone who has the ambition to live (and look) like certain celebrities to follow their healthy lifestyle. Some celebrities have been elevated to a status of health guru as a result. Some even grasped the opportunity to build an entire business empire on this Mini Trend.

> *Gwyneth Paltrow, who started her wellness brand **Goop** back in 2008, now leads a company valued at USD250 million. Jessica Alba's **Honest Company**, which offers chemical-free baby products and natural make-up is valued at USD1 billion. These two celebrities are probably the most successful examples of the Mini trend in which people aspire to become as healthy and perhaps as happy as celebrities. And there are many others too. Former top models Elle MacPherson and Cindy Crawford each launched well-being products that might persuade women to drink and eat like them. Hillary Swank and Beyoncé are known for their focus on fitness routines, and these stars both launched activewear collections that allow customers to move like them. No matter who the adored celebrity is, fans need not only admire them from afar; they are now able to learn from and live like them.*

While the above examples might last several more years, other products and services that come with Lifestyle, and perhaps some of the Well-being decisions, are more at risk of disappearing quickly. Walking around holding a smoothie might go within a couple of years. Wearing activewear during the day will not remain as fashionable as it is today. Both are riding the wave of the Macro Healthusiasm trend but should rather be considered Micro trends. These are the leaves annually growing on the Trend tree. We discuss and obsess over these every day. They are the lifestyle decisions that showcase the identity we want to create, so these decisions tend to evolve and shift quickly, as do other hyped products and services. These products and services are rapidly disseminated, and become less attractive just as rapidly. The same is true for some well-being decisions, which have been as much part of Micro trends as lifestyle decisions. Think of all the different diet fads that have come and gone in the past 100 years, the Gwyneth Paltrow endorsed popularity of cupping massages 10 years ago or (perhaps) the recent boom in breathing sessions.

Healthusiasm is a long-term Macro trend that finally answers the desire to be in good health. This need has always been prevalent, but the information and tools have now pushed it beyond the turning point of the S-curve. Becoming as healthy and happy as possible is the new normal. It's no longer a hidden secret, nor is it dependent on belief or prayers. Reinforced by the Transformational Economy, self-actualisation and the possibility to become who you want to become, Healthusiasm is the achievable aspiration to be as healthy as possible.

Because the healthier you are, the happier you can become. People strive to go from sick to healthy, from healthy to happy.

From sick to healthy, from healthy to happy

Healthusiasm is a Macro trend because it answers an aspiration that is relevant for many people. This aspiration is the life-long personal desire to become as healthy and happy as possible. The graph below visually maps the Healthusiasm trend and how Healthusiastic decisions go beyond the typical customer or patient decisions.

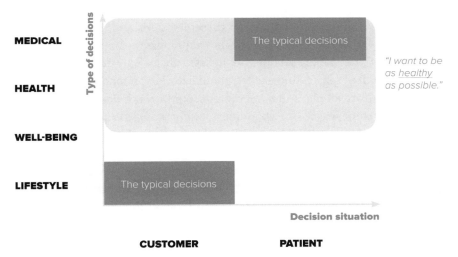

Healthusiasm model: Decisions people take to be as healthy as possible.

Health and Medical decisions are generally taken to stay or become healthy. Sometimes, even specific Well-being decisions can contribute too. They help both patients and customers to achieve the level of physical and mental health they would like to attain, maintain or prevent from becoming worse. It is obvious that everybody wants to be healthy, but it is rather new that we actively want to impact our health as much as we do today. But in a time where digital disruption has taught us that we can become who or what we want to become, we desire that same level of impact on our own body. That is one of the main reasons why people want to impact their own health with Healthusiastic decisions: It's our damn body and we want to have an impact on it.

Knowing that the customer wants to impact his own health, is your company doing everything possible to help him with it? Or are you shying away from taking as much responsibility as your own customer?

More intriguing, however, is why people are making Healthusiastic decisions to become happy. What is the link between these decisions and happiness? So it might be worthwhile to look deeper into what happiness means for us. It is critical to understand that happiness does not necessarily (or only) mean having fun at a party, the thrill of sex, feeling excited about a new experience, or the joy of a tasty meal. These are all pleasurable moments, but they are fleeting. They may all contribute in some way to one's happiness, but happiness is not merely about chasing pleasure. Happiness is when life fulfils your needs. Therefore, happiness can be considered as a changeable state of general satisfaction with your current situation. Happiness is not a long-lasting, permanent feature or a personality trait. It is dependent on multiple factors such as income, family, social relationships, environment (for example, safety), values and, of course, health. You might rightfully recognise these factors as the needs of the Maslow Pyramid, regrouped earlier in this book as Functional and Emotional Needs. Having these needs fulfilled makes you happy. But even if these needs are largely fulfilled in the Western world today, it remains a challenge to keep them fulfilled over time. Often, the effort is not only in attaining but also in maintaining happiness.

> *Imagine the life of someone in her 30s who is married to the man of her dreams four years ago. Together they have a two-year-old daughter who requires a lot of attention and time-management from them both. She has a career that really kicked off a couple of years ago and promises a rosy future. Running is one of her passions. It makes her forget about everything for a moment, and keeps her in shape. She has a really good bond with her friends from college. Being with them brings laughter and joy, as ever. With all these functional and emotional needs fulfilled, she really considers herself happy with her life. But it might be quite a challenge to keep these needs fulfilled over time. She has to be a well-organised mum, a loving partner, a*

> *productive colleague, a friend who is always available... This often comes with a lot of stress that drains energy. So it is really important for her to maintain her physical and mental health and have enough energy to meet all these expectations. That is exactly why she focuses on being as healthy as possible. Because healthy means happy. A healthy body helps her attain the highest possible energy. This energy will help her in maintaining what she has and who she wants to be. Energy will make her happy.*

Instead of selling product features or service levels, how can your company actually sell true happiness?

Depending on your personal situation, one or the other of the needs mentioned above may play a more important role. It will define happiness as a more concrete aspiration to be fulfilled and an additional reason to live healthily. *Energy* facilitates happiness for the young woman in the example. *Beauty* might promote happiness for the young adolescent. *Balance* might aid the parent in being happy with becoming older. Most likely, *enjoyment* means happiness for the retired senior with grandkids. Whatever one's life situation, each of the functional and emotional needs will have a different degree of importance and result in a specific driver for being as healthy and happy as possible. If you want to enjoy your experience as a grandparent, being healthy will certainly help you. If you aspire to radiate beauty, good mental and physical health will help you achieve that.

LIFE SITUATIONS DEFINE WHAT HAPPINESS MIGHT MEAN FOR YOU

Beautiful
(15-30 years old)

Energetic
(30-45 years old)

In balance
(45-60 years old)

Enjoying
(+60 years old)

Example: the potential drivers for different people to live healthily and become as happy as possible.

Whatever the specific personal driver, Lifestyle and Well-being decisions are the ones predominantly taken to impact happiness. Some health decisions can also contribute. People may not have to deal with a disease yet, or they might not think specifically about preventing diseases, but they are keen to be as healthy as possible. They will actively try to live healthily, because it helps them to be happy.

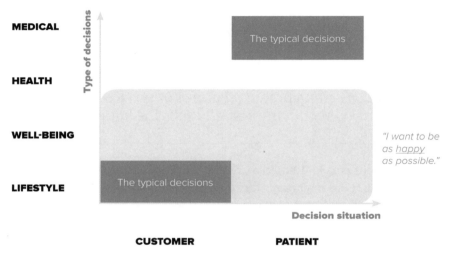

Healthusiasm model: Decisions people take to be as happy as possible

Self-care & wellness

In the Healthusiasm model depicted on page 129, people make different types of decisions that are health-related. Medical decisions help us to take care of our (future) diseases by *managing* or *predicting* conditions. With the many everyday Lifestyle decisions, we *establish* our identity, and when living with a disease, even *maintain* our identity. But we really "care about our self" when taking Well-being and Health decisions. These are the decisions that either make us feel good or help us maintain our health. Self-care is the over-arching name of the driver behind these decisions, and it's hugely popular today.

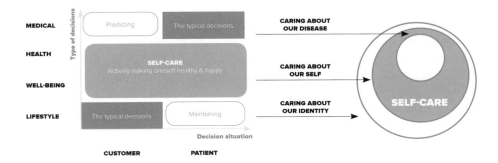

But self-care hasn't always been so popular, because it implies putting yourself first. In the past we were conditioned to believe that this is wrong, or even selfish, because the word "self" seems to be about the individual only. We were meant to suffer and endure hardship. People like Gandhi and Mother Teresa were examples to our society because they exemplified self-sacrifice and suffering. Self-care, on the other hand, was considered indulgent.

Self-care became increasingly important as more and more people reported anxiety, sleep troubles, and irritability. Often, people feel that they aren't ageing well, don't feel good physically, or simply feel exhausted. These symptoms have always existed, of course. But our perception of this, and the way we deal with it, has changed radically. During the Renaissance, exhaustion was seen as an inherent weakness. When monks, for example, went through spiritual weakness (which is what exhaustion was called), it was a sin they needed to cope with. And melancholic people were said to suffer from the impact of Saturn. It is only since the mid 1800s that doctors and philosophers started pointing to the changes in society and the demands of modern life as additional causes of exhaustion. In current society, these demands have not decreased: relentless emails, chattering social media, the lack of boundaries between work and private life can eventually bring us to the edge of exhaustion, or cause us to feel unwell or experience sleep troubles. With the oversupply of information today, an additional cause may lurk. We are now aware of both Mariah Carey and Pope Benedict XVI suffering from burnout. We know about the pregnancy struggles of Beyoncé and the heart failure of Luke Perry. Even within our very own environment, we now sometimes feel as if everyone we know is sick to some extent: someone has poor digestion, someone's son has autism, another is burned out... This ubiquity not only makes it socially more acceptable, but also gives the impression that it will eventually happen to you too. This drives us to act. But we are very confused about the right thing to do. We want to eat healthily but herbicides are used on all our foods. We know we lack vitamin D but we have to wear tons of sunscreen when we go out. No wonder people are increasingly looking for answers to take better care of themselves. Nothing really showcases this need for answers more effectively than the fact that the number of Google searches on the term "self-care" have doubled in the past two years.

SELF-CARE

Actively making oneself healthy & happy

Relative amount of search terms across years

Google Trends Data April 2019

Technology does indeed offer answers to questions and, as in any other domain, self-care is also highly influenced by it. As we keep our smartphones close to us, we can rely on them for moments of self-care. Think of the popularity of running apps, meditation apps (like the aforementioned Calm), or food apps that offer information, coaching, or tools to keep records. Self-care was in fact the most popular app theme in 2018, according to Apple. These self-care apps turn our phone into a device that is perhaps less about likes and filters, and more about you and your happiness. Perhaps it's no coincidence that the rise in screen time runs parallel to the popularity of self-care. But it's not enough to just feel better. These apps are also here to affirm that we are doing the work, that we are indeed improving ourselves. Self-care apps could be regarded as a new and more impactful delivery system than the CDs, books and videos that were already proffering self-help. They now allow us faster and easier access to tools and knowledge to take care of ourselves. That said, self-care is not limited to these apps.

Business consulting firm Stella Rising (2018) reported that 95% of people link self-care with healthy habits. It's no longer considered as pampering or indulgence, or as "selfish". Self-care is the key to a healthy and happy life. It is really about becoming the best version of yourself (self-actualisation), which in turn fosters good relationships with yourself and others. Stella Rising (2018) disclosed that more than half of the respondents believe that self-care is important for their own well-being. The report also states that these people are proactive in caring for themselves. It could be as simple as going to bed earlier on a specific night, or as hard as changing your habits to live more healthily overall. It's manifested as a group of different behaviours that are often also labelled as "wellness" activities. They range from eating healthfully or indulgently, to spending time alone or seeing friends, and working out or taking a rest day, depending on your personal needs. Wellness is the active pursuit of self-care. But it also refers to the overarching term for businesses that offer products, services or experiences to support people in actively taking care of themselves.

"Wellness is not a word that you hear every day," Dan Rather said in 1979, during *60 Minutes*, one of the greatest TV shows of all times. Back then, wellness and the people who were proactively taking care of themselves were presented as a cult. Today, however, wellness is pervasive: on television, in magazines, and in any store you might walk into. This industry helps a broad range of people to become healthy and happy. Euromonitor called wellness one of the top global consumer trends in 2017. It is used to make hotel rooms more pleasant, to transform flights into a moment of self-care, or to make co-working spaces more attractive for health-conscious workers. These are the type of businesses Healthusiastic people choose when making well-being or health decisions.

Wellness is the answer to the increasing desire to take care of oneself. It is a part of the bigger aspiration of be(com)ing as healthy and happy as possible. This Healthusiasm trend is influencing all industries. It offers a new range of opportunities to connect with customers. But it also contains the potential pitfall of becoming irrelevant if the expectations of the growing group of Healthusiastic customers are not met. Much as companies that still use plastic 10 years from now will have become irrelevant for their customers, companies that don't feed into the Healthusiasm trend will be eradicated as well.

The Healthusiasm business

The objective of this chapter is to offer a glimpse into how Healthusiasm affects various industries, their size and segmentation, and how it influences the dynamics within and beyond the boundaries of these industries.

Healthcare and medical Industry

In 2017, the global healthcare and medical business was worth about USD8 trillion, making it undoubtedly one of the largest in the world. This industry consists of healthcare services (hospitals, care institutions, diagnostics laboratories), pharmaceutical drugs, medical devices, biologics and the up and coming DNA sequencing business. With the growing and ageing population, clinical and technological innovations and rising labour costs, this business is expected to grow to between USD10 and 12 trillion by the year 2022, depending on the reports consulted. It would then represent about 10% of global economic output.

As the healthcare and medical business is primarily funded by governments and payers (like insurance companies), this growth puts its financial viability under enormous pressure. That's why the objective of the industry is no longer limited to improving care and health, but to a reduction in spending. This imperative will impose radical changes on its functioning because it is likely not possible to charge patients more. The industry will need to innovate and experiment with new business models and care delivery to realise affordable, high-quality healthcare solutions.

One of these changes is the intention to switch from a fee-for-service model to an outcome-based financial model in which payments will be based on the actual value delivered to the patient. Another considerable change is the switch from costly hospital care to convenient home care. Both these changes promise to make the healthcare industry somewhat less expensive, but this will entail efficient collaboration from all stakeholders. Their patients will be held responsible for their decisions and actions, which will motivate them to focus on prevention and care. Patients will be accountable for their own medical condition to a greater degree than before.

Although this change induces fear within the healthcare industry, the increase in responsibility assumed by the patient does fit well with patient involvement in medical decisions within the Healthusiasm trend. Today, about half of patients are actively involved in medical decisions. But with greater involvement, patients are also becoming more demanding. They expect similar experiences to those they receive in other industries. And currently, people are really dissatisfied with the access, the poor information and the service they receive within the healthcare industry. They increasingly insist on transparency on price, quality and safety. Patients demand more impactful customer service from their healthcare provider. These accelerating patient expectations are putting pressure on the healthcare sector.

Healthcare organisations certainly have become somewhat more patient-centric in the past couple of years. Challenged by the different waves of digital disruption, more organisations look into seizing the opportunity to serve people better. But this necessary change does not come easily to the industry. After all, healthcare providers have not really been trained to deal with demanding customers, regulations are not a good fit with an agile technology-driven world, legacy infrastructures are not easily replaced, and, above all, the healthcare industry is simply unused to dealing with customer-centricity. The industry has always been predominantly preoccupied with medical care as an internal process or a scientific practice. Pushed by the financial imperative and the Healthusiasm trend, the patient should no longer just be part of the processes or the scientific context but put at the centre of healthcare. Patient experience should become a core value. To be successful in this patient-centric environment, a deeper understanding of people's expectations is vital.

This new patient-driven dynamic in the healthcare and medical industry will unlock the opportunity of establishing a more fruitful two-way relationship between the healthcare provider and the patient. It will engage patients far more. Establishing involvement and customer service will improve the overall patient experience, and even increase convenience for healthcare providers. With non-traditional companies slowly infiltrating their industry, customer experience will be mandatory for the business outlook of these healthcare and medical businesses. Technological companies like Amazon, Google, Walmart and Apple, which are particularly known for their customer experience, might slowly but surely substitute parts of the current processes and tools. Simply because patients will request their healthcare solutions. The medical industry needs to be prepared for these major changes in the back end (processes and infrastructure) and in the front end (patient-driven dynamic).

With people increasingly expecting organisations to help them become healthy and happy, is the patient really at the centre of your business? Or is he part of the context without really understanding his deeper expectations?

Self-care and Wellness industry

Traditionally, people only took an interest in their health when they were unwell. These customers were part of the healthcare and medical industry that revolved around treating rather than preventing disease. But healthcare costs are rising faster than the GDP of most developed countries. Knowing that modifiable behaviours account for 71% of annual deaths globally, it becomes increasingly important to deal with those behaviours. As described in the previous section, the healthcare industry is therefore increasingly focusing on self-care and prevention, not least in introducing outcome-based models. But customers themselves are also increasingly aware that their health problems are related to their health and well-being decisions. The wellness industry could be very useful in the area of prevention.

But the wellness industry isn't driven primarily by doctors and governments. Wellness is mostly customer-driven. If our contact with the wellness market was previously limited to an occasional visit to the gym or sauna, in the past few years consumer behaviours have changed profoundly. For more and more people, self-care and wellness is evolving from rare to daily, from episodic to essential, from a luxury to a dominant lifestyle value. From sunup to sundown, people want to be(come) and feel healthy. It affects their decision-making when purchasing food, reducing stress, or incorporating exercise because they expect it to improve their happiness in terms of having more energy, feeling beautiful, or being able to enjoy life.

Today, the self-care and wellness industry is one of the most lucrative businesses to be in because everybody wants better health or strives to be as happy as possible. The Global Wellness Institute, a non-profit research centre that represents 10 sectors under its overarching umbrella, reported that the global wellness economy reached USD4.2 trillion in 2017 far surpassing the pharmaceutical industry. Today, it makes up 5.3% of global economic output. With growth that is twice as fast as global economic growth, it is bound to remain one of the world's biggest and fastest-growing industries.

GLOBAL WELLNESS ECONOMY:
$4.2 trillion in 2017

Traditional & Complementary Medicine **$360b**

Wellness Real Estate **$134b**

Personal Care, Beauty & Anti-Ageing **$1,083b**

Wellness Tourism **$639b**

Workplace Wellness **$48b**

Thermal/ Mineral Springs **$56b**

Preventive & Personalised Medicine and Public Health **$575b**

Spa Economy **$119b**

Healthy Eating, Nutrition & Weight Loss **$702b**

Fitness & Mind-Body **$595b**

Source: Global Wellness Institute

In our daily conversations, wellness is most easily linked with healthy eating, weight control, fitness, mental health, and the spa economy. However, these only make up 35% of the self-care and wellness industry. Both Personal and Beauty care, as well as Preventative and Alternative Medicine each make up another 25% of the wellness cake. The biggest growth is realised by sectors such as Wellness Tourism, Lifestyle Real Estate, and Corporate Wellness. These might be less well-known but are becoming immensely popular.

> *With about 830 million wellness trips in 2017, Wellness Tourism already represents 17% of total tourism expenditures. The global Spa market is expected to accelerate and grow by 35% in the next five years, according to Technavio (2018). "Wellness tourism" is the fastest growing travel sector*

(Lonely Planet, 2018) while wellness real estate developments make up about 2% of the annual global construction market and are tipping from niche to mainstream (Global Wellness Institute, 2018).

Driven by their Healthusiasm, people incorporate more wellness values into their lives. This makes their interaction with the wellness economy more holistic and integrative. For example, customers who shop in one particular sector are more likely to buy wellness services in other sectors as well. They approach their health holistically. If you exercise, you are most likely interested in healthy eating as well. If you like spas, you might be interested in wellness trips too. This makes it interesting for different sectors of the wellness industry to blend or to expand from one to another. Think of the yoga classes that now also offer retreats, or how the mental health app Headspace successfully partners with apparel brand Nike.

People also want wellness to be integrated into the different parts of their lives. Fitness, for example, is no longer solely relegated to the gym. It is now integrated into your vacation, workplace, technology or beauty routine. The choice of hotel you book on a business or holiday trip might be determined by the availability and quality of the fitness facilities. At work, you can participate in yoga classes or sit at a "biking desk". Your make-up preference might be one that is sweat-resistant for your after-work workout. As it is part of our daily ambition to live healthily and happily, we expect self-care and wellness to potentially be part of the different moments of our (daily) lives.

With self-care and wellness becoming an integral part of our values, do you know which of your products or services can blend into the different moments of the (daily) lives of customers?

Lifestyle industry

The Lifestyle industry is composed of brands that attempt, through marketing, to embody the values, aspirations, interests, attitudes, or opinions of a group.

Typical Lifestyle brands range from sectors such as electronics, beauty and clothing to furniture and food. They seek to attract customers by positioning their offering in line with the customer's lifestyle. By choosing these brands, people confirm their style of living. Customers establish their identities by choosing brands whose stereotypical users are perceived to be similar to their own self-images. In doing so, brands become a way of life. They sell a lifestyle.

Healthusiasm suits lifestyle brands just perfectly. Earlier, I described how Healthusiasm is not only about managing or predicting a disease, nor is it only about maintaining health or feeling good. In fact, Healthusiasm is also about the desirable image of health-consciousness. Lifestyle brands can play into that specific desire by positioning themselves accordingly. Fitness wearables can confirm someone's healthy image as much as buying that cool bike for the ride to work does. Customers can opt for paint without harmful particles, they can walk around daily in activewear, and can pretentiously buy healthily. Many sectors can be influenced by the Healthusiasm lifestyle because it simply is "cool" for people to be health-conscious today. One of the biggest industries in the world, the food industry, is certainly impacted by the aspiration to be healthy and happy.

Since the early 1980s, nutrition-related behaviours have emerged as one of the most frequent activities that support health. This behaviour or interest in health is a key motive in the choice of food and gives products with health claims noticeable advantages over competitors. That's why food retailers and manufacturers have eagerly positioned themselves as health friendly, targeting those health-conscious consumers. They responded by increasingly selling healthy food options, providing nutritional information on labels and reviewing the use of additives. Back in the 1980s, Tesco established a list of contentious additives to remove from its products and had labels on all of their products by 1987. Other food corporations soon followed that example as companies like Pizza Hut stopped using artificial flavours and colours.

Today, food and beverage companies still focus continuously on making products healthier. But in the meantime, with an annual growth of 8%, organic food has replaced "sugar free" and "low carb". Kraft Heinz recently spoke about giving their well-known brands a health update, because sales of their non-organic products like Capri Sun have declined in recent years. Suntory, the company that brings you Orangina and Schwepps, among other consumer beverages, changed their company's mission to "growing for good" and aims to contribute to a healthy lifestyle through products and services. Deloitte confirmed that 88% of companies have launched products that were formulated or reformulated to support healthier diets and lifestyles.

Technavio analysts forecast that this trend will not stop any time soon. The healthy lifestyle food market is expected to grow 6% annually in the next five years. In fact, the entire USD13 trillion food and grocery retail industry will continue to develop at a similar pace, with non-packaged healthier foods at the forefront of the market. Failing to establish a health-conscious image certainly puts food companies under heavy pressure. In fact, revenues of most of the US-based traditional packaged food producers have fallen considerably since 2017 compared to the overall S&P 500 Index.

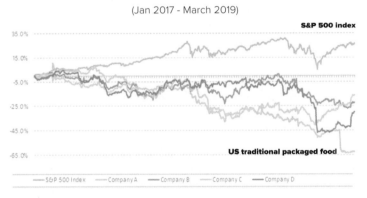

US TRADITIONAL PACKAGED FOOD VERSUS THE S&P 500 INDEX
(Jan 2017 - March 2019)

Source: Robeco Trends Investing

It is very difficult to put an exact value on the Lifestyle industry. There are so many sectors involved, even more brands and products, and desired lifestyles vary. Intelligence provider GlobalData, then called Conlumino (2014), analysed the UK retail market, attributing certain brands to the Lifestyle industry. They reported that between 2008 and 2013, the lifestyle brand segment in the UK grew almost 12 times as fast as the overall market. Actually, the main growth within the retail market came from the Lifestyle brands that identified themselves with the characteristics that matched aspirations like be(com)ing healthy and happy. From its position as the smallest segment in the market, the Lifestyle industry grew bigger than the Luxury segment. Brands that help customers to confirm their health-conscious image are now more attractive in the market than traditional luxury products.

What attributes of your business play rightfully into the health-conscious image of your customers? What actions can you take to sincerely speak to their health concerns?

Healthusiasm Business

Healthusiasm is here for the long haul. It's very much present within different industries and requires companies to approach their customers' aspiration to be(come) healthy and happy more strategically. But while Healthusiasm is changing the dynamics within the Medical, Wellness and Lifestyle industries, it also creates new opportunities beyond the boundaries of each industry. Customer expectations towards a company don't just stay within industry boundaries. After all, Healthusiasm is now ingrained in our lives. Companies can mean something to their customers beyond the offering of their typical industry-related products and services. That's why many companies from one particular industry are now expanding their offerings into other industries. Lifestyle brands are moving into the Wellness and Medical industry, as much as medical companies are moving into the Wellness business. The three following examples will showcase how companies or brands can address expectations that were previously met by different industries, or not all. This drive to help people be(come) healthy and happy is typical for the Healthusiasm business.

Supermarkets

Supermarkets from around the world now offer several services or experiences that meet the typical customer expectations within the Lifestyle, Wellness ànd Medical industries: an entire section of their store is dedicated to healthy foods so that health-conscious customers identify themselves with the space. To offer their clients convenience within their hectic daily schedules, the retailer has extended opening hours. Wallmart, for example, organises several times a year a "health day" during which customers have their health analysed and can discuss it with professionals. For shoppers with particular sensory needs, like patients with autism, PTSD or dementia, it has already been mentioned that retailers start offering a sensory-friendly shopping experience with noise-cancelling headphones or even open the store exclusively to these customers at specific times. Patients with Crohn's disease can easily find recipes that are appropriate for their bowel syndrome. The same goes for diabetic patients, arthritic patients and many others. The in-house pharmacy can then again allow patients to shop for everything in one location. No longer is the supermarket just a place where customers can buy goods, but where they can experience services tailored to their specific needs. Both patients and customers can purchase products, services and experiences that make them healthy and happy. Retailers are expanding their offering in the light of the Healthusiasm trend.

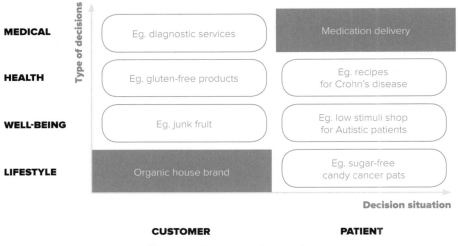

The cross-industry supermarket example

Pharmaceutical companies

Today, pharmaceutical companies no longer sell only medications to patients. A company with a medication for Crohn's disease now also offers recipes that help sufferers to avoid symptom-inducing ingredients. They help patients to deal with disease-related fatigue by providing them with insights into how to feel better physically. In collecting and sharing tips from other patients, they motivate them to continue to live the lifestyle they desire. Travel tips, work-related documents, or conversation starters can all contribute to improving the patients' lifestyle. With their expert knowledge of the functioning of the intestines and the potential development of bowel syndromes, pharmaceutical companies can also advise people on how to live more healthily. They can even put their scientific knowledge of the bowel at disposal of all people out there. No longer are they purely manufacturers of medication. They are providing patients and non-patients with the necessary help in taking Healthusiastic decisions every day. However, these services are still largely contained within the medical industry, but it should not necessarily be the case. Channels outside the medical industry, like supermarkets, wellness centres, or beauty magazines are sometimes even better placed to reach people with that information.

The cross 'industry' pharmaceutical company example

Dr. John's Healthy Sweets

Finally, single products are meeting expectations beyond the boundaries of a single industry. Dr John's candies are a good example. When dentist Dr John Bruinsma realised that sugar-free sweets tasted terrible, he started a company to create great tasting sugar-free sweets. His intention was to bring an alternative to patients with many cavities, within the boundaries of the dental industry. About 20 years on, this company has become the most innovative and healthiest sweet manufacturer in the world. By creating the world's first xylitol-based lollipop, he actually created the first popular sweet that prevents cavities. Thanks to the use of xylitol, the bacteria in the mouth that cause dental decay decrease in number, lessening the chance of a new cavity forming. Just recently, Dr John's company also released a nutritional line of sweets that contain fibre and probiotics. This allows children with cancer, for example, to enjoy a "sweet" and experience a normal childhood delight. And the added fibre and probiotics are critical in both preventing the child's health from becoming worse and managing their compromised immune system. What started as a sugar-free sweet for people with lots of cavities grew to become a popular sweet sold on Amazon, meeting expectations far beyond the boundaries of the dental industry. Thrive Ice Cream is a similar example of a product in the healthcare industry that not only addresses malnutrition in the elderly, but also helps athletes to perform better and supports customers with weight management.

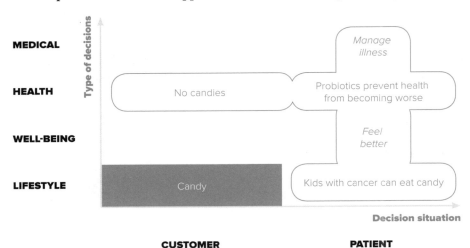

The cross 'industry' candy example

*What expectations that previously were met by business
from different industries would organically fit
or extend your business expertise or knowledge?*

Healthusiasm summary

In a world where technology increasingly meets our needs, people are becoming more aware of their health and happiness. At least half of the population, regardless of whether they are sick or not, actively manages their health. But in fact, everybody is more health-conscious today than they were in the past. More than ever before, both men and women are focused on living healthily. And while each generation may have their own background and current reality as a source of motivation, today they all strive to be(come) the healthiest and happiest version of themselves. Every day people are making decisions to be(come) healthy. Every day, they are making decisions to be(come) as happy as possible. While this often may look like a very cool and fashionable thing to do, this trend is certainly not short-term hype. It is actually a radical societal shift that has been growing on us for many years. Being healthy is a fundamental need. We've always believed we could positively influence our health, even by praying to the gods. But digital disruption has finally made it possible for us to have an impact on our own body. We can go all out to become the person we want to be. This empowerment has slowly changed our society and has become the new normal. Customer expectations have changed because of it and are even altering the dynamics within each industry.

Today, companies are looking for ways to make their customers healthy and happy. They offer the products, services and experiences that mean something to their customers, and won't let the industry boundaries limit them in doing so. The only way to truly connect with customers today is by bringing transformations to the market that fit their aspirations and values. That's why marketing is evolving from being product driven to being meaningful to the customers and their aspirations.

In the next chapter will be explained how marketing evolved into something transformation-driven. Health marketing will then be elaborated upon as the version of transformation-driven marketing that fits the Healthusiasm trend. With examples from different industries will be illustrated how companies and brands are meeting the customers' need to be(com)ing healthy & happy. Finally, a specific focus will be held on how the healthcare and pharmaceutical sector are growing towards transformation-driven health marketing.

Health Marketing

Marketing evolution

Marketing is a widely used word. Most people today are probably able to explain what it means. "Activities to sell more products and services" would likely be most mentioned. That definition is immediately associated with a prevalent negative connotation. Marketing is seen as something that lures them into buying stuff, like the snake oil salesman who throws arguments at the naïve listener to trick them into the purchase. But should it really be considered a bad thing today? Isn't marketing playing into the actual needs of customers?

There are many different theories about how marketing is evolving. Many are structured in line with how technological evolution is facilitating marketing. I prefer aligning the marketing evolution with the evolution in customer needs as described by Maslow.

Product-driven marketing

Of course, attempts to sell are as old as civilisation itself. The development of persuasive communications to sell goods and services has been around since the times of ancient China and India. However, it wasn't until the Industrial Revolution that marketing really came about. In that era, it became easier for people to buy goods instead of making them. Mass production created a growing need for products, and many producers wanted to serve these customers' needs. It wasn't until the late 1940s, when competition became more intense, that using techniques to sell goods became part of competition. Companies had to explain how great their product was. The goal was to convince customers that the goods from one company were better than the ones from another company that actually sold the same thing.

By the 1960s, markets were so saturated that marketing became a discipline that was needed to survive in the business world. Companies reflected on how best to sell products. As markets grew with the increasing wealth in Western society, companies started bringing different products to different customer segments. In the 1980s, market research enabled customer differentiation by life stage or social standing (*socio-demographics*). Companies then defined the *product* that specific customers might want, the *price* customers would need to pay, the *place* to make the product accessible to the customer, and the *promotion* of the product. This 4Ps marketing model, introduced by Jerome McCarthy and Philip Kotler, was widely used during these years.

Product-driven marketing strategies addressed the customer's *mind* with product-related arguments by using a mega-phone approach. It was about how certain products outperformed others based on features. Product-driven marketing answered the functional needs of customers. In the following decades, marketing turned these performance statements into branding. Strengthened by recognisable logos, colours and slogans, brand reputation made customers want brands even more. Volvo was about safety. Mr Proper was the most efficient way to clean. Marketing created brands with an identity based upon the products features that matched a socio-demographic customer segment. As customers could identify themselves with this brand identity, they were more easily persuaded to buy the product.

Customer-driven marketing

In the 1980s, different customers started to adopt particular lifestyles in search of status. They were motivated to understand to what extent brands matched their lifestyle needs and behaviours. The value of the product was no longer solely determined by the main product feature of a brand. The value of the product became increasingly defined by how it matched the customer's emotional needs. Could they identify the brand with their lifestyle? Does the brand confirm their status and feed their self-esteem? It was all about the customer's attitude and perception. The customer became king and companies became more customer-focused. In that period, market research enabled companies to better understand their customers, structure them into different *psychographic* segments, and identify products and brands tailored to their needs and motivations. Different products were brought to market so that customers could choose from a wide range of functional features and corresponding identities. Customer-driven marketing did not only address the functional needs of its customers, but it also spoke to the emotional needs of people. It was about appealing to the minds and the *hearts* of the customers.

But just like technology facilitated mass production and the consequent need for product-driven marketing, technology amplified the need for customer-driven marketing as well. The first waves of digital disruption empowered customers more than ever. They could then research and compare the quality of a product before buying it. By 2006, research by Forrester indicated that 76% of people used comparison sites or customer reviews. With the rise of social media and the widespread use of smartphones, this trend was amplified. Brands were created or at least confirmed within the communities on social media. Typical one-way marketing promotion now even evolved into online conversations on social media and within customer reviews. Customer decisions no longer relied solely on brand advertisement but were much more influenced by friends, network connections or influencers. A mega-phone approach could still help to create brand awareness (minds) but probably wouldn't suffice to convince customers emotionally (hearts).

What part of your marketing strategy speaks to the hearts of your customers to the extent that it actually initiates conversations among them?

Digital disruption allowed the empowerment of customers even more. And the evolution of market research is a good example. Market research was typically used to create customer segmentation in the early days of customer-driven marketing. But brands could now target specific customer communities and actually co-create with them. Brands conducted more immersive research to not only listen with empathy to the members of the communities, but to open up direct dialogue with them. By collaborating with the community, brands are co-creating products, services and experiences directly with their customers. Putting the customer at the centre of everything made brands and companies evolve from being customer-focused to being customer-driven. Lego is a very good example of this approach. They state that 99.9% of the smartest people work outside their company and therefore are structurally collaborating with them.

Marketing communication transformed into two-way customer conversations. Research became a vehicle to co-create. Digital and mobile solutions amplified customer-driven marketing and customer experience became the main field of competition, according to 89% of the business leaders surveyed by Gartner (2014). But Artificial Intelligence will play an even more significant role in customer-driven marketing as it will impact the entire customer experience. Data, connected devices and automation may not be that visible, but they will reinforce customer-centric strategies. Data will feed algorithms to help customers make decisions (for example, Zalando makes specific suggestions based on your previous choices), as well as learning what innovations to bring to the market, and for whom. Connected devices learn about your personal behaviour and generate contextual customer services in real-time. Automation will facilitate digital relationships and manage the purchasing process. This enhanced experience defines the value of the brand. A good experience will make the customer have enjoyable memories and make them loyal. Customers will feel understood and properly treated. Bad experiences will discourage the customer from investing time again in the future.

Customer-driven marketing answers the emotional needs of customers. In the past decades it extended from lifestyle-confirming products into experience-enhancing solutions. However, both will continue to coexist and will require additional skills and expertise within the marketing team. For the brand to be recognised across all channels, it needs to be consistent in the customer-focused experiences it offers. A visual depiction of a logo and a slogan that states a product performance will no longer suffice to create a recognisable brand.

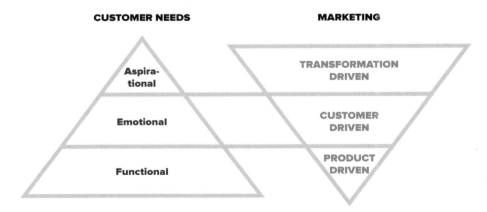

As customer needs evolve, marketing needed to evolve to answer these needs.

Transformation-driven marketing

In a third shift, marketing really becomes human-centric. In this evolution, customers are seen as having a mind, heart and *soul*. This means that marketing no longer communicates only product features (mind) or customer-driven experiences (heart), but also speaks to their *soul*. Customers don't want products to just answer their functional and emotional needs, but they expect brands to help them in their search for self-actualisation. It's perhaps the most humane evolution of marketing, in which brands actually focus on the entire person. This means marketing is now addressing customer concerns that go beyond the product, the quality, the attributed status or the customer experience. Customer-driven algorithms within the AI-first reality, may (soon) have the power to automate customer decisions (as explained in a previous chapter), but customers are very unlikely to allow it from brands that don't support their own core beliefs and aspirations.

Would your customers let your algorithm make a decision for them, because they fully believe in the values and aspirations of your company?

Driven by concerns about their health, societal issues or environmental despoliation, people are increasingly looking for answers and solutions governments can't seem to solve. In fact, the Earned Brand study by Edelman (2017) reported that customers believe brands can do more to solve these concerns than government can. Customers expect that brands will take on issues that matter to them. In fact, 86% of customers want brands to take a stand on social issues, according to Sheldon Group (2018). You could justifiably say that customers "believe" that brands could be considered an alternative democracy because they enable them to vote with their wallet or smartphone. They feel they can control their relationship with a brand more easily than with a polarised, paralysed government. As mentioned in earlier chapters, customers are indeed seeking companies and brands to help them transform their environment (Ecotional trend), their lives (Societeam trend) and themselves (Healthusiasm trend). Marketing is expected to answer these aspirations and values. More than ever, marketing needs to bring hope. In differentiating themselves from other brands (and governments), they will connect with customers on a deeper level. They will earn their trust.

*Looking at your recent marketing activities,
which one of them brings hope to your customers?
Which one really earns their trust?*

It's important to note that transformation-driven marketing goes beyond what we know as Corporate Social Responsibility. It's not only about ethical communication, contributions to charity or giving back to the community. Customers need to recognise a consistent brand personality that confirms its aspirations through everything it does in this world. Therefore, this personality should be ingrained in the core of the company and in each of its products. Transformation-driven marketing should live within the entire organisation and leave the employees even more proud than the customers who choose these brands. It is no longer only about brand lobbying or creating awareness. It's actually all about brand activism. Companies should have the ambition to make a difference where others can't.

Patagonia, a privately-owned outdoor clothing brand, has a distinguished record of environmental philanthropy and investment. For about 10 years now, the company has run ongoing campaigns to encourage a national conversation about the threat posed to the planet by a global economy that depends on relentless growth and consumerism. Back in 2011, it created a memorable full-page advertisement on Black Friday that said: "Don't buy this jacket". The text of the advertisement broke down the environmental footprint of one jacket and urged customers to think twice before buying this, or any other product for that matter. The company is well known for similar campaigns that encourage customers to think about a responsible economy. The company itself promises to make products that last longer, and to repair, resell, or recycle them as necessary. In fact, repair and recycling is a growing part of its business model. The company even

tours around the States to help repair outdoor gear and sell used Patago-
nia products along the way. In 2018, their initiatives moved beyond cus-
tomer-facing communication campaigns. Patagonia sued the US Federal
Government for downsizing Bears Ears National Monument by two million
acres (shrinking Bears Ears by 85%) to expand oil and gas extraction.

This transformation-driven marketing allowed Patagonia to deeply con-
nect with a largely untapped market of sophisticated customers who sup-
port the brand's anti-consumerism in thoughtfully consuming its products.
So, while the company is reducing the environmental footprint of the cloth-
ing they produce, it increases the footprint of the company as it grows. But
Patagonia strongly believes that the new economy must grow from be-
neath the old one. They are allowing customers to live a more responsible
life with the apparel that they choose.

Health marketing

Health marketing is a form of transformation-driven marketing that feeds
Healthusiasm. By adapting their offering, it solves customers' health and happiness concerns. It helps people in achieving their health ambitions by putting
relevant products, services and experiences at disposal. Health marketing is
the creation of value for customers who aspire to be(come) healthy and happy,
regardless of whether they are sick or not. It's about "helping" them to make
healthy decisions in everyday situations, from establishing a healthy lifestyle
to managing a (future) disease.

How do you help your customers to make decisions
that positively impact their health?

There are many examples today of the way companies are playing into Healthusiasm with health marketing strategies and tactics. Some industries have made major strides, while others are taking their first baby steps. But embarking on health marketing often starts with smaller, tactical initiatives, like removing artificial additives from certain products. But what is first an isolated tactic, will slowly spread across the company like a healthy virus and become an overall strategy. As with all additives, artificial colouring and e-numbers are currently being removed from about 10 000 different products retailers offer to confirm their Healthusiasm strategy. But neither does it stop with adapting or launching products, services and experiences. Slowly companies will understand they need to create a brand identity to which Healthusiastic customers can relate. Their own Healthusiasm needs to be summarised in their promise to the market. That's exactly why we've seen retailers change their slogans from price-focused claims to mottos that put a good and healthy life first. Walmart changed their tagline from "Always low prices" to the more aspirational "Save money, live better". But many other retailers have brought their life-altering ambitions to the forefront of their brand identity too.

Walmart's *previous mission statement was about being the best retailer in the hearts and minds of customers. The retailer now focuses more on experiences that actually transform their customers. They now also speak to the soul of customers by addressing their aspirations. Already five years ago, more than 10% of their revenue derived from health-related products and services. To answer this increasing demand, in 2014, Walmart launched a "Healthcare begins here" event. For one day, it offered their 150 million weekly visitors a guide to a healthier life by offering free access to several preventative services such as blood pressure measurement, immunisation and food advice. The success of this event has made it a re-*

curring theme in Walmart's experiential marketing strategy. Walmart really strives to transform people by uniting a wide range of Health and Wellness products and services (4 500 pharmacies, 3 000 vision clinics, 1 000 digital health kiosks, and several emergency clinics) while expanding into new programmes and products based on customer needs (for example, health literacy tools, insurance assistance, and food recommendations). They really want their customers to "live better".

It may sound like a very obvious strategic move for a retailer to focus on health marketing, but this started with a tactical action several decades ago. Similarly, we now see other industries making their first moves into health marketing. Lego launching "Mia's Organic Food Market" building set is obviously no more than a confirmation of the importance of organic food today or a way to address the lifestyle of health-conscious people. But in the next examples, it will become clear how some brands are making their first conscious steps into health marketing, while other industries are shifting gear more radically in addressing the aspirational needs of their customers.

__Netflix__ has become a household name in the past couple of years. It is essentially a storehouse for all types of content, ranging from movies and documentaries to TV series, that is available for a flat monthly subscription fee. But the online platform actually changed the way people watch television. In a time marked by on-demand services, Netflix created the best experience for a night on the couch. By collecting data on its users' preferred series or movies, an algorithm will suggest the titles that best fit your personal taste. And once you click "play", the episodes will roll one after the other without you having to leave your couch. Binge watching, the phenomenon of watching multiple episodes, has existed since series were distributed on DVD. But it wasn't until Netflix hit the home screens that over 60% of the population using on-demand services actually began binge watching. Of course, staying glued to your couch can't be good for your health. In a world that has been focusing on obesity for the past few decades, this new trend is not welcomed. Studies have even shown a correlation between binge watching and depression. The image of Netflix suffered quite a bit from this, because its link with binge watching was that strong. In fact, in October 2018 an Indian binge watcher made the news globally for having himself institutionalised for his addiction to Netflix. It was time for Netflix to come up with a first tactical health marketing move: you can now make your favourite series character into a personal – yet digital – coach that will oblige you to work out before the next episode can be unlocked, or that will pause your episode if you don't keep up with the tempo of your exercises while watching Netflix. With this innovation, Netflix makes it possible to personalise your experience into a transformation. It's unclear whether other health initiatives will follow, but this one surely was needed to manage their image in an increasingly health conscious world. In a similar fashion and at approximately the same time, the NBA 2K game offered additional credits to gamers once they've done 10 000 steps in a day. **Google** and **Apple** also introduced screen-time functionality into their operating systems as a similar health marketing tactic. Just as people risk being glued to their couch, people are easily glued to their phone. Operating systems now calculate average weekly screen-time to promote awareness in their users and enable them to improve their habits.

In an industry characterised by cold transactions, **Alfa Bank** in Russia initiated health marketing by rewarding their most healthy clients with higher interest rates. After connecting an activity tracker to their Alfa Bank account, money is automatically transferred to another account each time the customer logs an activity. As this account offers exclusively the highest interest rate at the bank, this marketing strategy not only attracts new "healthy" customers, but also motivates current customers to exercise (and remain with the bank).

L'Oreal is meanwhile also known to heavily focus on health marketing. Of course, skin care by definition is a form of health management. But L'Oreal is helping their customers in making the right decisions everywhere they are. After all, our skin reacts to our environment. If you or your child spends too much time in the sun, you protect yourself with sunscreen or look for shade. In 2016, L'Oreal began offering their customers patches to help parents monitor sun exposure. The company later launched a clip-on device, My Skin Track UV, to not only monitor and analyse environmental exposure to UV but also to offer information on exposure to pollution, pollen and humidity. The accompanying app then helps customers make appropriate decisions related to their skin care, making sure customers manage their skin in the best possible way in each condition or environment. The recently launched pH tracker complements *this data with insights on the acidity levels of the skin itself. As varying pH levels do cause inflammatory skin conditions like eczema and dryness, this tool becomes of interest to dermatologists. By offering new tools to its stakeholders, L'Oreal is creating value by transforming their customers into people with the best possible skin.*

PRODUCTS – SERVICES – EXPERIENCES – TRANSFORMATIONS

*Netflix and Apple acted from a PR strategy to counter a negative image. Alfa Bank initiated a customer acquisition and retention strategy with health marketing. L'Oreal is making skin care choices well-founded and personal with health driven innovations. **Mercedes-Benz**, on the other hand, embarked on health marketing to take advantage of a huge opportunity for its drivers. People spend on average a little over an hour a day in the car. Next to our home and our work environment, the car is probably the place that we spend the third greatest amount of time. It has actually transformed the car into a personal "living" space in which people seek and enjoy comfort. Early in 2017, at the Consumer Electronics Show (CES) in Vegas, Mercedes-Benz launched a concept car that will improve driver experience, comfort and health through the use of data. The Fit and Healthy car not only syncs with fitness trackers and other external health sensors, but the steering wheel itself has sensors that monitor the driver's vital signs every time they hit the road. Together with other external data, like traffic data, weather info or scheduled commitments, the driver will be presented with a tailor-made offer for enhancing their well-being such as seat massages when driving for a longer period, stimulating or relaxing music to suit the driver's mood*

> *and traffic conditions, and matching climate control including fragrance and suitable ambient lighting. Mercedes believes that drivers should arrive at their destination feeling better and fitter than when they got into the vehicle. It's no longer about driver experience, it's about transformation. Many of these features are present in the latest S-models. But Mercedes wants to continue to create value with their health marketing strategy. Through a strategic partnership with Philips, a leading provider in the field of healthcare technology, it jointly researches future health applications. If you still doubt the dedication Mercedes-Benz currently applies to health marketing, take a look at the many health and well-being articles that are to be found on the Mercedes-Benz.com website. A website from a car manufacturer might not be your top-of-mind source for health information, but many magazines or blogs would envy the amount as well as the quality of content to be found there.*

Companies from various industries are applying Health Marketing to create value, bringing products, services and experiences to the market that feed the aspirational needs of their customers. This is a new approach for industries that previously were not focused on the health and happiness of their customers. But don't be mistaken in thinking that Health Marketing has been exercised by the healthcare and pharmaceutical industries for decades. These industries have of course been applying marketing tactics to "sell" their health services, but they are also making their first marks on this new transformation-driven marketing. The healthcare and pharmaceutical industries are facing their own challenges. But they do realise that Health Marketing will be necessary to remain relevant to their customers.

Healthcare marketing

Health marketing is easily confused with healthcare marketing. But health*care* marketing refers to the efforts by hospitals, care institutions, patient associations and associated doctors to communicate about their services with patients. Do healthcare institutions need marketing? Well, it is true that patients in Europe are still largely referred to care providers by general practitioners. But the importance of properly communicating about their services has become more important than ever for care institutions. After all, patients increasingly shop for health services. They might seek a second or third opinion, they might opt for the easiest and earliest appointment, they might prefer the experience that has been praised within their own (online) network. This new dynamic, often called the consumerisation of healthcare, has truly made the healthcare market increasingly competitive. Hospitals and care institutions are therefore putting in more effort to attract new patients or to satisfy the current ones and keep them "loyal".

In fact, for 80% of all healthcare needs that drive someone to choose a doctor or hospital, people begin with (online) research. From a sudden cold to excruciating abdominal pain, more and more people are searching the internet to find out what's wrong with them. Within that search they are now more likely to look for solutions as well. What do I need to do? Where do I need to go? Who is trustworthy? If possible, people will even book an appointment immediately.

How is your care institution appealing to the emotional and aspirational needs of your patients?

However, it is now not sufficient to approach the patient as a someone who simply needs their problem taken care of. It is still necessary to inform patients about the services available but communicating the features or characteristics of a service is the bare minimum. Care institutions will have to answer more than the functional needs of patients in order to attract them and differentiate themselves from other healthcare institutions. People will only be engaged if they feel the care institutions bring the emotional and aspirational value they are looking for. It's about reassuring patients about the experience and the overall focus on health management. Only then will people be engaged.

Patient experience

As patients are actively involved in their healthcare choices, patient satisfaction has become paramount for healthcare institutions. But this does not mean that doctors need to meet all the expectations of the patient. It's not about keeping the patient happy by ordering tests or prescribing drugs that are unnecessary or carry risks. It's not about avoiding difficult conversations like the need to lose weight, quit smoking or cut down on alcohol. It's first and foremost about ensuring a good experience for patients. For example, nurses could check up on the patient every other hour to establish the perception of availability but hamper the patient's rest in doing so. Patient experience requires focus on the technical as well as the emotional benefit for the patient. Understanding both the patient's functional and emotional needs is therefore essential. Little wonder that in recent years many hospitals have appointed a Chief Experience Officer and that patient experience has become one of the most important internal measures. Care institutions are now putting the patient at the core of everything they do because it's as much about the outcome of the service as the experience with service delivery.

For each of your services, how can you optimise the emotional benefit for your customer?

Within healthcare, even though a lot of things are out of our control, care institutions can control the way they make us feel. Patients typically face situations that generate a lot of anxiety. Every step in the patient journey can be characterised by uncertainty. This is very impactful for patients and, more often than not, this is simply because information is lacking. Information and communication have always been the biggest needs for patients and their caregivers. The fact that they rely so much on the care team for information means that trust in the healthcare professional is a determining factor of the experience with the care institution. Healthcare institutions are therefore focusing on strengthening the bond between the patient and the healthcare professional (HCP). But that does not mean that each HCP should bring all the answers. Neither does it mean that they should be at the disposal of their patients at all times. Communication as a one-way push is long gone. Ideally HCPs should facilitate a consistent two-way conversation, and refer patients to channels optimised for specific support, such as YouTube videos, leaflets, patient groups, and advanced digital tools. Patients should not take their own notes and make their own action plan. The hospital should be helping them to access the information they need, when they need it.

*Hospital marketers at the **Mayo Clinic** crafted one of the first customer-driven social strategies. The world-renowned medical institution created a YouTube channel that offered interviews with doctors, how-to videos and stories about everyday-people receiving care. Patients get firsthand reports of the experience at the Mayo Clinic, from check-in to follow-up care. It's an effective means of educating patients about their entire journey while promoting the hospital as a patient-centric institution. Video marketing is an easy tool that has been widely followed by other hospitals. But even though those firsthand reports are based on true stories, the related pre-produced videos might not feel authentic. Real-life experiences are perhaps more trustworthy. That's why the Mayo Clinic even allows patients to share their real-life experiences on the hospital website. This initiative goes beyond the typical 'Office of Patient Experiences' that answers your calls or complaints. It allows patients to share their experience with others, in social media style. Healthcare providers can learn from these firsthand stories, while the hospital is provided with opportunities to improve quality. One of the improvements based on this type of patient feedback was related to the use of tablets and smartphones: to make the patient feel cared about and establish that two-way conversation as much as possible, Mayo Clinic has installed "a cultural norm" that healthcare providers don't look at their smartphones or tablets when near a patient. That way the doctor's gaze isn't directed downwards, but rather towards the patient. Based on patient-driven suggestions, the Mayo Clinic now manages to better deal with the emotional needs of patients. "The best interest of the patient is the only interest to be considered."*

Even if two-way communications are being established, healthcare will always remain an emotionally driven environment that impacts each person individually. It has become critical for healthcare institutions to not only provide their patients with memorable experiences that inform and delight, but to also invite action. Patients have always desired a stress-free experience, but they now require influence and impact. For a start, patients can be given some sense of control over their physical environment and access to information they need about their diagnosis. But taking matters into their own hands has never been as prevalent as today. Patients want to have the knowledge, but also the control and the tools to impact their own body. Healthcare institutions should therefore explore where, when and how much patients could help themselves with certain activities, decisions, and self-care. To succeed in this patient-centric objective, however, the only way is this: healthcare institutions should be intensively involving patients and caregivers to co-create the best experience together.

> *Perhaps the most remarkable hospital experience is offered by **Bornriget Children's Hospital** in Copenhagen. Several hundred children, parents and employees gathered on a two-day camp to focus on the future hospital building. They were involved in user panels, eye-tracking research, workshops, simulations, steering committees and management meetings. With this direct input and intensive co-creation, 100 different patient pathways were identified and gathered in several design principles. These principles served to build a children's kingdom (Bornriget in Danish) that primarily focuses on every single experience of the patient and their relatives, while guaranteeing professionalism, excellence and expertise. Because children don't stop playing when they are sick, the hospital emphasises the power of play as an integral part of medical treatment and patient experience. It will create an environment where the family can stay close to the patient to have a life as close to what they are used to. The entire architecture will implement the vision that physical surroundings and sensory experiences can soothe patients and aid their healing process. Because it is very hard to predict future changes with the exponential impact of technology, the entire building is being built with flexibility in mind. If you are interested in knowing more about this exceptional project, the hospital has created a 100-page guide that explains their approach to parents and other hospitals. It is worth visit-*

Entrance at the Bornriget Children's Hospital in Copenhagen.

ing the rigshospitalet.dk website to discover the incredible, well thought-through experience they have created with patients.

Improving patient experience does not mean that healthcare institutions need to reinvent hot water. They can easily take cues from within retail, airports, hotels or even experience champions like Disney and Airbnb. Should they go for a parking valet, an entry waterfall, live music in restaurants, custom-ordered room service meals, kitchenettes or VIP lounges? After all, Destination Medical Center (DMC) research shows that in-hospital patients have four to five hours of free time per day. That is time they might want to spend doing other things besides waiting for appointments. Having 10 chairs in a waiting room simply does not scream "good patient experience". Improving patient experience is about finding the right comfort for patients because comfort is all about being patient-driven.

Would you want a hospital to have the comfort of a hotel, Airbnb, Disney World or an airport?

Wellness focus

The first time that people really wanted to actively impact their fitness and health was during the fitness craze in the 1980s. Most people were absorbed by a popular culture now remembered for lycra, up-tempo beats and home fitness videos. At the time, hospitals did put in the first considerable efforts to answer the rising needs for education and information. Wellness and perhaps even prevention actually enjoyed their first initiatives in that decade. Fast forward 30+ years, and this early attention really accelerated into a shift in focus in the entire industry. Driven by an imperative of reducing costs, hospitals are now increasingly concentrating their efforts on a holistic approach from prevention to overall health management. When done right, it's a focus that speaks to the aspiration of their patients. It's not just about the right service (*minds*) with the right experience (*hearts*), but it's about offering a transformation (*souls*) for people to be(come) as healthy and happy as possible.

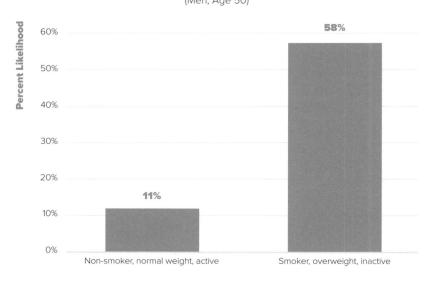

LIKELIHOOD OF DEVELOPING HEART DISEASE, STROKE OR DIABETES BY AGE 65

(Men, Age 50)

Source: Centers for Disease Control and Prevention (2003).
The Burden of Chronic Disease and the Future of Public Health.

Avoidable chronic diseases remain the principal reason to see a doctor, which means they take a lot of time in doctors' schedules. The importance of this can be illustrated by the impact of cardiovascular diseases, with about 85 million people in Europe living with this. Knowing that cardiovascular diseases are almost six times as likely to hit an inactive, overweight smoker than a healthy person, prevention and health management becomes unavoidable for the healthcare system. Care institutions know they have a responsibility to educate and inform patients. But those care institutions that understand they have a role to play in managing people's lifestyles might have figured out that wellness centres could be 'the front door' of their institutions.

While most have not yet taken it that far, wellness is already being integrated into the core functioning of care institutions and largely used as a transformation-driven marketing tool. Exercising, together with nutrition and relaxation techniques are used to set specific goals for their customers, holding them accountable for their own health. Acupuncture and aromatherapy are used to make patients feel better. Some institutions even have demonstration kitchens where people are taught how to prepare and cook nutritional foods as part of a holistic approach. Care institutions are now being designed to facilitate relaxation or enhance physical activity. Accessible gardens, either on the roof or the ground, provide healing spaces. Playgrounds and libraries allow people to interact with one another. Stairways are no longer hidden in the corner of a building but are integrated in the design to encourage people to move. It's all about offering the right transformation to their patients. And Healthusiastic people will demand such transformations. We've already seen it happen within the food industry where people demand healthier options.

What wellness habits should be part of your own care pathways?

Obviously, technology plays an important role as a wellness tool. It encourages people to take ownership, facilitates earlier discharges from a hospital, and prevents readmissions. Its importance is best proven by how clinical care continues to expand outside the walls of institutions. In fact, it's estimated that 50% of revenues that previously were managed within the confines of a care institution are now considered outpatient services. Soon, care institutions will be reserved for the sickest patients requiring the most critical care. Less needy patients will have the luxury to recover or to be treated while being in the comfortable environment of their own living room. After all, people feel and heal better at home.

Mercy Virtual is arguably the world's most advanced example of clinical care outside the walls of a hospital. This institution can actually be considered a real virtual hospital where specialists care for patients remotely. In fact, the hospital does not have any beds at all. Instead, nurses and doctors monitor patients on screens. An even more radical change is that this hospital does not wait until sick people come to them or end up in an emergency room. Through technology, they are able to reach out to people before they actually have symptoms, or before nurses would even have been able to pick up on them. This means that quarterly doctor visits are no longer required if patients are constantly followed up. However, this

> *does not mean that contact with the care team is limited. In fact, quite the opposite is true considering that touchless regular tele-consults are done every time the smallest change occurs. Of course, a tele-consult is never as good as a real encounter. But the speed and the frequency of the contact makes the overall experience exceptionally better for both patients and caregivers. Patients do not only feel and heal better at home. They also have a far better and more intimate relationship with their care team that positively impacts their health and well-being.*

Wellness is becoming an integrated part of the care delivered to patients in or outside institutions. But how much of an impact can care institutions actually have on the community around them? Currently hospitals are constructed in such a way that local residents don't enter the facilities unless they are sick or injured. Both the location and the large parking lots do not really invite people in. As a transformation-driven effort, it is not impossible to imagine that care institutions could open their doors to people who want to live healthily. What if care institutions could become health villages that serve their communities with wellness? What if hospitals became open environments, instead of closed practices, where people could be engaged in day-to-day activities driven by wellness? It would indeed make wellness the front door of care institutions. Healthy cooking classes, smoking cessation seminars and medically supported gyms would be part of the extended early care pathways. Such health villages, focused on community wellness, would answer aspirational needs. Such health villages would have wellness facilities as an open 'front door' to their institutions.

How can you open up your care institution and invite local residents to be part of a wellness-focused community?

Pharmaceutical marketing

If marketing has been considered "a bad thing" to some degree, it certainly has been the case for marketing that involves pharmaceutical products. As these products are largely paid for by public or private health insurances, the question is, to what extent is promoting greater sales actually acceptable? What makes this setting even more unique for marketers is that doctors have always been the main customer making the product decisions, while patients merely "consume" the product. However, a patient remains the same person as a customer of consumer products. They might find themselves in different situations, but their personal needs remain very much the same. It's logical to assume that people who find themselves in a situation as a patient will have the same expectations as they do when they are a customer. If you want "consumer brands" to care about environmental, societal or health concerns, why would you not expect this from pharmaceutical or medical companies too? This is why the same marketing evolution is to be seen in pharmaceutical marketing.

Do you care about and address your patients'
main concerns?

Pharmaceutical marketing was originally product-driven. Through huge numbers of sales people, they endlessly repeated the performance characteristics of their products. Efficacy, safety and tolerability were the pharmaceutical equivalent of the 4Ps when promoting their products to healthcare professionals. Product performance arguments would speak to the minds of healthcare providers. When dealing with payers (authorities or health insurance companies) they would justify the price with studies about the financial benefit of the product. But in both situations, it was about proving to be different to the competitor. Visual aids that used brand colours and presented simplified graphs highlighted when a particular pharmaceutical product showed the slightest "significant" difference compared to other products.

Patient-driven marketing

To understand what characteristics were desired by healthcare professionals when choosing between products from the same therapeutic class, pharmaceutical companies conducted prescription behaviour surveys. This type of research investigates what makes the average doctor choose one or the other product. For several decades, the efficacy, tolerability and safety of the product were constantly in the top three, closely followed by the "impact of the sales representative" and the doctor's own "prescription habit". But in the past 10 years, "patient services" have consistently entered the top three reasons to prescribe a product. The "reputation" of the pharmaceutical company was also mentioned more often than before.

This radical shift was induced by patients. Since the advent of Dr Google in the early 2000s, many patients became more demanding and sometimes left the doctor baffled by their demands. Doctors were now dealing with both the 'old' patient who would listen and gladly accept a solution, as well as the 'new' patient who had many questions and sought a way to manage his condition. It's been a long time since the doctor was one of the most respected people in the village. The paternalistic role of the doctor has crumbled. Arguably, doctors have not been educated to deal with this empowered patient. Little wonder then that physicians preferred prescribing pharmaceutical products that were accompanied by appropriate patient services. By speaking to the *hearts* of patients with these services, physicians were convinced to prefer one pharmaceutical product above the other.

Another important change in the relationship between doctor and patient came in recent years. In all the patient researches I have conducted in the past years, I have always included one question about the role of the patient in the choice of the pharmaceutical product. Across all pathologies, it's fair to say that, on average, in about 50% of the cases, patients have an impact on the final choice. In between seven and 15% of the cases, the patient claims that he predominantly selected the product to be prescribed. While the reality might not always fit with this, it does show patient perception of the importance of his role in this process.

Patients are no longer just recipients of healthcare but active participants. They used to listen to healthcare providers; now they interact with them. It's about choice and influence. In an era where time spent with a doctor is decreasing, technology is bolstering the patient's confidence and improving their relationship. This means the value of pharmaceutical products is being determined by the patient and his experience. So it is important to pay him attention.

Do you deeply consider the emotions, information searched, doctor contact, symptoms and expectations in each step of the journey of your patient?

It would be too strong a statement to say that pharmaceutical companies have never taken the patients into account within their marketing strategies. But mostly, the patient was only part of the context. The patient's interest was always at heart, but actual patient preferences, experiences, or inclusions were often omitted. Even though slogans like "putting the patient first" were present in the missions and visions of almost all pharmaceutical companies, patients were rarely the core of the conversation or the focus of the strategy. In Europe, this was partly due to regulations that prohibit patient marketing that might offer an expected return on investment. Patients are not to be persuaded by marketing to choose products that are paid with public money. The fear of non-compliance and adverse event reporting when directly communicating with patients also prevents patient inclusion. But the fact that the physician is considered the one who makes the final decision probably reduced the importance of the patient as a stakeholder within their strategy. That's why patient-driven marketing has not received enough attention within pharmaceutical companies until now.

Patient-centricity

While many pharmaceutical companies have been rather hesitant to put the patient first, there have been several initiatives to turn the tide in recent years. Several pharmaceutical companies have created the position of Chief Patient Officer, a Global Executive Director in charge of helping employees to enhance patient initiatives throughout the company. In an interview with EyeForPharma back in 2016, Sanofi's newly appointed Chief Patient Officer Anna Beal explained that the added value of this approach is still unknown.

Sanofi is continuously trying and learning. Failures are allowed if dealt with quickly. No company has ever done this before. The creation of this type of mandate clearly shows an increased focus on patient-centricity, even though many employees still wonder whether this is really going to help, or whether it is yet another responsibility that is simply being piled on top of others.

Early in 2016, Paul Simms, chair of EyeForPharma, and Jill Donahue, author of EngageRx, created The Aurora Project, a volunteer group designed to bring the industry together to focus on patient-centricity within the industry. In 2016 The Aurora Project set up a first global benchmark survey comprising 2 346 pharma industry respondents from 84 countries. One of the key insights of that benchmark survey was that about 86% of participants ranked the importance of delivering on patient-focused missions as greater than eight out of 10, but only 21% ranked their confidence in their own company delivering on these missions. Another striking finding was that 78% stated that they don't know how to train people to behave in a patient-focused manner. There is a clear will to focus on patients, but not many feel comfortable doing so.

The **IMPORTANCE** of Pharma to deliver on their patient-focused missions

The **CONFIDENCE** in being able to deliver on their patient-focused missions

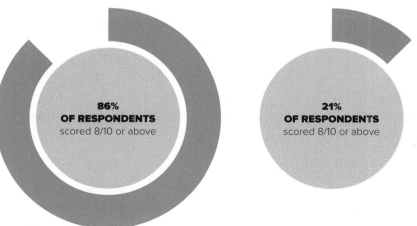

86%
OF RESPONDENTS
scored 8/10 or above

21%
OF RESPONDENTS
scored 8/10 or above

The Aurora Project: *Pharma's Global Patient Centricity Survey & Analysis*, EyeForPharma, 2016.

---

*Do your colleagues feel comfortable putting the interest
of the patient first in every business decision?*

A second Patient-Centric Benchmark Survey was conducted in 2017 by Ipsos. The results from the previous years were confirmed but were now compared with patient perceptions. The survey asked participants the degree to which they considered Pharma to be patient-centric. Patients in the survey consistently rated pharma companies lower than participants did who were employed by the biopharmaceutical and medical device industry. In other words, pharmaceutical companies believe they are more patient-centric than they actually are. For example, the majority of the pharmaceutical companies may believe they listen to patients, but only a minority of 38% agreed with them.

---

*Are your patients convinced you listen to them
and really act on their deepest and most pressing needs?*

Pharmaceutical companies are certainly becoming increasingly patient-focused, but many can hardly be called patient-centric yet. This would mean that the patient would be considered the core customer, not the doctor. Each and every business decision would need to be taken first with the patient in mind. It requires gathering (online) data and building intelligence about their preferences and experiences. Companies need to constantly engage with patients throughout specific key moments in the lifecycle of medicines. Just as consumer businesses focused on customer-driven marketing, pharmaceutical companies will need to build an always-on dialogue with patients to really get to know them. Because patients are part of a changing cultural, societal and technological reality, and their needs constantly evolve as well. You simply can't expect to know what the patient expects without consulting them at all times.

> Since **UCB's** 2015 annual report, the "patient value" strategy has been identified as central to UCB's path for sustainable growth. This means that success for UCB is when they enable patients to live the life they choose, rather than one dictated by the disease. The company is dedicated to creating value and improving the lives not only of the patients living with severe chronic diseases, but of their families and care providers as well. That is why the "patient value" strategy creates a sense of accountability and ownership across the entire value chain of the company, from R&D to production, from sales to marketing. Since the needs of patients are highly specific and often changing, UCB puts the patient at the centre of all their activities, which allows them to be agile and respond to change swiftly and appropriately. A large-scale patient satisfaction survey has even been put in place to track patient satisfaction as well as the elements that impact that patient satisfaction most. This innovative piece of research really measures the impact of UCB's patient value approach. This is extremely important because the patient-focused approach is only a real success story for UCB if the results show increased satisfaction in patients. That's why it was widely shared across the entire company through different channels.

Reservations about a patient-centric strategy were always linked to whether putting the patient first was in contradiction with making sales. One of the purposes of The Aurora Project by EyeForPharma in 2016 was to prove to the industry that patient-centricity and profitability can indeed go hand in hand. But for pharmaceutical companies to succeed in this patient-centric endeavour, it is important that the entire company understands the strategic importance. It demands a clear key performance indicator that can and will be translated through every department of the company. At UCB, every single employee knows what role he or she plays in creating value for the patient. This is very important because having a positive impact on patients reconnects people with the purpose of their work. It makes employees want to make a difference as they know they are speaking to the *hearts* of patients.

*Does every employee at your company speak
to the heart of your patient?*

Trust and reputation

In a world where people turn to companies and brands to solve their concerns and help them with their aspirations, you might expect the health-focused pharmaceutical companies to be in a unique position to easily deliver on this. However, research by Gallup (2018) shows that the reputation of governments is the worst across all sectors, and that the pharmaceutical industry comes in at a close second. On top of that, trust in pharmaceutical companies has decreased as much as trust in governments today. The Edelman Trust Barometer (2018) reports that global trust in pharmaceutical companies has declined year-on-year. In a time and era where self-actualisation and aspiration-driven marketing become increasingly important, this is far from an ideal situation.

But how can someone trust something if they are not familiar with it? As only 20% of the population claims to be somewhat familiar with the pharmaceutical industry, according to the Reputation Institute (2018), it is difficult to create a good reputation. Media coverage on monopoly pricing, blocking generics and biosimilars, supply chain controversies, and political lobbying certainly don't help either. But the fact of the matter is that the majority of people don't really know whether the pharmaceutical business is ethical or not. Within this confusion and unfamiliarity, pharmaceutical companies meanwhile tend to chase trust by relying heavily on regulatory and legal compliance.

Say the word "pharma" outside the industry and mentions of life-saving drug discoveries rarely come up. The pharmaceutical industry simply does not get enough credit for the positive influence it has on society. Instead, the general perception is that it puts sales before patient welfare, and company profit before good health. One of the main reasons is that they are communicating to the wrong audience. As long as they consider regulatory bodies to be the most important stakeholder in building trust and reputation, it will be difficult to change the public's opinion. But another reason is that they don't communicate in ways that are relevant. Pharmaceutical companies fail to communicate about their activities with authenticity, openness and transparency. The results of a study by PatientView (2017) should then not come as a surprise. Only 34% of patient associations gave pharma a "good" or "excellent" rating for reputation. Eyeforpharma (2017) came to the identical conclusion: only 36% of patients said they trust pharmaceutical companies.

What is the authentic personality of your company that you openly and transparently want people to know about?

So, while pharma is making its first marks in patient-driven marketing and patient-centricity, it has yet to deal with the challenge of transformation-driven marketing. But it would be foolish not to be somewhat optimistic about its chances of success. Today's start-ups often originate from scientific innovation around a significant customer need, and pharmaceutical companies actually started with similar ambitions too. Knowing that these ambitions match people's desire to actively impact their health and happiness very well, there simply has to be an authentic way to speak to their *souls*.

Making customers healthy & happy

As people's needs are becoming more aspirational than ever, companies should increasingly focus on transformation-driven marketing strategies. In a previous chapter, Health Marketing was described as a specific form of transformation-driven marketing that answers the desire of people to be(come) healthy & happy. But how can companies really make their customers healthy & happy? How to best go forward with Health marketing? This final chapter will elaborate upon the Recurring Expectations customers might have towards the products, services and experiences that companies and brands are offering. It will also highlight what Contemporary Evolutions are critical for the survival of your company and brands in this aspirational world. But first, let's start by explaining why customer expectations are so important.

Customer expectations as the golden nugget

Customer needs

Every customer has desires and wants. As previously explained, using the Maslow pyramid, we all have needs that can be categorised under the same umbrellas. We start by fulfilling functional needs, like food, water, warmth and rest. People can't live without those. Safety, stability and security are basic, functional forms of comfort that allow us to live without external worry, and to feel at ease. We simply need all this to function normally. It is what survival is about. It's what our *minds* focus on.

Emotional needs, on the other hand, are defined by our relationships and our personality. This is the theme of romantic movies. We want to feel loved, to connect with someone, or, at least, to be part of something because this largely defines who we are. It forms our own identity, which we like to see confirmed or recognised in our social interactions. It is what speaks to our *hearts*.

Nowadays, both our functional and emotional needs are increasingly being met. People aspire to become the best version of themselves, to develop and grow into the person they really desire to be. Documentaries about successful sportspeople, musicians who made it on their own, or universities calling for students all speak to our aspirational needs. People want to achieve something that makes them feel good and even proud about themselves. Healthy and happy? Socially engaged? Involved with our planet? It's about our own *soul*.

Beyond the theory of basic needs, there are specific needs that apply to your business. Generally speaking, companies know the needs of their customer. And if you look closely, each of these needs is likely to fit into one of the above categories. The question is, however, how can your company create value for your customers by answering these needs?

Customer experience

The majority of business owners confirm that experience is the main site of the battle to win customers. Products and services no longer cut it. People generally value experiences a lot more. And if experiences become personal, they can even transform customers into becoming a better person. Is there anything you could want more? That's what really creates value for your customers today: memorable experiences and personal transformations.

With companies in turmoil as a result of rapidly changing technology and the different waves of disruption, a common misunderstanding arises: that customer experience is the experience customers have when they use your website, application or bot. Of course, customer experience is driven by digital disruption. But customer experience is not at all about the experience with one touch point. It's not the experience with an online onboarding form that defines the experience of your customers with your company, just as it is not the experience of someone pointing you to another gate that defines the experience of your flight transfer. It might have a clear impact on the overall experience, of course, but customer experience is also defined by the moments that precede and succeed that specific touch point. It's the entire experience that counts.

In fact, customer experience is determined by all the moments that people consider being influenced by your company. But it is not a summation of those experiences. It is about the overall experience with your brand or company. It's not only the length of the queue when entering a theme park. It's not only the friendliness of the staff at the park restaurant. It's not only the thrills during a roller coaster ride. Neither is it all of the above added together. It's the entirety of all experiences that creates the actual customer experience. It's not about one or the other job that is being done properly, it's about all the jobs you expect to be done properly.

Still, each separate experience needs to be consistent with another. Only then will customers value the good experience you've offered. Easily subscribing online for health insurance might be enough of a good experience for a customer to prefer one company above another. The positive user experience – in gaining time – is worth the cost. Failing to perpetuate these experiences afterwards will however negatively impact the customer experience with your company, even if the actual insurance is the best in the market. That's why "mission statements" are becoming even more important for companies. It should clearly be stated what you do, how you deliver it, and to whom. Because that is the real foundation of the consistent customer experience you are supposed to be offering.

Being consistent in the customer experience offered also means that each separate experience needs to deliver on the respective customer expectations. More often than not, experiences are designed from an immediate internal capability and not from customer originated expectations. Companies generally lack this knowledge because – they claim – customer expectations are changing too rapidly in today's society. Knowing what your customer expects has become the golden nugget for business success today.

Customer expectations

Customer expectations are all the preconceived ideas or assumptions that customers have about dealing with your company. A couple of decades ago, it was merely limited to quality, service and price. But that all changed dramatically in recent years. The expectations are evolving in line with the exponential growth of technology. Expectations therefore seem to be rising faster than ever before and seem to have become a moving target.

Forrester (2018) reports that almost two-thirds of decision makers at enterprises consider rising customer expectations as a high and critical priority for the success of their business. This may not come as a surprise, as whether or not customer expectations are met will indeed determine the customer experience with your company. The experience customers desire is composed of their needs and expectations. As customer experience is the main competitive battlefield for today's businesses, meeting expectations becomes exceedingly important.

Customer need(s) x **CUSTOMER EXPECTATION(S)** = Customer experience

There is a gap between customer experience and expectations. PwC (2018) assessed that the biggest gaps are in heavily regulated industries like airlines, healthcare, pharma, and banking. Stringent regulations make it much more difficult to adapt to new expectations and to optimise experiences. But all industries are actually looking for ways to close that gap because 76% of customers require companies to meet their needs and expectations. If not, they can (and will) easily take "their business" elsewhere.

 Understanding and meeting customer expectations is indeed critical. Companies assume that as every brand is different, customers have different expectations. It is also assumed that it is hard to understand what specific expectations might impact their business next as customer expectations are moving so fast. That's why companies often lack confidence that they are going to cut it in the future. However, customer expectations are not changing as fast as you might think, nor are they that brand or industry specific.

In fact, expectations are forged by customer experiences with leading brands across all types of industries. Most of all, they are being forged by companies that really excel in customer experience, like Amazon, Apple, Google, Facebook, Uber or Netflix. If you order a pair of shoes online, it will be delivered to your door the next day. But if you order a new debit card online, it might take up to eight working days to arrive. Why would customers have different expectations towards a bank than when ordering from Amazon? Customer expectations remain (largely) the same across all industries. New expectations that might hit an industry are much more 'predictable' than one might think, because they are often already present in other industries.

In the final chapters of this book I've assembled a series of dominant customer expectations. While they are certainly applicable to different trends and situations, they have been elaborated on to answer the Healthusiasm trend described in this book. They will help you to make choices within your transformation-driven health marketing strategy, and support you in creating the right experiences and transformations for your customers, whatever business you are operating in. These Recurring Expectations are structured in such a way that you can distil the ones that are relevant for your products, services and experiences. In the final sections these expectations will be completed with the Contemporary Evolutions that companies and brands need to reflect upon when moving forward with Health Marketing.

Recurring Expectations

Recurring expectations are the ones that matter to customers when you are putting a product, service or experience onto the market. It's what they expect when they want something to be done. However, not all these expectations may be relevant to your particular business. It's therefore important to understand where and when it might suit the experience of your customer. Some expectations might be critical, others might be nice to have. Some expectations you might already excel in, others might require work (alone or in partnerships with others). They are regrouped in such a way that they showcase how certain expectations are currently accelerating, evolving or simply linked to one another. Here again, it is important to see those accelerations in the broader context of the dominant needs of your customers, as well as in your own business focus. But it will surely serve as an inspiration to challenge yourself on where your business should be heading.

Just a couple of remarks before deep-diving into the recurring expectations: if some examples sound ludicrous to you, then they most certainly are. But try to think past them to see how they might (or will likely) change expectations in the future. It's also important to note that the expectations are not mutually exclusive. One particular product, service and experience can answer different expectations, just as one technology can be used to meet different expectations.

From near-by to real-time

Because health services required a physical presence, customers were expected to visit a specific person or a certain location. If you needed something, you needed to go somewhere. In today's reality where customers are increasingly used to being put at the centre of attention and focus, this dynamic has shifted.

Customers now expect health services to be offered where they are. Neither will they wait to be served. Being accustomed to on-demand services, they expect that every part of their current journey will be shortened. Being able to deliver a health service where and when your customer wants it is a basic expectation of your customer today.

Near – expecting nearby products, services or experiences

In the recent years of smartphone domination, location-based services have played a huge role in our habits. Think about how Waze helps us to navigate through traffic, how Google maps suggests where to go for dinner, or how we check in to notify places of our presence. We even checked in at our favourite location so often that we would become its mayor on Foursquare. By pinpointing our physical location, we now realise everything it can offer, from a vegan restaurant and a sunlit terrace, to the connecting bus stop and friends partying nearby. We have come to expect something in our vicinity. And that's no different when it comes to health services. In fact, Google searches for health services that are "near me" have grown 20 times in the past five years. If we might previously have benefited from a certain health service at a particular moment, it would likely have been postponed if we did not have the opportunity nearby. Today, we expect it to be exactly where we are, where we go, or where we pass by.

Which of your services or experiences would people appreciate discovering in their vicinity?

Pharmacies are a typical example of nearby health services. The international Pharmaceutical Federation (2017) calculated that there is on average one pharmacy per 2 000 people in the world. In Europe, the average pharmacy density is even higher with one pharmacy per 1 200 citizens. Bringing health services close to people is a clear mandate for pharmacies. CVS Health alone is within five kilometres of 70% of the US population. But it is supermarkets that really have long understood the importance of bringing everything nearby. Grown out of local grocery stores, the success or failure of a supermarket still depends on its location and its ability to offer almost everything customers might want to buy. Little wonder that health services are now part of these one-stop-shops too. From pharmacies to retail clinics and eye doctors, supermarkets are bringing these close to where people are or often go. Supermarket Migros in Switzerland even has the biggest fitness chain on their premises, making it effortless for customers to combine a workout with their daily or weekly errands. One-stop-shops have transformed into one-stop-places.

Digital health kiosks allow you to engage with your health, know your risks, and make positive lifestyle changes. People can easily conduct a non-invasive biometric screening that includes key health indicators such as weight, blood pressure, BMI and pulse rate. **Walmart** *offers several hundreds of these digital health kiosks within their stores.* **Ping An Good Doctor** *in China went even further in their nearby ambitions. They now offer over 1000 "one-minute-clinics" in the neighbourhood of supermarkets. These AI-driven unmanned units provide basic diagnosis and advice for over 2 000 common diseases and really put health services where the people are.*

People love finding everything in one place because life moves at a breakneck pace. If you can't buy earbuds, get your blood checked and book your next trip in one place, then it might not get done at all. That's why new initiatives are now applying that same one-stop magic by housing several health services under one roof – as a supermarket dedicated to health services.

> **The Well** in Manhattan gathers yoga classes, health coaches, trainers and functional medicine practitioners in a café where people first and foremost meet with friends. From food as medicine, to sleep advice and managing stress and anxiety, The Well is bundling all services under one roof. WeWork created **The Rise** because they believe that exercising, relaxing and hanging out with friends can all be done in the same place. Its complete wellness experience drives a cultural shift toward greater well-being. This vision is shared by **Clean Market**, a Manhattan-based market slash bar slash apothecary slash wellness centre that aims to optimise the way people feel. You can shop for supplements, beauty products and organic food while you wait for your IV drip, infrared sauna or cryotherapy session.

Would it make sense for your customer if you bundle some of yours and others complementary services in one location?

Supermarkets are built on easily-accessible locations. Advertising billboards are placed at locations that lots of people pass. Product-driven marketing is no longer the only marketing strategy. Billboards no longer take the main chunk of the marketing budget. However, a location at a crowded place might still serve to create awareness for certain health-related topics. The NHS is using billboards to drive blood donations in relevant areas, while others are being used to livestream the need of nearby donor centres or local air pollution. But many commercial companies also use smart billboards to bring their own health services close to people.

*Billboards are now alleviating stress **(ClearChannel)** throughout the sub-way network of Stockholm or offering a great break with back massages in Bogota **(KitKat)**. Smart billboards are also being equipped with diagnostic tools. Through technology, they are now able to detect a cough or sneeze **(Boehringer Ingelheim)**, fever **(GSK)**, or even germs **(Lifebuoy)**. The perk of it all? These nearby billboards will refer you to nearby solutions. In Nordic countries, where daylight is very scarce in winter and leads to population-wide vitamin D deficiency, Pharmacy brand **Apotek Hjartat** provides light therapy within a display window. This spark of light not only creates awareness of the pharmacy, but also of the need to take care of oneself.*

Source: Saatchi & Saatchi IS, Poland

By being nearby many people, supermarkets and billboards offer health services exactly where people are or often go. However, sometimes it is not necessary to find convenient physical locations. Certain frequently used objects are almost always close to people. Think of how we rarely separate ourselves from our smartphone, our watch, our glasses or our jewellery. Other nearby objects are in the places we find ourselves in most often, such as our house, our work, and our car. Many technology companies are already incorporating additional features into these widely used objects so that they can be leveraged as health services. But less obvious companies are also starting to feed into the proximate expectations of Healthusiasm.

> *What in-house objects are most spread around the world? It has to be IKEA furniture, of course. No wonder **IKEA** started selling products like sensuous posters with lavender-scented ink and a white noise speaker to help the 40% of people who are sleep-deprived to get a great night's sleep. With reports increasingly stating that indoor air pollution accounts for significantly more deaths than the outdoor kind, IKEA has also designed air purifying curtains that destroy the toxins in your house. But other frequently used objects might do the trick as well. The **Asiri group of hospitals**, one of Sri Lanka's largest healthcare providers, transformed a bus ticket into a free piece of soap. As public buses are a mainstream form of transportation in Sri Lanka, they have become a hub for spreading germs across passengers. The "soap bus ticket" functions as a sanitiser and prevents viruses from common colds to hepatitis from spreading across the population too easily.*

What ordinary objects that are frequently used could bring your mission closer to people?

These widely used objects are present where we are. They are designed to offer us the right health service when we are near that object. But when no billboards, supermarkets or pharmacies are around, or when there is no 'healthised' object nearby, we expect these services to come to us. In a time driven by on-demand services, a press of a button should yield the right health service at the right place.

> *In collaboration with St John's hospital, UK-based taxi company **MyTaxi** has trained and equipped drivers to perform first aid in case of emergency. After all, taxis are widely distributed across a city and are therefore potentially even nearer emergencies than ambulances. Uber partnered with the medical bot Practo to rapidly transport patients to a healthcare professional in case of emergency. Other ride-hailing apps like **Gojek** in Indonesia or **Grab** in China also offer health services on demand.*

Health services will be brought near you, or you are brought near a health service. And we are yet to move into the era of drones and driverless cars that will make it even easier, faster and better. Zip-line already offers urgent medical material to deserted areas in Rwanda using drones, and they are planning to do the same in rural areas in the States. Ambulance drones, flying at a speed of 120km/h, are also being tested in both The Netherlands and the US to bring faster health services to you. It is now possible to envision driverless ambulances or driverless doctors' rooms or clinics coming to you. They can pick up low risk patients or perform early diagnostic tests wherever you are. In fact, several governments are already exploring the possibilities and the necessary regulations for this.

AIM is a self-driving clinic that uses AI to diagnose patients. Images courtesy of artefact.

Fast – expecting speedy delivery

We have been pampered with on-demand services. At any given moment, we can immediately stream the latest episode of *Game of Thrones*, listen to the newest album by Arcade Fire, or have a pizza Napolitana delivered to us. It has dramatically changed our expectations and willingness to wait. Uber was originally chosen over traditional cabs because of its convenience, not least because its services were simply a lot faster than mainstream taxis. And our expectations of speedy delivery have risen ever since. The longer Uber offers their services in a city, the less people from that city are willing to wait for an Uber. We no longer accept a 10-minute waiting time. Uber is now expected to pick up their customers in no more than six minutes. And in some cities people are even picked up after no more than 3 minutes. Spoiled by on-demand services, we often expect almost real-time service now. But how does this play out for health services? In their everyday decision-making, people seek ways to make themselves healthy and happy. And when it comes to their health, they are definitely no longer patient. People expect it fast, or even in real-time.

A typical approach in trying to understand health-related expectations is to map out the patient journey or the disease pathway. In open discussions with patients and healthcare professionals, the different phases of a typical journey are described and aligned to each other. In the course of my career, I've designed many patient journeys with input from patients from across the globe and for all kinds of diseases ranging from chronic diseases to mental illnesses, and from acute conditions to under-diagnosed pathologies. The common learning through all this research was that patients have to wait a long time at several moments in their journey. In fact, in the top three things that patients would improve in their experience, three are related to 'waiting', according to Deloitte (2017). "Having access to services faster" is arguably the most pressing health-related expectation.

What part of your customers' journey would benefit from speeding things up quite a bit?

In many countries today, the number of general practitioners has decreased so much that it has become practically impossible to schedule a doctor's visit within two weeks. This means that your flu-like symptoms might disappear before you actually see a doctor. For specialists, this 'waiting' might even go from several more weeks to several months, leaving the patient in the unknown for a very long time. Various online calendars have been facilitating online appointment for many years but have not been able to significantly decrease the waiting time. Telemedicine and telehealth solutions are starting to offer patients a faster service by getting them in contact with doctors remotely. These solutions are very promising because they offer both flexibility and speed. But in a third wave of digital disruption, algorithms from medical chatbots are now offering patients medically graded answers to their symptoms in real-time. Through a series of pre-programmed questions, patients learn about a potential diagnosis or the need to see a doctor. Some chatbots even book an appointment automatically. Others set up an immediate call.

While offering some real-time initial answers, these bots also materialise a triage to the doctor's office. How great would it be if the "not-so-sick" would refrain from seeing a doctor? Could it even make waiting rooms redundant? Nobody really likes to wait, let alone hear the words, "Have a seat in the waiting room". Entering a room packed with sick people is utterly discouraging. And, chances are, you are not feeling well in the first place. This will surely negatively influence even the best service the doctor could offer. In a world driven by expectations of promptness, waiting rooms should be avoided or transformed into "energise rooms" where our time is actively used to improve, educate or prepare. Healthcare surely can get some inspiration from airline business lounges, where people enjoy 'waiting'. Now, bring to that experience some value-added services and something annoying will soon become valued.

> *The Belgian start-up **Bingli** is a consultation preparation bot. The algorithm can ask between 60 and 100% of the medical questions in advance so symptoms are accurately communicated to the doctor. This prevents rushed appointments, frees up valuable time, and allows doctors more time to listen and interact with patients. This not only turns waiting time into useful time, but optimises consultations.*

Another pain point in the patient journey is related to the time needed to get a diagnosis, but several innovative solutions are tackling this expectation. Theranos was one of the first to (almost) have disrupted the diagnostics business by allowing faster and easier access to blood tests. Through the automation and miniaturisation of blood tests (using microscopic blood volumes), Theranos claimed to conduct valuable blood tests but was never able to scientifically prove the validity of the results. The company was sanctioned and declared bankrupt shortly after. In full Napster style, many other start-ups were inspired to follow in the footsteps of Theranos and are on their way to offer fast and broad tests based on small blood samples. But while these start-ups aren't yet operational, other diagnostic companies are already focusing on providing the patient with diagnostic results more quickly than the ones currently available.

> One way of doing so is by eliminating the inclusion of overbooked physicians. **MyMedLab** and **HealthCheck** in the US, and **Werlabs** in Sweden, are allowing customers to purchase diagnostic testing online 24/7 without the blessing of the doctor's oversight. But while these still require the planning of a visit to the diagnostic centre, **Everlywell** and **Thrive** allow customers to conduct the tests themselves within the confines of their home. After sending back the samples, results with medical comments can be quickly accessed online, avoiding a wait for another appointment. In the next phase, start-ups like **CueHealth** and **Apollo** will bring self-diagnostic labs directly to the home of the customer and even omit the effort of having to send samples back. Once installed as a customer habit, these and other start-ups will also facilitate home-based health monitoring. **Apple Watch** and **AliveCor** are meanwhile famous for monitoring patients with atrial fibrillation. But many other handheld devices are being invented for home monitoring. A very useful example that will certainly meet customer expectations for real-time health services is the handheld whole breast ultrasound device **Monither**, which keeps an eye on the breast tissue of at-risk or recent cancer patients. Many women dread the long waiting times between those medical check-ups. Now they can perform frequent tests at home.

The diagnostics market in the US alone is a USD70 billion market that is bound to increase radically with these Direct-To-Consumer services. That's why many existing companies are also jumping on the bandwagon of fast and real-time health services.

Warby Parker is an American retailer of prescription glasses and sunglasses. Through the use of their app, they now offer a telehealth service that allows an optometrist to assess how you're seeing through your glasses and provide a real-time updated prescription. In a completely different industry, the Japanese **Matsumoto Apple Association** needed to boost their declining apple sales and unveiled a line of apples that include free personalised dental consultations. Customers were invited to take four bites of an apple and upload a photo onto the Dentapple application. Within no more than 24 hours, customers would then receive a free diagnosis by a professional dentist. Many others soon followed. Medical device company **Cochlear** has created an online film that in real-time doubles up as a hearing test, while **IKEA** debuted an advertisement about baby furniture that also functions as a pregnancy test when urinating on it.

Campaign made by Hakuhodo Inc, a Japanese advertising and public relations company.

Can you help people to be in the know?

From informative to supportive

In world that is experiencing an explosion of information, we feel less and less overloaded by it. Instead, it has become exactly what we expect in order to be able to make an informed decision and live a good life. We want specific and detailed knowledge that transparently unravels each aspect of your business, your product and your service. Only when it fits our aspirations, will you be able to attract our attention. But sometimes information won't cut it and we will require more direct support from parallel health services. In any case, we expect companies and brands to help us in achieving our aspirational needs.

Informative – expecting to be informed

This book is just one of the more than two million books published globally in 2019. That's a whole lot of pages filled with information. If you are searching for information today, you can surely eat your heart out. In fact, more information has been produced in the past 30 years than in the previous 5 000 years. But of course, most of this information is not to be found in physical books today, but rather in an undefined physical space called "online". When that online information became popular and always-on in the early internet years, it was named "the information highway". Internet was the fastest source for all your information needs. Once its mobile version launched in our pockets, we could even feed our addiction for information at any given moment and place.

Only this time round, pocket size does not mean less content. Online information is growing massively, at a speed of 571 new websites launching every other minute. Yes, every other minute! Terms like "information overload" have been used to indicate that people are not able to handle all this information. But PEW Research Center (2016) reported that almost 80% of people like having all this information at hand. They also stated that over the past 10 years, fewer and fewer people feel overloaded by information because it really helps them to simplify their lives. And that's exactly what people have grown into: a feeling of control thanks to relevant and useful information available exactly when they want it. It allows them to make the right decision at any given moment.

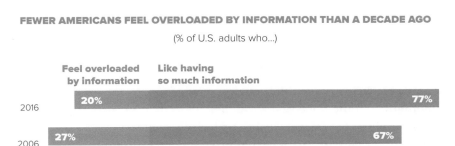

FEWER AMERICANS FEEL OVERLOADED BY INFORMATION THAN A DECADE AGO

(% of U.S. adults who...)

Feel overloaded by information **Like having so much information**

2016 20% 77%

2006 27% 67%

Source: Survey conducted March 7-April 4, 2016 – 'Information Overload', PEW Research Center

Certainly, at a time when increasing numbers of people actively want to impact their own health and happiness, health information is a more valued good than ever. Seven out of 10 adults (70%) say they are interested in information about health and medicine. That is more than any other topic, mentions the PEW Research Center survey (2014). Little wonder then, that each offline or online magazine offers health-related information today. Whether it is a magazine about fashion, technology, sports, food or travel, they all have a "health section". Even in the Trends report from Facebook (2019), "health" was a trending topic that ran across different popular categories like food, sports, and leisure time. Health-related information that feeds into this Healthusiasm trend is found literally everywhere.

Where can customers find the health topic on your website?

But people are no longer interested in general or superficial information. They expect in-depth and specific information. The latest annual trends in Google searches also demonstrate this. General health searches have largely disappeared in the past decade, while more targeted searches have soared. Even though you are not a professional athlete or model, this does not mean you don't want the best or most specific knowledge to optimise your health at your disposal. The recent popularity of health websites with in-depth content like HealthHunt, MindBodyGreen, and EveryDayHealth shows that they are feeding perfectly into those heightened expectations. The rise and fall of the wearable fitness tracker is another example of how people expect more in-depth information today. They want it. They need it. But for some, the tracker is just not offering enough yet, because they want more information and insights than it can currently offer. But soon, when new features are added, they'll give it another try in the hope that it will live up to their expectations this time. As soon as biometric trackers do live up to these expectations, I expect almost everybody to wear them because they offer in-depth insights.

Do you allow your customers to become a specialist on a subject?

People will embrace products and services that bring them in-depth information in an intuitive and actionable way. Information now needs to be complete, accurate and at a professional level. Words like "nutritional value" or "sugar to fibre ratio" are no longer Martian expressions. For example, easily digestible health slogans on food packaging are now not enough. As stated by Nielsen (2015) earlier, most people read the small-print on food labels before making their purchasing decision. Ingredients are very important; for example, seven out of 10 US customers are willing to switch food brands to those that do not contain artificial ingredients, according to the Food & Health Survey (2018).

> *In a bold move that feeds into this insight, **Heinz** Brazil changed their 140-year-old brand label by putting the six (natural) ingredients found in ketchup front and centre. Tomate. Açucar. Vinagre. Sal. Cebola. Aroma Natural. No more small print. Putting the real deal in real font sizes, where the recognisable brand logo once took pride of place. Heinz has let go of its distinctive brand assets to put forward this piece of health marketing focused on details (and transparency).*

*Are all parts of your products or services worth
being shown publicly to customers?
If not, why do you still have them?*

Customers nowadays simply want to know everything. But in a world that is awash with fake news stories and misinformation, people consume information with a dose of scepticism. Transparency has become hugely important because the distinction between fact and fiction has faded. In fact, 86% of Americans say that transparency is more important than before (SproutSocial 2018). When making health-impacting decisions, people definitely want to know about your business. But even when not making the healthiest of choices, people want the facts in order to make an informed decision.

*Since 2014, **McDonald's** Canada has offered their customers a chance to publicly ask questions about its food and ingredients. The campaign is ongoing and has garnered over 42 000 questions and answers that have generated more than 3.8 million views to date. In one instance, McDonald's even shared video footage from inside its Canadian beef pro-*

197

cessing plant, showing that its burgers are indeed made from real cows. Unless you are a vegan, it's that type of transparency that could make you confident when making decisions. Even when that decision is rather "unhealthy".

Supportive – expecting to be supported

Information serves people in making an informed decision. This is stating the obvious. But why are people no longer making decisions until they are armed with enough knowledge? Because they want to take care of themselves. For some brands, this means putting the relevant information about their own products and services out there. For other brands, it means introducing health boosting services that are complementary to what they are offering. It can help attract customers, reinforce your positioning in the market, or clean up your image. But as a customer, it makes us wonder, "Why aren't we always supported by such parallel services"? Good intentions are pervasive. But we want more. We want to become the healthier and happier person we aim to be. Intentions paraphrased in hollow slogans are not of value any more. We expect to be supported in our pursuit.

To maintain their health, people are primarily focused on sleeping better, eating more healthily, and exercising more regularly. This can be considered the holy trinity of healthy living. Many sectors now swear by this religion and find ways to develop parallel offerings that speak to these devotees. One of the most discussed examples is the travel and hospitality industry, which has grown into a sanctuary for Healthusiasm.

Not so long ago, hotels were evaluated by the sizes of the beds, the choices during breakfast, or the grandeur of the entrance. Today, however, guests more often determine the choice of their hotel on the presence of an alluring gym and healthy options on the menu. Health and wellness amenities are now simply part of the guest experience, regardless of whether people are travelling for pleasure or for business.

Yoga mats are part of the refurbished hotel rooms and yoga TV channels are included in the price. But it might as well be fitness apparatus, medicine balls, resistance bands, city running maps or paid access to a nearby gym. The fact that guests of the **Camelback Mountain Hotel** *can book one-on-one chats with an in-house nutritionist shows how hotel staff are*

> *becoming wellness savvy. At **EVEN Hotels**, every member of the person-nel is trained to help guests with their wellness routine. The hotel was in-tentionally designed to empower guests with a wellness experience that feeds into the trinity of healthy living and makes their guests accomplish more: Eating Well, Resting Easy and Keeping Active. The **Four Seasons Hotel** in Los Angeles has wellness rooms that, on top of the "usual fitness equipment", also offer healing lights, showers with dechlorinators and air purification systems that reduce allergens.*

Just as people don't want to give up on their wellness routine when travelling, nor do they want to abandon their healthy living ambitions when working. To find greater balance between private and work life, people have started work-ing from home or from nearby coworking spaces. Long gone is the time when a coworking space was merely a location where you could drink coffee and plug in your laptop. They have been converted into places for self-actualisation, self-improvement and a feeling of community.

> ***Werklab** in Vancouver offers a meditation zone, beauty bar, and access to energy-healing practitioners within their work place. It aims to be a hub for personal and professional development. **WeWork**, the American company known globally for its shared workspaces, has now appointed a head of Wellness. Since 2016, workers at WeWork are offered fitness classes including spinning, yoga, meditation, dance, and kickboxing. But just as WeWork is becoming "a work place with a gym", the **Equinox** gym chain has added communal spaces with wifi, making it a "gym with a work space". It has become so common for coworking spaces to include health services in their approach that the only ones not offering these today are probably 'libraries'.*

Within the hospitality industry or the coworking sector, health services rein-force their image and positioning in the market. However, this perfectly fits their customers' aspirations, and makes total sense as a transformation-driven marketing strategy. It perfectly fits the Healthusiasm trend. Even cities are now devoting parts of their centre to support their citizens' aspirational needs. From inviting stairs that count steps to motivate activity, to paved running tracks with drinking fountains and distance marker posts, cities are being redesigned to encourage people to move. But many other health-related initiatives are tak-ing place all around the globe. The examples are limitless.

*The city of **Kilis** in Turkey is distributing free bicycles to children. Fast-food advertising is strictly controlled in **Amsterdam**. **Copenhagen** launched stress clinics that offer subsidised nine-week courses. **Newcastle** has introduced dementia-friendly cinema evenings. **Turku**, in Finland, offers people six months' discounted access to sporting facilities, theatre seats and concerts. **Sydney** has built a dozen swimming pools. **Lisbon** paved hundreds of kilometres of bicycle tracks into the city. **Vienna** holds joint exercise classes for preschool children and older people.*

If you highlight all the (even distant) touch points in your customers' journey that are about food, sleep or exercising, where could you make a transformational change for your customer?

The holy trinity of healthy living clearly offers plenty of ways to present Healthusiastic people with parallel health services. It's an obvious choice that might easily fit any existing self-care routines people have or want to start. It's about adding better services to the parts of their life that are already rather good. Another way to go about supportive services, however, would be to improve the least healthy moments in their lives. Stress, commute, air pollution, loneliness or partying – just to name a few – take an unhealthy toll on our lives. So why don't we tackle those as well?

*Loneliness is becoming a world-wide epidemic. A little while ago, UK chain **Costa Coffee** introduced "chatter and natter" tables at 25 of their outlets. A simple sign on top of the table indicates that the person sitting there is happy to chat. This initiative creates a safe space to strike up a conversation. A similar initiative to tackle loneliness was made by the **Montreal Museum of Fine Arts**. The museum motivated doctors to prescribe a free visit to the Museum for people who needed to get out more. This action was followed and extended with a workout by the **Metropolitan Museum of Art** in New York. Before visiting hours, the world's largest and finest art museum organised tours that included workout choreography that left the audience* *both sweaty and inspired after exercising their way through the exhibitions. Fashion designer **Stella McCarthy** opened a store with an air filtration system that removes 95% of all air pollution and traffic fumes. Grab&Go is a service offered by ride hailing app **Grab**, that lets customers buy personal care products directly during their ride to alleviate commuting stress. Heartburn and indigestion relief brand **Gaviscon** makes late-night stops at various attractions and festivals with a neon-light truck that serves pH-neutral food like watermelon burger, a hazelnut fried fish sandwich, burnt chipotle broccoli tacos and zucchini fries.*

Picture credits by Metropolitan Museum of Art.

The Gaviscon pH-neutral food developed by Borderland London.

What situations in your setting are worth making healthy?

*What are you known for that could mitigate
typical "unhealthy situations"?*

Whether serving customers with better ways to sleep, eat or exercise, or relieving customers from typical health-impacting situations, all these initiatives meet the expectation of becoming healthier and happier. They often run parallel to the core products and services of existing companies, but fit rather well with the expectations of their customers: to help them achieve their aspirational needs.

From convenience to impactful

In our search to become the best possible version of ourselves, we seek information and support. But this should not be cumbersome and marginal. From the other experiences in our lives, we expect these to be just as convenient and impactful. We want limitations to be removed as soon as technology allows. Let it happen automatically and serve us with the benefits. We will gladly accept it. We are all for handling technology when it has the desired impact of helping us change our behaviour or battle loneliness. Bring it on.

Pragmatic – expecting convenience

When looking for the best experience, customers are comparing your business to the best experience they have ever received from any company they buy from. They know what they want and are expecting no less from you. Convenience is one of those expectations. People want to have things made easy. And why shouldn't they expect this? It's a trend that has been going on for decades. A car is more convenient than the maintenance of a horse. A supermarket is more convenient than – a convenience store. Buying online is often more convenient than having to drive to a supermarket. And how about walking in and out of stores without passing the checkout with purchases, like Amazon Go in the US, or Taobao in China? In any of the decisions customers make, they will always try to maximise pleasure and minimise pain. It's about avoiding friction and unpleasantness in their experiences.

The aforementioned expectations are existing examples of improved convenience. Nearby services are more convenient than services at a distance. Real-time services are more convenient than delayed services. Building knowledge is more convenient than lacking information. However, convenience is such a universal draw that it requires a specific topic in this book. Not least because within the health(care) industry, internal processes were generally the drivers of health services, instead of a patient-centric perspective, which often resulted in a dreadful experience for patients. But convenience is no longer an alternative. It's an imperative for any type of business. No longer is it just about saving time or energy. You need to understand the pain points and difficulties in the day-to-day lives of your customers. When customers feel that the company or brand has considered their reality, they are more likely to prefer that brand.

Do you know the actual pain points in your customers' life that go beyond making it easy to do business with you, but radically improves their lives?

Amazon is a trailblazer when it comes to convenience. It's not only "open" 24/7, but it allows you to find pretty much everything you are looking for. From an afro wig for a dog to plantar fasciitis insoles, it requires just 'one click' and your order is on its way to be delivered to your door the next day – if not the same day. I loathe clickbait articles or conference lectures on whether healthcare will be "Amazoned" some day. The fact is that there simply is no other way than to make things more Amazon-like in convenience. Whether it is the choice, the availability, the smooth processes, the delivery, or the customer service, all customer expectations are being set by the convenience that companies like Amazon deliver. But the fact that convenience will help people even more in be(com)ing healthier and happier, should be an even bigger driver.

> *For example, take the way the popularity of medical tourism is driven by the expectation of finding what you are looking for. From the best surgeon to the cheapest treatment option, people are travelling increasingly for medical procedures. Growing at a speed of 22% annually, medical tour-*

> *ism is set to be worth almost 180 billion euros by 2026. Taking a page out of the book of Amazon, **Heal2Go** created a global "online shop" for treatments. The site facilitates convenient searches by treatment, destination and package, clinic and price comparisons, quote requests, access to patient reviews and online bookings. Much as you would do when buying a pair of jeans.*

https://www.heal2go.com

What part of your processes is no longer on par with the expectations of the average spoiled Amazon customer?

Another reason to particularly pay attention to convenience is that health services are more often about making things convenient once again. Convenience is focused on minimising pain or removing a negative. And isn't that arguably the *raison d'être* of healthcare? Most patients have to deal with limitations every day, while they expect their life to be more convenient. The MySugr app, for example, brought simplicity to aspects of diabetes management that were previously cumbersome. It took care of the pain points in their life. There are many more examples of how the lives of patients are made easier today. The possibilities of new sensors in combination with artificial intelligence certainly create a range of opportunities to alleviate limitations.

> *Parkinson's disease is an incredibly difficult experience for both those living with the illness and those caring for loved ones. One of the common issues for Parkinson's patients is that at times they become stuck and immobile for no reason. To bypass this situation, the **Albert cane** emits hap-*

tic feedback as soon as it detects a freezing of gait. The rhythm can be felt through small vibrations in the handle. This interesting trick "awakens" the patient and prompts them to continue moving. It helps patients avert potentially embarrassing situations so that they are no longer limited from going out.

*The **Chronolife** vest is embedded with sensors that can predict the onset of a heart attack before it happens. Designed for patients diagnosed with chronic or congestive heart failure, the vest slips on easily and is meant to be worn daily. Even though it contains sensors that measure six different physiological parameters in real-time, it is fully machine washable and does not need charging. Without the need for internet, it connects to the smartphone of the patient, where it can be transmitted to a healthcare professional. By warning patients ahead, it provides the convenience of living a normal life that is not beset by the fear of an unforeseeable event.*

Convenience requires specific attention because technology is continuously making our lives more pragmatic. Each wave of digital disruption has already done so, from the ubiquity of information, to real-time written conversations with bots. But more is yet to come. Speech is rapidly becoming the new interface and standard for convenience. With the launch of the iPhone, touchscreens replaced plastic buttons. But by eliminating the need to use our hands and eyes, vocal interactions allow us to perform commands while driving, walking, exercising, cooking, or operating other devices. As people pick up their phones about 300 times a day, there is quite some "eliminating" to do indeed.

Apple's Airpods, Google's Home, and Amazon's Echo are most responsible for the massive uptake of voice-controlled interactions today. More than 40% of the users of these type of smart speakers say they have already requested product information by using voice interaction only. A little over two billion euro of online shopping was effectively conducted through smart speakers in 2017, according to OC&C Strategy Consultants. But the potential is massive. If you take into account that almost 10 billion digital voice assistants will be in use by the year 2023, it should come as no surprise that voice-initiated online shopping is expected to grow to 80 billion euro by then (Juniper Research 2018). That is a growth of 4000% in less than five years. Then we haven't even discussed the use of speech to command houses, cars or work appliances, which is actually the easiest and most popular use of voice-controlled interactions today.

What part of your business could literally be "called" upon?

This new, increasingly popular interface will also generate huge opportunities for health services. When smart speakers are addressed, this will facilitate a real conversation. And soon, these voice assistants will listen without being addressed.

> *The **Alexa** platform from **Amazon** has lightweight healthcare apps from institutions like the **Mayo Clinic** that offer medical answers, help communicate with caregivers or send alerts in case of emergencies. The **NHS** also announced a collaboration with Amazon's Alexa that will allow people to receive NHS-created health advice directly via their smart speaker. It's not difficult to imagine that Alexa will often be used for medical adherence by reminding people to take their medication. But Amazon's patents now hint at permanent health monitoring by continuously listening to its surroundings. When a recurring sneeze is noted, Alexa can suggest ordering Over The Counter medication. When the user's tone of voice is unusually unenthusiastic, Alexa might one day be able to detect diseases like depression or burnout. No wonder Amazon, together with Google, is considered to be one of the Tech Giants that will have the biggest impact on health by 2025, according to CB Insights (2018).*

While voice is clearly on the verge of becoming very important in our lives, facial technology is following its lead very quickly. Our phone unlocks by seeing our face. KFC in China launched a "smile to pay" terminal just like Alibaba allows you to "pay with a selfie" online. Now check-in, room access and elevator calling in Alibaba's FlyZoo hotels fully employ facial recognition. Similar convenience initiatives are being taken in healthcare.

> *Health insurer **Cigna** lets customers in China file and sign insurance claims using a photo. **Hospitals** are experimenting with facial technology to access patient records, streamline patient registration, detect emotion and pain in patients, and even help identify certain genetic diseases. **AI-***

> ***exa*** *has also filed patents that would allow monitoring of blood flow and heart rate through the presence of a camera. Facial technology will make things a lot more convenient in many different use cases.*

The ultimate convenience will be achieved if health services become ambient. Much like sensors and cameras are integrated in tools and devices to scan their nearby environment, or smart speakers are constantly listening when people are around, health services should ultimately become integrated into our environment. It would omit all limitations to creating healthy spaces, monitoring health parameters or commanding responsive behaviour. Ambient health is the ultimate convenience.

> *Just as curtains by **IKEA** and **Colt Chow** are ensuring a healthy space by purifying air, health services should ideally be integrated into the environment to initiate interactions without any effort or consciousness. For example, the **Qatar Airlines** fleet is fitted with LED lights that change colour to resemble sunlight, corresponding with the natural circadian rhythms of passengers. It was also already mentioned that hospitals are also implementing circadian lighting. The **Philips** EnergyUp lamps at **Starbucks** in The Netherlands are designed to have a mood-lifting, revitalising effect after around 20 minutes of use. These are examples of ultimate convenience that will truly make health and well-being an intrinsic part of our life. How much more pragmatic can it get than this? Whatever situation or health decision it will feed into, ambient health services can't but reinforce Healthusiasm.*

How can your health services disappear into the ambient to make them even more pragmatic?

Impactful – expecting to be able to make an impact
Pragmatic services are removing limitations by disappearing into the background. Persuasive services, on the other hand, are moving into the foreground to create a

meaningful impact. People don't necessarily expect these services to be ambient, they expect them to be (t)here. Of course, health services can be meaningful or impactful in multiple ways or forms. This section mostly refers to the way certain services make an impact that was never previously accomplished. Many of these are obviously technology-driven. But it does not need to be that way.

> I admire the way **Beagle Street**, a start-up life insurance company in the UK, managed to accommodate one of the most recognisable problems: finding the right policy documents to know what you are insured for. According to research, the insurance policy is among the top three most frequently lost objects in UK households. Beagle Street wanted to make an impact. Once people sign the policy online, Beagle Street will allow them to choose from several dozens of artworks. This artwork will then be printed on the front of the policy and placed in a nice frame to hang up in your house. That way, people will never forget where to look for their policy documents. A very impactful, non-digital way, of literally moving into the forefront.

Now, when it comes to impacting our health, changing our own behaviour is often considered the holy grail. It may perhaps determine only 30% of our health (WHO 2008), but it's the single most meaningful thing we can actually do ourselves. Scientific studies correlate cigarette smoking, low physical activity and poor dietary habits with bad health, disease and mortality. It's common knowledge that these types of behaviours are extremely bad for you. Yet very few people manage to change those behaviours. Unsurprisingly, people are expecting health services to make *behavioural change* less daunting for them. By being near, smart or immersive, technology now has various means to alleviate some of these burdens.

Previously, I mentioned that running apps like Strava or Start to Run are successfully built to make people persevere in their running ambitions. Perhaps there are not many conclusive large-scale clinical studies that cement the scientific impact of these applications, but many digital behaviour change programmes are being used and appreciated nonetheless. However, more and more digital therapeutic programmes are the subject of peer-reviewed clinical studies and are entering the field of treatment.

> *Quit Genius*, for example, claims to help people kick a smoking addiction for good. Smokers are guided through step-by-step cognitive behavioural therapy that consists of a mobile application, a connected breath tester and unlimited remote one-on-one coaching. With 36% of their users having quit, that is perhaps not particularly higher than certain other intensive methods, but it is considered the best digital addiction treatment in several recent clinical studies. But more importantly, it impacts those who do quit.

Virtual reality is also a proven new technology that is increasingly used to alter behaviour. Alleviating arachnophobia by gradually exposing people to virtual spiders is probably well known by now. Its uses in pain distraction and (pre-) operative anxiety have also been widely shared on different media. But how much of an impression would it leave on you if you could actually see your future self? This goes beyond looking at a mirror image. How meaningful would it be if you could interact with your future self about your failure to take action (now)? By putting on a virtual reality headset, you can be immersed in a world where you discover the future results of your current behaviour, and where the 'future you' gives a motivational speech to inspire you to take action. Time travel has never been so close.

> While virtual reality certainly would add to the experience, other technologies are generating similarly meaningful impact. *Healthy Selfie*, from the company Medical Avatar, generates a three-dimensional representation. It then ages you realistically, using inputs from your health trackers. The technology makes it possible for you to see how skin might wrinkle by smoking, for example, or how your waist might thicken without exercise. The *Future Self Mirror*, from the Copenhagen Institute of Interaction Design, also extrapolates the data from fitness devices and smartphones to augment one's mirror reflection with visual predictions.

How do you make it easy for your customer to change their behaviour?

Loneliness is also proven to impact health considerably. A meta-analysis conducted by the Brigham Young University (2017), showed that loneliness, isolation, and living alone all had a similar effect to obesity on a person's risk of early death. We live in the most connected age, yet rates of loneliness are assumed to have doubled since the 1980s. With more than 20% of the global population stating that they are lonely (Kaiser Family Foundation, 2018), loneliness is now considered a health epidemic globally. Question how real this is? Britain has appointed a minister of loneliness – the first nation in history to do so. Many cities have already followed in their footsteps, and other nations surely will too.

Facilitating 'emotional companionship' can therefore be another meaningful way of creating the expected impact for your customers. For those who were shocked by the movie *Her*, in which Joaquin Phoenix's character develops a relationship with an artificially intelligent virtual assistant personified by the voice of Scarlett Johansson... well that is exactly what it could be. People start to feel that it is not impossible to have meaningful conversations with virtual persons that entertain, educate or heal. Apple has even hired psychologists to optimise the human-to-computer interaction. People are starting to talk to Siri about all kinds of things – when they're having a stressful day, when they have something serious on their mind, or in case of emergencies. Siri can really help people when they need guidance on living a healthier life. When conversations are that meaningful, artificially intelligent speakers become our virtual companions. So why not turn them into robot-like objects with a personality? They will no longer be in the background, but be present in our home or in the hospital.

> ***Pillo Health*** *is a voice-activated assistant that is already offering the services of a doctor, pharmacist, fitness coach, Google search engine and nutritionist all in one. Through facial recognition, video conferencing and machine learning, it functions as a personal health assistant that provides the tools and information to keep you healthy. Pillo can recognise each*

user's face and voice, have a conversation with you, learn more about you as time goes by, dispense the correct pills at the appropriate time, and conveniently reorder medicine before it runs out.

https://www.pillohealth.com/

*But what if personal artificial intelligence could help you express and witness yourself by offering a helpful conversation? Well, **Replika** offers exactly that comfortable space where you can safely share your thoughts, feelings, beliefs, experiences, memories, and dreams with your own self/bot – a mirror image of your own personality. The chatbot, which learns to imitate the user's speech patterns, now even has a voice recognition feature so you can call your bot-friend to see how you yourself are doing. It was launched as a form of mindfulness and constant companionship to make you feel better.*

*If you think this is all too far-fetched for your type of company, then consider this virtual companion. Insurance company **Aflac** created a robot duck as a companion for children with cancer. They experience joy playing with this cute, fluffy, stuffed little animal. But it also helps improve their psychological well-being by producing soothing sounds and calming heartbeats. Through medical play, children are to treat their duck*

> *just as they are being treated, which reminds them of health-related tasks or health goals.*

Between 2017 and 2018, the use of home assistants such as Amazon Alexa or Google Home almost doubled among people aged 50 and older, from seven to 13 percent. This is no surprise for three different reasons. First of all, voice-interaction is indeed more convenient for the elderly than clunky keyboards or too-sensitive screens. And older people are also more in need of assistance. But most of all, the elderly often really crave *emotional companionship* as they are typically disproportionately affected by severe loneliness.

> ***ElliQ*** *looks much like EVE from the Pixar movie WALL-E, a computer ani-mated movie for kids. But ElliQ is in fact designed for the elderly as an aid to healthier and happier ageing. It might look like a table light, but its mov-ing cylindrical head can make animatronic movements and hold vocal interactions with people. Sounds to spacey? Try this. The voice-enabled assistant helps seniors to make video calls, sets medication reminders and arranges doctor's visits. And of course, it plays bridge. Is there any better companion possible?*

As OECD figures suggest, Japan is possibly the loneliest nation on Earth, and many inspiring initiatives can be found there. And they are an astonishing sign of where all this could lead. The Blue Leaf Café in Sendai, for example, hosts an augmented reality experience where guests can interact with a digital charac-ter sitting on the other side of the table. But even experiments with personal holograms are no exception.

> *The Japanese popular messaging app **Line** has brought its ambition to make loveable artificially intelligent characters to life by launch-ing **Clova**. This AI-driven hologram functions in similar ways to **Alexa**, but really provides intelligent conversations about the weather, news, music or, simply, your day. This virtual interactive friend can cer-tainly feel like a great companion against loneliness. At least, as soon as you overcome the initial self-conscious weirdness of talk-ing to a projected anime character. But be aware, she will· contact you via phone to ask you when you actually will be home tonight. The bright side is that she will already have turned on the lights and heating for you so that you don't need to enter a dark, cold house.*

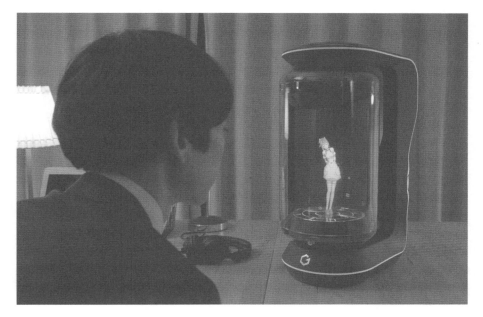

When you've initiated digital or automated health services that reduce human contact, have you thought about the impact it might have on the loneliness of people?

Changing behaviour is the single most important aspect of impacting (future) health oneself. Loneliness has become a global health epidemic that demands *emotional companionship*. But at the same, we live in an age where technology can really expedite short term *physical or mental improvements*. And people are indeed increasingly looking for ways to impact their own physical and mental performances. The Zombie Run app in which you need to outrun a horde of zombies certainly was a fun way to outperform yourself. But virtual or augmented reality can easily apply similar gamified techniques to make you push yourself physically. About 30% of virtual reality games now on the market are exercise driven, which is radically changing how we are exercising. From boxing to biking or flying-fruit slicing, it's expected that each fitness discipline will soon have virtual reality available because it creates such a big impact. It even can improve relaxation or cognitive abilities. However, beyond these rather gimmicky examples of how we can improve our physical and mental performances with virtual fruit-slicing, breakthrough technological inventions really can establish a physical or mental improvement.

> *Products like **eSight** can restore sight of the visually impaired. Paralysed people can walk again with the **ExoSkeleton** frame. **Cochlear** implants can make some people hear again. In the way that medicinal breakthroughs in the 1960s made us feel like we could actually impact our health for the first time, technology is now amplifying this feeling of impact even further. And that's exactly what people are looking for.*

What part of your business can make your customers (feel) physically and mentally improved?

From "for me" to "about me"

There are many ways to create impact, but there is one that is almost always a guarantee for success: personalisation. When products, services or experiences are made for me, they are more likely to make an impact. It's an evolution we see happening in all the industries around us. But it is of the utmost importance for Healthusiastic decisions. Because we all differ so much, personalisation is in fact the only certainty that will influence our health status. When this personalisation is used to predict the future impact of our current choices, it will actively influence our health and happiness.

Personal – expecting products, services and experiences made for me
From the first black Ford Model T in the early 1900s to the abundance of Amazon's offering, we've seen markets evolve in the past 120 years from a One-for-All to an All-for-One model. The choice is now so infinite that you'll always find something. I feel that this effort to offer "something for everyone" can be considered the first wave of personalisation. It ensures that at least one of the products and services appeals to the individual. But it came

with a huge downside. If you search for something as banal as, let's say, a carnival mask, you can scroll away half of your weekend to find the one that appeals most to you.

Algorithms have meanwhile created some order in that chaos, or in that excess. Based on previous purchases, recent search activities or your personal customer profile, that excess is now being narrowed down to what you most probably would choose anyway because that is exactly what customers expect. Research by Salesforce (2018) concluded that 76% of customers expect companies to understand their needs and expectations. And companies are putting in huge efforts to engage with their customers by offering products and services that fit their customer's personal needs and expectations. Ever noticed how your Spotify Weekly playlist is specifically generated to establish a personal engagement with the service? You can now also engage with fashion retailers to have clothing matched with your own style, size, lifestyle and existing wardrobe, sent in regular time frames to your house. Those algorithms narrow the options for you personally. "It's nothing personal, it's just business" has now turned into "It's personal, it's no longer just business".

For which products, services or experiences can you truly say "It's personal, no longer just business"?

I am fascinated by how the fashion industry is tackling the expectation of personalisation. It's no longer about customisation of clothing, nor will it remain about purchase-based recommendations only. Each body is literally so different that those types of personalisation are simply not enough to engage customers. With a growing 27% of the fashion industry being bought online (Forrester, 2018), we all know today how difficult it is to find clothes that fit perfectly. The day e-commerce manages to send clothing that always fits perfectly is the day we will see the remaining 73% of the fashion industry evaporate into online air. And that day is looming.

Echo Look, Amazon's new Alexa-enabled device, allows customers to take full length photographs and videos of the themselves to be analysed for fashion advice. As the customer creates lookbooks of their daily style, Alexa will rate the looks with algorithms made with fashion specialists. Customers will then receive personalised styling advice from the smart speaker.

More personalised than tailored styling advice is of course custom-fit clothing. US apparel brand Ministry of Supply uses a heatgun to shrink clothes to fit. For a while, Japanese fashion retailer Start Today even assured customers that apparel bought online would fit them perfectly at the first order. By using a garment called ZoZoSuit by Zozo Technologies Inc., embedded with 150 sensors, they've collected 15 000 body measurements per person to map their bodies. Customers definitely did make a statement on the need for clothing personalised to their body as over one million ZoZoSuits were ordered within the first six months. The suit is no longer available today because ZoZo Technologies now has enough data to produce custom-sized clothes for customers without creating 3-D models.

The Zozo suit by Zozo Technologies Inc.

Now, if customers value personalisation of the *outer* body that much, how critical must the *inner* body be for them then? One thing is certain. The Healthusiasm trend will only make it even more critical. People are expecting health and wellness solutions that are personalised around the individual. Because having services and experiences tailored to you makes a real difference in accomplishing what you aspire to achieve. It's that important. And for those who aren't yet Healthusiastic, they will certainly become so as soon as they are introduced to this level of personalisation. Amazing will become expected.

> *From **Sally**, a salad-making 'vending machine' that can prepare 1 000 different salads while calculating the respective calories, to **Vita Mojo**, the restaurant where you use a tool with sliders to determine the exact grams of ingredients and their respective nutritional value, they all help in personalising your food choices. Self-adjusting diet algorithms, like the ones offered by **Suggestic** and **FitGenie**, will help simplify nutrition planning. This type of Artificial Intelligence will personalise recommendations for people wanting to achieve a certain weight or fitness goal. And for those who still prefer personal coaching over Artificial Intelligence, mobile solutions like **Rise** can connect customers to a nutrition coach who then will provide personalised dietary suggestions on their actual food diary. That same remote personal coaching approach is being applied in exercising as well. Data collected by the wristband **GOQii**, for example, can be shared with one of their qualified trainers, who then provides personalised workout plans.*

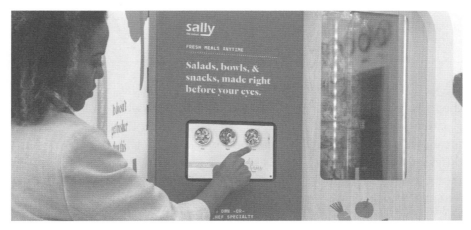

Sally, a salad-making vending machine that can prepare 1000 different salads. Picture courtesy of Chowbotics.

A ton of new initiatives is making it possible to make personalised health and well-being decisions. However, when it comes to medical choices, we have been treating our health with averages or over-simplified methods for many years. Ever wondered why pillboxes are mostly a multiple of five or seven? Think no further than the number of fingers on your hand, or the number of days in a week. We also consider a temperature surpassing 37 degrees centigrade as a fever, right? Well, that belief is based on "research" performed by Carl Wunderlich on 25 000 patients. A pretty solid sample indeed. However, it's interesting to understand that this study was conducted in 1868 with a thermometer of about 30 centimetres in length that measured temperature in the armpits of patients. This method of measuring fever is currently not the standard. The fact that it was impossible to read the temperature while this device was in place must surely have led to quite some variation. Recent studies comparing the measurements with that "museum piece" to current clinical thermometers indicated that the average temperatures were two degrees centigrade off. But beyond these facts, the simple reality is that the normal body temperature is individual. It differs from person to person. In fact, only 8% of the population has a normal temperature of 37 degrees. On top of that, it also varies by one degree through the day. Yet we still apply 37 degrees as the threshold for fever today.

Do you frequently contemplate what habits or routines are totally worth re-evaluating?

If 84% of customers expect to be treated as an individual (Salesforce, 2018), then why would this change if these people find themselves in a situation as a patient? One thing is sure: patients are no different than customers. This means that they have similar expectations, even if they find themselves in a different situation. In fact, as this situation is typified by anxiety and uncertainty, it is highly likely that they will claim personalisation to an even greater extent. Because it's about their body. And we all know that each body is different. Our muscle mass, our fat mass, our weight and other measurements, all should determine how much medication needs to be taken.

We are all unique, just as everyone else is. And our DNA proves it. Little wonder that a wealth of genetic tech start-ups is fuelling an even more important type of health personalisation: DNA-driven personalisation. And a wealth it is indeed. In fact, estimates from the genetic testing data company Concert Genetics (2017) have shown that there were more than 65 000 different genetic tests available on the market by 2017. So, DNA personalisation is now available for a wide range of applications of dietary and nutrient advice, fitness regimes, beauty care products and even medication. All of these types of applications will make a major contribution to the way we can impact our own health. But DNA-personalised medication will certainly have a huge impact on the way we will manage diseases. If you take into account that about 70% of the patient population does not respond well to a certain class of cancer or Alzheimer's drug, it is clear why pharmacogenomics plays such a crucial role in managing our health. Even asthma medication, diabetic medication or anti-depressants are ineffective for about 40% of the patient population (Spear BB, 2001). And while we are at the early stages of these insights, similar findings are expected in other therapeutic areas.

> Medical tech start-up **Genomind** helps people to understand how they will personally respond to different psychiatric medications. The testing kits are now made available for customers nearby the US grocery stores of retailer **Albertson**. Although there is still some debate on the availability of scientific evidence to back up these types of personalised medicinal recommendations, **Mayo Clinic**'s genotype testing already guides selection of mental health drugs for individual patients within their own genetic testing programme. Start-ups like **Genelex**, **Admera Health**, **OneOme** and **Color Genomics** are also making strides in the pharmacogenomics space. Pharmaceutical giants **GSK** and **Pfizer** have even partnered with **23andMe** to learn first-hand about pharmacogenomics.

People will welcome personalised medicine so that they can have the best possible impact on their condition. This will radically change the way medication will be delivered. Medication delivery will be a personal thing. Personal pill dispensers are already invading the market. But these are still focused on multi-medicated elderly. Some are blister packaged, validated by the pharmacist and oriented for industrial use in senior residents. Other robotic devices are for personal home use and offer a simple and automated way to manage multiple medications with 24/7 monitoring.

*The previously mentioned pragmatic solution **Pillo** is one of those home-use devices that dispenses personalised medication. The **Philips** Medication Dispensing Service, part of the Philips Lifeline service, is another personal home-use device that allows the elderly to live independently in the comfort of their own home. It is marketed as a monthly subscription service for 24/7 monitoring that also provides daily reminders and instructions and can function as an alarm if in need of assistance. The personal dispensing scheme makes an anomaly of missing doses, taking incorrect amounts, or taking medicines at the wrong times.*

The next wave of pill dispensers will start from the pharmacogenomics of each individual. Instead of swallowing the typical standard doses, people will be able to take personal doses of the active ingredient. The era of precision medication is finally upon us. It is the ultimate personalisation of medical decisions. Patients will take personalised pills that are built and optimised to their particular pharmacogenomic need. But if each individual medication is constructed on-demand, then it will even be possible to integrate different medication needs into one poly pill – which is easier to take and likely to improve adherence. These personalised "poly pills" would then have to be composed with a dispenser that is able to combine micro doses of the necessary active ingredients. Daniel Craft of IntelliMedicine has created a prototype "printer" that can produce the exact combination of active ingredients needed by any individual. From the different cartridges with active ingredients, the personal poly pill is 'printed'. This is the real initiation of an era of precise, on-demand medication that can truly personalise the way we manage our own conditions.

Predictive – expecting to know how to impact my own (future) health
Predicting the future has always fascinated people. Nostradamus, the medieval equivalent of a doctor, is known to this day for his predictions. Tarot cards, numerology, palm and crystal ball readings, or even horoscopes are still popular in today's incredible era of technology. And consider that in 2012 the world was preoccupied with the Mayan prediction that the world would end in that year. We wish to know what will happen to us or perhaps even when we might die.

__The Tikker Watch__ is a device that counts down to your estimated life expectancy. Through a simple medical survey, an estimate of your life expectancy can be calculated. Or, in other words, when death may oc-

cur. However, the Tikker watch is not about death expectancy. It's about encouraging people to lead a life they never would have thought possible and about leading a healthier life.

The Tikker Watch makes you think consciously about how you'd like to live today and in the future. It is indeed one (particularly strange) way of amplifying some people's Healthusiasm to make more Healthusiastic decisions. But what are all those correct decisions that will ensure the healthiest future for us? We don't yet know exactly. However, hardly anyone doubts that the right data, used in the right way, at the right time, will indeed enable more predictive, more efficient and more individualised Healthusiastic decisions. It could enable us to understand the likelihood of certain outcomes and ease the processes. Imagine if machine learning, instead of a doctor's opinion, could predict the likelihood of someone waking up from a coma. Wouldn't that inform a family's stance on continuing life-sustaining treatment? Or what if we knew the exact impact on our health for every single Healthusiastic decision we took – wouldn't that be powerful? Of course it would. Each of us simply wants to make the most of his own life. But we all walk a unique path based on so many decisions of which we don't know the results. Deep down, we all expect to be able to predict the implications of our actions. Gone are the words "If only I had known".

Can you free your customers from the feeling that they should have known something upfront?

__iCarbonX__ is a Chinese data company that aims to do just that: create a map of human health that guides people through their decisions. To achieve this, they are collecting both biological and behavioural data from millions of people from around the world. The biological data would comprise RNA and DNA, proteins and antibodies, microbiomes and metabolites. The behavioural data would contain exercise, diet, environment, and medical treatment. All this information in combination is then analysed to learn from birth to old age how we age or why we get diseases. By digitising every aspect influencing our health, we will be able

> *to learn from the effects of all our choices as never before. It will help people to make smarter choices, every day. It becomes a GPS of our health, so we can choose the path that is right for each one of us.*

From participation to sharing

As a result of technology and digital disruption, people can now take control and participate in things they weren't involved in previously. How great is this? It has become so easy to do things ourselves that we don't have to depend on others. We can more easily take matters into our own hands, even our own "health". And that's exactly what we are doing, because we want to be in control of our own body. If we can do it ourselves, we will do it. If we depend on someone else, we expect to participate in the decisions. If we want more, we will reach out to whomever or whatever we'd like to. Sharing has already become part of our life, so why not do it for our health too? It has proven to be highly beneficial. Sharing not only confirms our value, or makes us express our emotions, but it helps us learn from the opinions or the insights of others. When it comes to our own health, we expect to be able to participate and to share. It gives us a feeling of control over personal matters we were previously not involved in.

Participative – expecting to participate

When we think about banks, the image that might come to mind is an ATM. These Automated Teller Machines have been around for over 50 years now and we deal with them more than with the bankers themselves. The number of ATMs around the world is still growing. In fact, there will be four million of these robot cashiers by the year 2021. The reason for this success is the desire for self-service. Research conducted by Nuance (2013) confirmed that 67% of customers prefer self-service over speaking to a company representative. It's fast. It's convenient. And it puts people in control. Mobile banking meanwhile may have replaced a lot of the ATM functionalities and smartphones may have turned into mobile wallets, but it all comes from the same place: the desire for self-service.

Is there a part of your business or processes that people would more easily or happily do themselves?

In similar fashion, people are now servicing their own health. We are just a Google search from finding health-related information online. This search is no harder than asking the questions out loud, for a smart speaker to hear and reply to you. It has even led to healthcare professionals putting up infamous signs in their waiting rooms saying that people should not confuse their Google search with the medical degree of the doctor. While those signs are debatable on so many levels, it does show how all of this self-servicing has led to a Copernican Health Revolution. No longer are healthcare professionals stationary at the centre of the patient universe. Observe that health solutions are now in rotation around a patient. It's their health ecosystem. From wearables and sensors to hospitals and doctors, from social media and artificial intelligence to alternative medicine and lifestyle changes, people are at the centre of all solutions that are boosting their health and happiness.

> *Walgreens have understood this patient-centric Copernican model very well and have even started to adapt the design of some of their physical locations accordingly. Walgreens is actually stepping out of the traditional drug store format. Instead, pharmacists are now literally circling around the patients. They are in front of the pharmacy counter where they are more empowered to engage directly with patients. They are one of the solutions that rotate around the patient. And they recognise it.*

THE COPERNICAN HEALTH REVOLUTION

No longer are healthcare professionals stationary at the centre of the patient universe.
Observe that health solutions are now in rotation around a patient. It's their health ecosystem.

In the mid 20ᵗʰ century, the role of doctors could be compared to that of a parent. They would obtain and protect the best interest of patients. A little shockwave first hit this paternalistic relationship between doctor and patient in the 1980s, when people became more health-conscious. This decade, characterised by a decrease in alcohol consumption, smoking cessation and a fitness craze, saw the first instances of criticism of doctors. Patients felt less shame about changing their doctor if the relationship was not as expected.

But it wasn't until Dr Google interfered with the distribution of medical information that patients really required involvement in the reasoning. Decision making was no longer expected to be unilateral. Doctors were influenced by the reactions, needs, and experiences of the patients who were more informed and demanding than before. In a way, it can be seen as an evolution from closed evidence-based medicine to an open experience-based decision model (that remains based on science of course). The paternalistic patient-doctor relationship is evolving into a mutual relationship in which the patient is an active participant. Patients should feel as involved in medical decisions as they are when looking for the right services in other industries. They might even feel in control, much as they are seeking this in other parts of their life.

In a time when people are accustomed to looking themselves for the right personal service, to what extent do you involve patients in medical decisions?

Sharing – expecting to be able to benefit from sharing
We share our lives on Facebook and our photos on Instagram. We pin our style on Pinterest. We build our career on LinkedIn. We participate in discussions on Twitter. We share our houses on Airbnb and our cars on Drivy. But why are people doing this? On one hand, we have a desire to share our thoughts and experiences with others because it activates the reward-seeking part of the brain. The attention makes us feel the same way we do if we receive food or money. How did it feel when you recommended something to someone? That is exactly why

people convey useful information. We do this to be valued, to increase our social currency or to shape the way people see us. It makes us feel intrinsically good.

That's also why we call friends and family to share exciting or sad news. It might not be about social appreciation then, but venting our emotions is also satisfying. On the other hand, we want to receive and learn from others too. It guides us in our decisions because we tend to do what others do. If you have to choose between two restaurants but only one of them is crowded, you are more likely to be attracted to that one. If everyone is going there, the food must be delicious.

Are you ignoring what people are sharing about your products and services? Or are you investing time and resources to help them share something valuable?

It's valuable to give and receive. This hasn't changed much over the past decade (since the surge in social media use since 2007). We still generally share the similar things. But we share it more broadly now, because we've come to realise that sharing is more valuable than keeping it from others. In the recent past, people were reluctant to share things too broadly because they would no longer possess the exclusive power of being in the know. They feared it would diminish their personal value. Exclusivity and privacy were king back then. Now it is the other way round. Your personality is in part determined by what and how much you share. Your value within the network and the extent of your entire network can grow naturally by sharing. But you also receive knowledge and insights in return.

This has been shown to be very valuable for our health. We can share our symptoms, treatments and other health solutions with others, while learning from their experiences. You spread information but build more knowledge. It helps in finding better solutions more quickly. It is simply an efficient and effective way to become healthier and happier. Little wonder patient communities like PatientsLikeMe, Carenity or any of the several dozen others are attracting millions and millions of monthly visitors who spend on average more than an hour sharing and receiving each day. In the past, you might not have talked much about your disease to other people, or at least not to that many. But now people realise they can harness the experiences and wisdom of people just like them. It's so powerful that over 90% of patients claim they feel more confident thanks to the information shared by others on patient communities.

> *I guess the demonstrated value of sharing and receiving is greatest within communities about rare diseases. If a doctor sees only a couple of such patients over the length of their career, then there is even less chance that patients will encounter them. In the past, those facing a rare disease could easily feel alone. Even the experience of doctors was often too limited to really help them to live with the disease. Social networks like **RareConnect** and **Inspire** are specific online communities for patients and families affected by a rare disease. It helps them to get in touch with people facing the same difficulties. They can share their experiences and treatments, express emotions and learn from others. It helps them to discuss their situation with their medical professionals differently. It even brings true friendship.*

People do not only rely on others for additional information, but they also consult doctors for a second opinion more often. They might wish to feel more in control, or to feel greater certainty about the diagnosis. After all, doctors are but human (for now), and can make mistakes. In fact, Arthur Elstein, a cognitive psychologist who studied clinical decision-making over his entire career, concluded that diagnoses are wrong 10–15% of the time (Butterworth-Heinemann, 1995). A research team at the Mayo Clinic confirmed this finding. For 21% of their referred patients at the internal medicine department, the diagnosis of the initial medical professional was in complete contrast to the new diagnosis. This shows that people rightfully take an active role in their health management by consulting with new or other healthcare providers. Sometimes they will feel relieved by the confirmation, other times they might be presented with new insights that can help them in taking the next steps.

> *Early in 2019, **Stanford Medicine** launched an online service that gives patients a second opinion about their diagnosis or treatment plan. Based on collected medical records, a Stanford Medicine specialist will write a second opinion for the patient and his doctor within two weeks. San Francisco-based **ConsultingMD**, on the other hand, promises to connect*

you online with top doctors in the medical industry to process your second opinion within 48 hours. No surprises that the latter service is about five times as expensive.

Cleveland Clinic *understood very well that it can indeed be worthwhile to review the initial diagnosis. They started an "online second opinion consult" in 2004 for patients who were looking for peace of mind or encouragement. Over the course of 15 years, they've learned that in only 75% of the cases did the doctors from the Cleveland Clinic agree with the initial diagnosis. This is approximately in line with numbers mentioned earlier. But the online platform **bestdoctors.com** that gathers 50 000 doctors worldwide, claims to correct even more regularly. Their website mentions that initial diagnoses are adjusted in 45% of the cases, and that treatments are even adapted in 79% of the patients.*

Modifying the initial diagnosis does of course not define its quality. But the fact that diagnoses and treatments so repeatedly differ has a significant impact on the trust patients have in a situation that is already dominated by uncertainty and anxiety. We are used to having all the information available. Self-service puts us in control. That is why this type of uncertainty is hard to accept. It might convey the feeling that the whole picture wasn't evaluated in making a diagnosis. People expect more. Often this simply means that they will look for even more information and complementary insights. They will share the information about their health with even more stakeholders.

Reaching out more often and more broadly to other people, patients or additional doctors is only a small part of the health ecosystem at our disposal. Today, people can share health information and medical records with dieticians, personal coaches, life coaches, osteopaths, acupuncturists – and even algorithms. Many Healthusiastic decisions can be taken to influence one's health. This holistic approach to health takes into consideration a broader range of elements like our physical health, nutritional habits, environment, attitude, behaviours and relationships. It helps patients to feel more comfortable about a potential diagnosis or treatment. It builds trust because it considers more information. It puts them at the centre of all the available health solutions. People expect to be able to share and receive information within the entire ecosystem that rotates around them. It makes them feel valued, allows them to express emotions, and brings more knowledge and insights.

How are you making it easy for your customers to share their health information?

From popular to relevant

People have never really been spoiled by health services. In fact, they were very rarely a pleasure to use. Customer products and services, on the other hand, have always been created to generate customer satisfaction first, but often lacked a tangible health impact (if that was the purpose). In impacting their own health and happiness, customers expect services that provide a sufficient trade-off between pleasant and useful. Only then will it be popular. But that is only on condition that it is really relevant to them and their communities.

Popular – expecting pleasant and useful services

Healthusiasm is popular. Many consumer brands are jumping onto this bandwagon to grasp the wealth of opportunities available. Attention is captured by popular marketing strategies these brands master so well. But now it's time to start integrating popular culture into the businesses that are dry, like science. Medical or pharmaceutical organisations should not shy away from making medical and health decisions popular to those in need of them. In a way, they have a duty to fulfil in supporting people on matters they should know most about. It's a void that risks being filled by others who are potentially less knowledgeable.

When searching for "psoriasis treatment", The Journal of Clinical and Aesthetic Dermatology came to the surprising conclusion that far less than one out of 10 videos on YouTube are from a medical institution, a verified medical professional, or a pharmaceutical company. In fact, pharmaceutical companies hardly ever attain 25 000 subscriptions on their YouTube channel. A number of US-based hospitals do better and sometimes broadcast to about 100 000 subscribers. However, several health vloggers easily reach over one million Healthusiastic people with their health advice. And yes, there are many obvious and well-known excuses to be made for this discrepancy. Nevertheless, it remains food for thought that so many

> single vloggers (individually) manage to create more popular health-related content than the armies of doctors and marketers that pharmaceutical and medical companies have at their disposal.

For what expertise that you claim to be an authority in is it your role and responsibility to make it "popular" and widely available?

Of course, it's not about the comparison between the numbers of followers. But the colossal differences in popularity start with the appeal of the content or service. That's where scientifically driven organisations often struggle. It will remain a research-driven environment with processes that are not adapted for today's agile, technology-driven world. Even when it is properly executed, it fails to be translated into something appealing. The focus is often on the service-driven aspects, rather than on the customer-driven or the transformational aspects. A couple of years ago, research was conducted to analyse whether exergames, like the Nintendo Wii or Xbox Kinnect, were a valuable option to make the elderly more active. There are plenty of studies on the impact or lack thereof on balance, mobility, walking endurance, or cognition improvement. But the conclusions of these studies hardly ever mentioned customer satisfaction. Did the participants enjoy it? Would they do it again? Can it be made more appealing? The focus is so scientific that we forget to ask how satisfied they were.

On the other side of the spectrum, customer satisfaction is the primary factor that is researched. Consumer businesses risk going overboard in winning popularity contests. They focus on short-term, hype-driven products, services or experiences that speak to the (new) lifestyle or well-being decisions of as many people as possible. Research is mostly lacking to back up claims or even to validate their reasons for existing. These types of "fads" have proven their commercial success in the past. But as Healthusiasm is claiming ground, people now settle less readily on these ambiguous, commercial tactics. People are tired of constantly changing from fad to fad, like Paleo to keto, or from quartz crystals to activated charcoal. And let's just forget about cow-cuddling now. Sure, it's fun to try something new. It certainly is motivating to believe in something new. But people are tired of unsustainable niche approaches that disconnect them from their friends. And short-term results don't cut it when you want to impact your health.

Every single product, service or experience that feeds into Healthusiasm should balance "pleasing" and "proving". When it is pleasant today and still trustworthy tomorrow, it will be popular. Some businesses will have to increase their focus on being pleasant. Other businesses will need to add proof points. But the chances of success are slim if you only focus on one, or if one overshadows the other.

If you look at your products, services and experiences, would your customers benefit from more proof points or more pleasure?

> *In the short term, Thailand is forecast to be one of the countries most affected by Alzheimer's disease because it will be an ageing society by 2021. As some research has proven that singing helps (some) Alzheimer's patients retain their memory and speech abilities, The **Alzheimer Foundation of Thailand** created the "Memo Oke Playlist" in 2018. It contains songs where lyrics are sometimes removed from the videos and the elderly then need to remember the missing words. Karaoke is very popular in Thailand, with most families having karaoke sets in their living room. The elderly won't have to change much of their behaviour to engage with this campaign, making it a light-hearted way to create awareness about the disease and the treatments. It's a perfect balance of pleasure and some (necessary) proof points to make it popular.*

Pertinent – expecting relevancy

We all want to be part of something, to belong, whether it's to our friends, our families, our culture, our sports club, a fan base, or to someone we identify with. Belonging is a basic human need (see Maslow). It improves our motivation, our health and our happiness, because it is inextricably tied to the feeling that we share common interests and aspirations. It is relevant to us.

That is exactly what people expect from brands and companies. People expect products, services and experiences to be relevant to them, or – in other words – to the community they belong to. It's important to balance pleasure with proof points to ensure a certain degree of appeal, but ahead of all of this, it should be relevant. Companies and brands invest USD76 billion into market research each year, according to the Global Market Research publications by ESOMAR and BDO (2018). But today, knowing your customer is less about research and much more about continuously keeping a finger on the pulse. Growth of traditional market research has therefore been flat for the past four to five years. But newer methods such as data analytics and AI-driven consumer research, which already take up 40% of the entire research industry, have grown 10% in the past year alone. These newer technology-driven research methods that allow continuous monitoring are a necessity in today's reality in which external changes occur faster than companies can imagine. If companies want to remain relevant, they need to know how the needs of their customer communities are constantly evolving.

Do you occasionally hunt for customer needs,
or are you thoroughly scanning the horizon at all times?

The pressure to remain relevant is greater than ever. Relying only on in-house experts to develop the expected products, services or experiences will no longer be enough. Customer insights are needed, but customers should even be involved in the early development process of solutions. Luckily, harnessing the intelligence of the crowd to solve problems is less complicated than before. It has been used by every industry at some point or another. In fact, it's commonly known to be the foundation of the successes behind companies like Wikipedia, PatientsLikeMe, Lego or even 23andMe. They all source information, insights, and even solutions from crowds. And yes, scientific researchers and medical scientists now crowdsource to better understand needs and incorporate the ideas of customers. It ensures that health solutions are relevant for the targeted community.

> *Early 2018, pharmaceutical giant **Johnson & Johnson** launched a Digital Beauty QuickFire Challenge to incorporate people from outside the organisation, who have a diverse set of experiences, goals and technical abilities, into its product development processes. Crowds were invited to send in solutions that address skin health management, skincare personalisation or anything related to stubborn skin issues. Winners would receive up to 50 000 euro along with a residency at its Innovation Incubator JLABS. The **American Heart Association** (AHA) also crowdsourced the wisdom of thousands of patients, caregivers, doctors and researchers to identify the biggest needs related to cardiovascular diseases. Prizes were granted to those who came up with the most relevant, scientifically solid and patient-driven ideas. It even led to an increased focus on the treatment of atrial fibrillation by offering a USD2.75 million grant to the Patient-Centred Outcomes Research Institute.*

*Do you tap into the abilities and experiences
of the crowds outside of your organisation to find
the appropriate solutions for your customers?*

Reaching out to existing communities has always been an important part of getting to know your customers and their ideas. As technology has accelerated customer needs, it has become more critical for companies. But now companies are starting to build actual (physical or digital) communities for their customers, to create the relevance that their customers are seeking as part of a community. It's no longer just about putting out a relevant offering based on the insights and ideas of a community. Now, it's about building relevancy by creating an actual community for their customers.

> *Vancouver Running Company is pushing the limits of how relevant a physical running store can be. In a time where running retail has suffered from online options, Vancouver Running Company created a much more experiential-based retail environment. Needs are very much the same for both the online and offline world, but physical stores can actually feed into the expectation of being part of a local community. The nearby experts for shoe choice and the training programmes with an Olympic marathoner all create a sense of belonging, inspiration, shared knowledge and resources for runners. The store's strong community has now become a test ground for brands like* **Nike** *and Stance. Meanwhile, Nike has also opened their own store in Santa Monica, California, as a community space for runners. Located at the site of one of the first Nike stores, people now gather and share running experiences there once again. In fact, the company – then called Blue Ribbon Sports – is now facilitating a community for and with running enthusiasts, just as it did in its very early days.*

It certainly remains important to bring people with the same interest, passion or need together, within a health-related context. It was always that way in the past. Healthcare was delivered within the community. The local doctor visited people's houses because that was where birth, sickness and death happened. The family was nearby and the whole town community was somewhat involved. People knew and cared for one another. It was relevant to them because people belonged to the community. It made health and healthcare closely integrated in their daily lives. But nowadays, doctors rarely do home visits. Healthcare migrated to within the walls of hospitals, which became specialised centres to which people travel from afar. Over time, health and healthcare have become less of a feature in our daily lives.

Nevertheless, a mass of research confirms that over half of our health status is caused by factors related to our environment or our habits. These are elements that communities can influence. There is a positive correlation between social connection and community, and reported health and happiness levels on the other. As a result, many cities are focusing heavily on building relevant smaller communities within the bigger one.

*Have you explored the possibility of building
a community for your customers that can bring them
the necessary relevancy?*

The company mission statement by the American multinational corporation 3M is "to improve every life through innovative giving in education, *community* and the environment". The relevance of communities is becoming more obvious. Some hospitals are initiating steps to build communities within their immediate environment. This could generate a relevant impact on the broader wellness approach hospitals are aspiring to. But even non-traditional health companies direct their attention towards health-impacting communities now.

__Lidl__ has long understood the relevance of building local communities. In 2018, it unveiled plans to build a community that contains 3 000 homes, a primary school, playgrounds and, of course, a supermarket. But it also communicated the launch of "The Bakery", a store providing a safe place to talk about mental health. __Marks & Spencer__ initiated a similar initiative and organised mental health meetups at the retailer's in-store cafés. Co-working spaces at __WeWork__ have become thriving communities that prioritise wellness and health services. Within their Flagship store, Athleisure brand __Lululemon__ opened up a library with over 1 000 books, to enable the yoga-minded community to meet and share relevant experiences. Last but not least, __Tencent__, the technology company mostly known for WeChat & Fortnite, has funded the Dancing Granny app Tang Dou. This cultural phenomenon of square dancing is a very important part of local communities. With over 4 000 meetups gathering over 500 000 dancing grannies per month, Tencent is contributing to both a relevant community and the health of elderly women in China.

Contemporary Evolutions

If Recurring Expectations are the expectations people have towards the products, services and experiences at their disposal, then Contemporary Evolutions are the ones they have towards companies or brands. These evolutions are societal trends that could have a huge impact on people's decisions. Even if your products, services or experiences meet Recurring Expectations, even then people might reject them if you don't meet their standards of what a company or brand should live up to.

As with Recurring Expectations, not all Contemporary Evolutions may be appropriate to your business. But it certainly is worthwhile to "stress test" your company and brand against these evolutions.

The company

Customers have become buyers who want to believe what a company is promoting. This calls for an authentic, meaningful purpose that is transferred through the culture of the company, so that not only customers, but also employees, are turned into fans of the purpose-driven company. Meaning creates happiness for customers, and certainly for employees. They are as Healthusiastic as customers. So Recurring Expectations also apply to employees, and companies need to ensure that their internal cultural helps people to be(come) the best and most productive version of themselves. Nowadays, people – whether customer, patient or employee – have high expectations of companies and brands. They want to believe in them.

Purpose – the evolution towards authentic meaning

In the 1940s, *Fortune* magazine polled business executives about social responsibility, which referred to the consequences of their actions beyond making a profit. This was the first time the concept of taking ownership of their social responsibility had come up. Back then, Johnson & Johnson was one of the very first adopters and created a credo (in stone) that required them to put the needs of the ones they serve first. But Corporate Social Responsibility, as we know it today, only really came about when Shell first implemented it in 1998 (Corporate Watch Report, 2006).

Corporate Social Responsibility has not undergone a radical change since. It remains a separate department within the larger organisation. Most initiatives are independent of the bulk of the business but do serve as proof points for the company's mission statement, showing that the company walks the talk. Some critics go as far as to claim that these initiatives are purely undertaken to distract customers from ethical questions related to their core business. Whatever the case, Corporate Social Responsibility in its current form is no longer sufficiently relevant. In the context of "fake news" as a pretty standard assumption, trust in businesses has suffered a major hit. In fact, 73% of global customers are afraid that "fake news" can be used as ammunition to achieve what a company wants to achieve (Edelman, 2019).

This is a very important fear for companies to note. People are looking for ways to be helped in their aspirations. So consuming a product or service from a company that is "fake" in its ambitions can lead to guilt. Edelman (2018) reported that 51% of customers avoid consuming products of companies that have a negative impact on society, the environment or themselves. The latest Edelman survey in 2019 highlighted that 64% of global customers make purchasing decisions based solely on a brand's position on social or political issues. The majority of customers are now "belief buyers". That is why they want to know what is real. Authenticity and transparency are the true values customers are trading with companies. They won't just buy *what* you do, they want to buy *why* you are doing it. Customers are selecting brands and companies as their change agents. Very often, that ambition for authenticity is why some people become entrepreneurs. They believe in something so much that they want to "change the world". And that authentic aspiration is exactly what their customers believe in too. Existing companies need to live up to these new expectations.

Are you giving your customers reasons to truly believe in you? Or are you to some extent avoiding taking an authentic and fully transparent position in society?

Corporate Social Responsibility can no longer be a communication strategy developed in an obscure department. In fact, social responsibility should permeate the entire culture of the company. Companies not only need to take a stand on social issues, they must also take part in those conversations. Only then will customers feel that they are engaged with purpose-driven brands that are authentically defending the same causes as they are. Achieving this is very powerful. It will turn your customers into fans, which is what Patagonia has achieved in defending a sustainable economy. But it is not without risks. Taking a strong position and delivering on it might put revenue at risk, as KLM is doing by suggesting that their customers could consider a more ecological alternative for certain flights, like the train. It might also drive customers away. Or does it?

In 2016, Colin Kaepernick, a National Football League (NFL) athlete, kneeled during the national anthem to protest against the racism, police brutality and social injustice that was prevalent in the country. Several other players and teams followed his lead and protested with him. The action received major media attention, with many people claiming it was disrespectful towards the flag and thus the United States of America. Whether influenced by President Trump's tweets or not, Kaepernick was eventually fired from the NFL. **Nike**, *the official sponsor of the NFL, stood by their athlete. In 2018, the company created a polarising marketing campaign that featured Kaepernick. It said,* **"Believe in something, even if it means sacrificing everything."** *It perfectly described what Kaepernick was doing. It also described very well what Nike was doing. Within the first 24 hours of the campaign, no less than 100 000 tweets were sent with the #boycottNike hashtag. Social media featured plenty of people burning their Nike apparel to show disagreement. Nike stock on the markets took a 3.2% hit on the first days (but eventually ended the year with a growth of about 50%). But the positive reactions totally outweighed the #boycottNike actions, as the campaign attracted more than a million positive responses, according to ListenFirst. Most large corporations avoid taking a stance that could make customers angry. But Nike has never shied away from being involved in political, societal or health-related debates. The 2018 "equality" campaign during black history month was one example that captured everyone's emotions wonderfully. But the Colin "believe" campaign was perhaps the most audacious and controversial of them all. And Nike knew exactly what they were doing. The campaign generated at least USD43 million worth*

> *of free advertising. Kaepernick's jersey was one of the most sold in the entire NFL, even though he was not even allowed to play. But more importantly, it turned the right Nike customers into Nike fans by daring to take a stance on subjects their customers value as much as Nike. Customers now believe in Nike and everything they stand for.*

What health-related issue does your company believe so strongly in that you are not afraid of potentially driving away certain customers with it? For what issue would you put a part of your revenues at stake?

Customers expect companies to have an integrated culture that takes a clear stance on issues that people can believe in. This means that related initiatives cannot be manufactured, in the way it seems Corporate Social Responsibility often is. These initiatives are about more than just generating awareness, they are actually influencing and changing (parts of) society. They come from within that company culture and are coherent with the overall mission statement. When done right, they can then even be championed by employees who feel they are empowered to do so. And that is exactly what employees are expecting – that employers will join and support them in taking actions on societal issues. Not only customers need to be fan of your organisation. Employees also need to be turned into fans that believe in your purpose.

> *The largest department store in the United States, **Kohl**, launched a clothing line for kids with disabilities and complex medical needs. The clothing made in sensory-friendly materials will have abdominal access as well as options specifically designed for wheelchair patients. It was an idea generated by one of Kohl's technical directors. Having a daughter with special needs himself, he gathered a group of colleagues with similar experiences to discuss solutions with the product teams. Together, they developed and launched a couple of clothing lines focused on inclusivity, one very particular social issue they've helped Kohl to take a stance on.*

These types of initiatives reinforce and demonstrate the authenticity of the purposes that companies and brands are vocal about. No more than a couple of decades ago, your brand was everything you carefully crafted in your media campaign. Some might come across it, others might not. Some might like it, others might not. Today, however, we live in a connected world that makes your brand a lot more transparent. Everything is pretty visible to everyone, and they all form an opinion in no time. The consequence of this radical transparency is that your internal culture also makes up a larger part of your brand now. Your brand is simply defined by everything that is visible to the outside world. So, it is all the better to be authentic, meaningful and in line with your purpose, your internal culture and your mission statement. Otherwise your entire brand will be seen as fake. And that cannot be the purpose.

Corporate wellness – the evolution towards self-care at work

It's one thing to create a meaningful purpose for the outside world, but purpose is important for your employees as well because it creates meaning for them. And when employees find meaning in their job, it will add to their happiness. It's no different to what was discussed earlier about happiness not being a permanent state but a result of fulfilling your basic, emotional or aspirational needs. After all, employees are also people, just in a different situation. All Recurring Expectations will certainly apply to them too. So, if you are focusing on the Healthusiasm of your customers, don't forget that your employees are as Healthusiastic as your customers or your patients. This means that you can't leave your employees out if you are serving your customers with health services.

Early on, companies understood that a healthy and happy employee is a more productive one. But it wasn't until the late 1970s (yep, that decade again) that true workplace wellness programmes really kicked off. Prior to that, there were companies that built employee fitness centres, but that was mainly in companies where good physical condition was a primary need. In other companies, it might have been available, but for the C-suite only. Other scattered examples involved support for smoking cessation or alcohol abuse. It was Johnson & Johnson (again) that established some sort of prototype for what a corporate wellness programme ought to look like. Started in 1979, their "Live for Life" programme provided support for weight control, nutrition and stress management while other companies were still focused on injury prevention and occupational safety. Health awareness at the workplace grew in the following years, and elements like stress, job satisfaction and sleep management were added by the mid-2000s.

When the Quantified Self came about at the end of the first decade of the 2000s, tracking tools also started invading organisations. It allowed ROI-driven, wellness-hesitant companies to measure the actual impact of their initiatives. It even motivated many companies to start wellness programmes as it helped them to understand the potential impact of corporate wellness – certainly in countries where larger companies are incentivised to self-insure their employees. Logging employee activity was an opportunity to measure against the potential reduction in their own health expenditures. But for companies that aren't self-insured, the returns of these investments are less tangible and the need for proof perhaps more desirable. After all, most illnesses are (unfortunately) not yet considered wellness-sensitive, and lifestyle-related conditions mostly hit employees only after they retire. That's why 'quantifiable' programmes were welcomed by companies. But while some companies are still attempting to prove the health impact of their efforts by collecting aggregated data of their employees, researchers at Harvard University (2014) had already reviewed 36 studies and found that every dollar spent on wellness programmes reduced absenteeism-related costs by about $2.73. Another meta-analysis, by the Chapman Institute (2012), found a 25% reduction in sick leave and health costs.

I had the opportunity to kickstart a diverse range of health and wellness programmes in different industries. They ranged from corporate-initiated programmes to HR-support companies with a growing, supplementary wellness service, and a number of start-ups that each offered specific services in their own speciality. Each offered their own approach around one or more aspects of the holy trinity of healthy living. I'll share two interesting Belgian approaches.

EnergyLab creates corporate-specific well-being services to encourage their employees to live healthier lives. Their goal is to give people the energy they need in their professional and personal life. Specialising in guiding athletes, EnergyLab's corporate programmes are focused on motivating people to combine their jobs with exercising. Physical workshops on healthy eating are combined with nutritional tips, training schedules and activity tracking within their digital platform. Public sporting events become corporate and individual challenges that can even unlock donations to good causes. It motivates many employees to move. It even creates team spirit.

> **emma.health** *is a medically founded insight into your health. Based on a questionnaire, and using algorithms, your lifestyle is mapped on a personal health diagram, to allow you to build a personalised action plan. emma. health can help people protect themselves from chronic diseases and mental health issues. The various elements of this preventive approach are the pillars of their client-specific employer pack that helps companies to personalise their well-being policy to the needs of their employees.*

Our work environment is considered our second home. It's indeed where we spend the second most time in a typical week. Any health services offered there immediately makes it very *nearby*. The corporate wellness programmes also go beyond providing *information*. They offer *supportive* health services that consist of *convenient*, often *personal* and sometimes *quick* assistance. Some are even taking their first steps in *predicting* how your health might evolve if not properly taken care of. Corporate wellness programmes meet Recurring Expectations very well. So it is no wonder that corporate wellness programmes have grown into a USD40 billion industry, according to the Global Wellness Institute (2018). However, just 9% of the global workforce has access to them. There is still a lot of potential, which means that this market is bound to grow significantly in the years to come.

But the market will not only grow but evolve. For example, tracking the activities of employees might undergo an evolution. One of the reasons is that its impact has already been quantified for many different types of programmes in the past. Another reason is that employees might not want to feel like lab rats. But the main reason for carefully considering whether to collect data through your wellness programme is that employees need to be willing to participate. Because even though, as explained earlier, people expect to *participate* in their own health, and even if they are therefore more open to *share* their health information, most are still rather reluctant when an employer "obliges" them to do so – even if the data is aggregated. The reason for this reluctance is largely related to the "Copernican Health Revolution" mentioned previously. People look at all the health services that rotate around them. As soon as they don't feel at the centre, there is a risk that they will withdraw. Even if people are part of a work community, that community is perhaps not the one they intrinsically want to build relevance with, specifically in relation to their own health. Such a programme should be designed for the benefit of employees as a tool at their disposal so that they feel that the initiative comes *from* their own desire.

*Are your corporate wellness programmes for them,
or by you? This may seem irrelevant to you,
but not to your employees.*

Corporate wellness programmes should not be financially coercive, as much as employees should not be 'hierarchically motivated' to participate. So why do it at all? But in a time when 48% of employees in the US have cried at work (Ginger, 2019), and 15.8 million working days are lost per year in the UK due to mental health issues alone (QBE, 2018), companies shouldn't hesitate to grant voluntary corporate health solutions. Whether to attract talent, to maintain happiness, to increase productivity or to decrease absenteeism, it should be available for their benefit first. That's the only way to succeed. Sounds confusing? Don't know how to 'manage' these investments? Perhaps it might help if you look at it in the same way as you go about the most low-key, basic example of corporate wellness: office plants. It's well known that plants remove trace toxins and carbon dioxide from the air. They certainly make our work environment more pleasant and can make us feel calmer. But research (Lohr, V.I. 2010) has even shown that plants reduce stress, increase pain tolerance, and improve productivity. Without a doubt, plants have increasingly invaded your workspace. That wasn't a difficult decision. Yet your employees will have benefited from it without it requiring a proven return or obligatory participation.

> *Start-ups like **The Sill**, an online/offline retailer of potted plants, frame plants as a form of wellness. **Greenery NYC** couldn't agree more. The botanic arts company, founded only in 2010, believes that plants are the antidote to everyday stress. The retailer has greened almost every major New York office, including Google, the New York Times, and Etsy. Plants make for a different experience. And the more plants, the more of a difference people will feel. That's exactly what **Second Home** must have thought when they conceptualised this coworking space for creative companies in Lisbon, London and Los Angeles. The design of this workspace is inspired by nature and biophilia, which stimulates connections with nature and other forms of life. The result? The open office in Lisbon*

is greened with 2 000 individual plants, ultimately living up to Second Home's mission statement to make people happier and more creative.

Second Home's new Lisbon outpost, designed by architects SelgesCano, is adorned with more than a thousand plants and trees.

Apart from the green 'feel', plants are perhaps not that different a type of ambient health service as the digital tools that measure and purify air quality. **Take Air***, a young Belgian start-up, is creating natural-like healthy indoor environments by injecting natural organisms into the air ducts of a building with a bio-disperser. Meeting people's expectations for the ultimate convenience, this ambient solution creates a positive effect on the health and happiness as well as the productivity of the employees. But the same thought counts for materials that improve their posture and overall health, or health food options in the company restaurant. These are obvious choices that employees would gladly benefit from.*

Of all the things that are ambiently present for your employees, what has the potential to improve their health even more?

The Workplace Wellness survey (2017) by The International Foundation of Employee Benefit Plans concluded that 66% of employers reported increased productivity from their wellness efforts. The survey also found that 75% of employers offer wellness initiatives as a way to improve the overall health and well-being of their employees. They want to do good. If your intrinsic motivation for putting out wellness programmes is to make your employees healthy and happy, not least because it is what you want to achieve with your customers, then it should of course be ingrained within your company culture. According to *Harvard Business Review* (2016), wellness programmes won't work unless the company culture allows and encourages to prioritise self-care. It's a critical part of making employees healthy and happy.

Telework and flex work can be a good way to illustrate how culture is indeed critical. Work has been organised from offices during the past 140 years, and entire company cultures were based on that reality. Modern life, however, is racing at a hectic pace, and people feel constantly under pressure. The daily commutes do not really bring you the desired rest either. It's not a surprise that a recent Gallup Survey (2018) indicated that 44% of employees have signs of burnout. It's the disease of the era. In May 2019, the World Health Organization even added Occupational Burnout to the International Classification of Diseases (ICD). Teleworking and flexible working were supposed to alleviate employees somewhat from the hectic burdens of life. Many organisations meanwhile have installed some form of teleworking or flexible working, for as much as the jobs allow. But if the company culture is such that employees are apologising about working from home, then to what extent does it create wellness? Flexibility should be reason agnostic and should not require justification. Very often teleworking and flexible working have caused more burnout, because boundaries are compromised. People don't set their availability hours themselves and stick to them. Instead, the company culture makes them feel that they should always be available. Even if the teleworking and flex working is set up for their benefit, it will never have the necessary impact as long as the company culture does not prioritise self-care.

Employees and customers are the same people, but in different situations. This means that both have the same Recurring Expectations. It's therefore perhaps not a bad idea to approach employees as your customers. Because you can't – and definitely shouldn't – oblige your customers to participate. At the same time, your employees could be an interesting test environment for something you might want to bring to the market. If it speaks to your most difficult employees, chances are it will speak to your customers too.

> *To create a wellness clinic for its employees at Cupertino, **Apple** is currently looking for nutritionists, sleep and exercise specialists, nurses and even care navigators. It is supposed to provide health services as a more holistic care experience and is rumoured to be an internal test before rolling out future customer health solutions. Early in 2018, **Amazon** announced it would be teaming up with **Berkshire Hathaway** and **JPMorgan Chase** to create joint solutions to reduce the healthcare spending of the more than 1.2 million employees and their families. This diverse group (socioeconomic status, geography, and age, among other factors) could be helpful when searching for solutions that work for specific use cases (for example, chronic disease management) and population demands (such as pharmaceutical delivery). This diverse group is certainly helping them in testing out, for example, the right health insurance products.*

For which health solution that you might want to bring to your customers would your employees be perfect to test and tweak it on?

People want to be(come) as healthy as happy as possible. And corporate wellness programmes are meant to encourage workers to achieve that. When taking into account that your employees have the same Recurring Expectations as your customers or patients, you'll be able to draw up the right programmes. They'll be made for the benefit of the employees within a culture that prioritises self-care of the person as a whole. It will reinforce the company culture, confirm the purpose of the company, and install true corporate wellness.

The customer

Earlier sections of this book emphasised how all generations are more enthusiastic than ever about having an impact on their health and happiness. There are still differences between generations but they are no longer as great as before. All generations, in principle, consume similar products, pursue similar things in life or build a similar identity. Age is no longer such a distinguishing factor in what people expect from brands and companies. However, brands and companies tend to focus on the most health-conscious generation ever: Millennials. Packaging is made "instagrammable". Services display young-sters. Experiences are about hipster events.

It is true that Millennials are more health-conscious than other generations at their age. Healthy eating, regular exercising and sleep have always been part of their lifestyle and even personality. Millennials also comprise one of the largest consumer groups, and together with Centennials, are bound to outgrow any other generation in the next decades. However, today, depending on the re-port consulted or the age threshold that is used, the number of Millennials has hardly exceeded the number of Baby Boomers. But more importantly, Ameri-can research by Epsilon Resources (2019) indicated that Baby Boomers would spend 70% more annually than Millennials, making them economically worth targeting. A focused study of Baby Boomers, compiled by AARP (2013), a US non-profit organisation that supports ageing Americans, found that spending by people aged 50+ is expected to increase by 58% over the next 20 years.

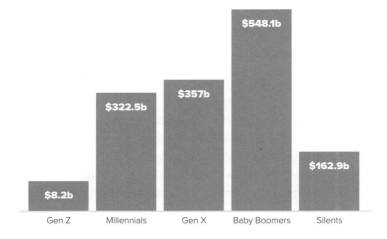

ANNUAL TOTAL DOLLAR SPEND BY GENERATION

American research by Epsilon Resources (2019) indicated that Baby Boomers would spend 70% more annually than Millennials.

Yet companies and brands are torn between focusing on the youthful Millennials or the senior Baby Boomers. Unless you are selling retirement homes or hearing aids, there has historically been a strong preference for young people. Especially because companies did not want to be seen as "elderly brands" for that could harm their image and reputation. But the new seniors, driven by the Healthusiasm Trend, are quite different to those who have gone before. Unlike their parents, they do not desire to relax during retirement. They want to go out and do the things they've always wanted to do. This generation, who grew up watching Peter Pan, still wants to explore what's beyond the horizon. AARP concluded that they still seek opportunities for personal growth. People in their 50s are taking up studying again, they start a business in their 60s, and why not get married again at the age of 70? PEW Research (2019) found that 70-year-old Chinese Baby Boomers still aspire to an active life with work, travel, leisure and even sexuality.

> Here are some examples of how Boomers are still active on several fronts. **McDonald's** is now not only employing 250 000 older workers, but it is also piloting a job-matching service for seniors. **Walmart** specifically employs seniors to welcome and help other seniors. On a monthly basis, 500 000 grannies tinder their way to dancing on corners in China with the **Tencent** funded app, Tang Duo. PEW Research and American Life project calculated that 80% of all luxury travel spending is done by people of 50 years and older. In fact, Baby Boomers spend more than any other generation (per capita) on errands, OTC products, and travel and leisure.

So, gear up for some transformation-driven health marketing to answer these aspirational needs. These youth-obsessed Baby Boomers are constantly looking for ways to live healthily. And unlike the younger generations, they have more time and definitely more money to devote to the health and appearance of their bodies. Baby Boomers are more active and healthier than before. They dress in activewear. They get themselves onto tennis courts or to spinning classes. It's all about living, not about ageing. That's also why Baby Boomers don't like the words "aged" or "elderly". They deny feeling or acting old until it is really inevitable, because they simply love life. And if 50 is the new 30, then maybe it is worthwhile for your company to target those new "youngsters". At least that is what they expect from you.

Helen Mirren for L'Oreal: "Are we worth it? We are more than ever!"

*In 2015, **L'Oreal** created a campaign that featured actress Helen Mirren wearing an edgy biker jacket and bright red lipstick. During the ad she says "The perfect age is now" – a statement that exactly embodies how Baby Boomers feel. L'Oreal's iconic slogan "Because I'm worth it" was even slightly twisted to fit the message the ad wanted to convey. With "Are we worth it? We are more than ever" it simply invites Baby Boomers to impact their health and happiness now. With this advertisement, L'Oreal reinforced their image with these Baby Boomers. And that's exactly what Apple has recently achieved as well. While 40% of Apple products are purchased by Baby Boomers, **Apple** enlarged its market for the Apple Watch by integrating fall detection and atrial fibrillation warnings. Electric bike company **Evelo** is primarily targeting a more senior population. With the slogan, "Live life to the fullest", it supports drivers in remaining active and independently mobile. Products are also launched specifically for Baby Boomers in the food and beverages market. **Perennial**, for example, is a plant-based milk with specific vitamins and nutrients for older people, to bolster brain health, bone strength and digestive function.*

*How is your company motivating your teams
to ramp up the focus on the active lifestyles
of these "don't-call-me-old" customers?*

Instead of automatically targeting the so-called most health-conscious generations, perhaps it is worth wondering what the former fitness craze generation could mean for you. They were the first to pro-actively do something about their health back in the '80s. And they certainly are the ones with the aspiration, time and money to do so now. Similarly, companies and brands should reconsider targeting the Wealthy, Worried and Well. What could your company mean for the more deprived groups of people, for patients, or for those who still require some education? Healthusiasm is a macro societal trend that is impacting the entire population. Find what fits with your purpose or existing offering and shift to a new audience that confirms or complements your own purpose. Help any population to be(come) as healthy and happy as possible.

> *Focused on people with disabilities, **Ford** adapted the trunk of their Ecosport SUV to double as a portable wheelchair ramp, while supermarket **Kohl** created clothing for people in wheelchairs. The **NBA store** was made accessible for people with autism. Noise-cancelling headphones were distributed, and the store staff were trained to deal with the special needs of this population. Also helping autistic persons, **Samsung** has created a tablet app PizzaAut to enable them to work autonomously in restaurants. For cancer patients who suffer with altered taste, **Life Kitchen** teaches them to cook nutritious meals that are more enjoyable. And **Lisa Marks**, associate professor at the Georgia Tech School of Industrial Design, created an algorithm that designs lace bras for women after they have undergone a mastectomy. It helps cancer survivors with comfort and symmetry, the two challenges most women were facing after having their breast removed. Would you bring it to the market?*

*So many different kinds of people who need tailor-made
solutions turn to you. Are you turning away
or is it your purpose to face them?*

The convergence of the two worlds

When looking for solutions to make themselves healthy and happy, people real-ise that these can be found anywhere. This changes the competitive landscape of companies and brands as much as it creates the necessity for partnerships. Choosing between beating them or joining them has never been so important for companies. In fact, it will largely define their strategy and success.

Competition – the evolution towards more competition

Earlier in the book the Healthusiasm model schematically explained how both the consumer world and the medical world are converging. The healthcare industry is moving into wellness, while consumer brands are helping people to self-care. It has made the dichotomy between patients and customers dis-appear. All industries have come to realise that patients and customers are in fact one and the same person with that one obvious aspiration: be(com)ing the healthiest and happiest person possible. This Healthusiasm is fuelling a rise in Healthusiastic decisions. Whatever situation people may find themselves in today, they will look for health solutions even if these are not from the tradi-tional healthcare players. Consequences can even be such that people move away from these traditional healthcare players for options they previously wouldn't even have considered. In Australia, for example, subscriptions for private health insurance policies have recently declined considerably. Younger, healthier people are no longer settling for expensive, non-transparent insur-ance cover they are not likely to need any time soon. They are investing their money in self-care instead. In that way, spending money on nutritional supple-ments, exercising, or sleep now seems to be competing with taking out private health insurance.

---

*Have you mapped what company is offering
an entirely different service to you, but might deliver
a similarly perceived outcome?*

Other competition in the Healthusiasm business is driven by the fact that brand boundaries are more blurred than ever. After all, customer expectations are not limited by industry boundaries either. As people expect *supportive* health solutions *near* them, many different types of business are crossing the boundaries of their own core business. This means that gyms are now competing with hotels, coworking spaces or even with people's homes. Hospitals are currently on the verge of investing in wellness centres to serve communities with gym-like experiences. And Reebok is even planning to turn the 114 000 American petrol stations into fitness hubs. "Nobody has died from some healthy competition" surely has a new meaning today.

> *Petrol stations are like the pit stops in racing. You want to be in and out in the least possible time. But that will all change as electric cars require more time to charge. Even Tesla superchargers require 30 minutes of your time. So instead of letting petrol stations fall to waste, why not make them a place to recharge yourself too? Petrol stations will become fitness hubs where you can find spinning, boxing, Crossfit, and even a running trail. Larger stations will even function as healing gardens with meditation, yoga, nutrition classes and healthy eating.* **Reebok** *is creating local wellness communities. But wasn't that something hospitals were also thinking about? And aren't coworking spaces health hubs as well now?*

---

*Health solutions are everywhere. Have you found the odd ones
that are creeping up on you yet?*

The collaboration between Reebok and Gensler to transform gas stations into places for self-care, where people can also recharge themselves.

The medical industry was long a fortress that wasn't easy to compete in. Regulations simply make it difficult to enter. It takes more time to cross those boundaries. Theranos did not succeed in disrupting the entire diagnostic business because it did not approach these regulations properly. But other tech companies are picking up steam now. Google is making huge strides in the field of devices and data. Apple is becoming a powerhouse in health data and medically graded wearables. Amazon is gradually challenging the delivery of healthcare with the acquisition of PillPack and with its own smart speakers. But even early initiatives by Nestlé and Campbell's are starting to assist people with medical decisions. Even if most of those innovations aren't yet at the brink of commercial success in 2020, things might speed up. Remember that five years ago, hardly anybody was wearing fitness trackers. Today about 30% of the population is running around with them.

Partnerships – The evolution towards new and more partnerships
With these boundaries blurring, traditional companies will need to make sufficiently early decisons on who their competitors or partners will be. The possibilities of technology are growing at such a breakneck pace that it has become impossible for one single company to keep up. They are not smart enough, fast enough or innovative enough. Dado van Peteghem and Jo Caudron, authors of *Digital Transformation*, paint that picture very well by comparing large corporations with giant tankers. They are gigantic, valuable and well on course. At the same time, they are slow and unwieldy when they need to

turn. It's therefore better to build a fleet with smaller, nimble boats alongside that can manoeuvre with speed. Many corporations are therefore providing accelerator programmes for start-ups, are establishing partnerships with them or are launching joint innovations. That way, large corporations can keep a finger on the pulse, remain nimble and keep evolving at a faster pace.

There are a lot of opportunities in combining complementary expertise. Those opportunities drive collaboration and strategic partnerships. And they do not need to be limited to accelerating or partaking with start-ups. Obviously even large businesses can work together to complement missing parts of their business and reach new markets with new products, services or experiences. It could give your company or brand a competitive edge, and grow your customer base into areas that were not easily attainable before. Or it could prevent your customers from leaving because you can't offer them what they expect. But it can also prevent your company from making investments into fields that others already excel in because it is their core business. They will do it faster and, yes, probably better and more cheaply than you.

*That was the primary motivation for **Nike** to halt the development and sales of wearables. It wasn't that they weren't convinced about the added value wearables could bring to Nike's customers or to the company itself. Nike realised it could achieve better results by partnering with **Apple**. The co-branded Apple Watch Nike+ series are pretty much the same as any other Apple watches. But not entirely. They have a perforated sports band that is supposedly more breathable, and allows you to choose from Nike-themed watch faces that facilitate a quick launch to the Nike+ Run Club app. And that's pretty much it. But it is just enough for Nike to reinforce their position in the market as the shoe made for people who love running, which was the initial goal of the Nike Fuel wearable anyway. Nike decided to partner with a company that was able to do things better, faster and more cheaply than them. A similar story is potentially unfolding in the car industry. In 2017, **Mercedes-Benz** launched its Fit and Health car and decided to become a health company that makes drivers healthier during the ride. **Hyundai**, **Mitsubishi** and several other car manufacturers are moving forward with similar ambitions. **Ford** has even set up their own wearable lab. However, the industry of biosensors and the car industry are obviously working at different paces. The recent collaboration between **Garmin** and Mercedes-Benz*

> *to use Garmin's Vivoactive 3 as the Mercedes driving companion makes total sense to beat the market in speed, investment, and performance. In another industry, I particularly liked how **Johnson & Johnson** reduced their time from development to actual market launch by partnering with none other than **Alibaba**, which is perhaps not the most obvious collaboration. But it allowed them to launch the new forms of Listerine in China within five months instead of the normal 18 months.*

Are you trying to reinvent the wheel? Or are you providing the best frame? Who needs to be in your network of partners to build the best car(e)?

Looking at the evolution in marketing, partnerships can help in bringing the right product to the market (product-driven marketing), as Johnson & Johnson managed to do for its Chinese customers by partnering with Alibaba. Nike's collaboration with Apple allowed for more runner-centric services (customer-driven marketing). But partnerships can even reinforce the purpose of a company and strengthen its transformation-driven marketing approach as well. For that, even collaboration with public health bodies might bring the desired impact.

> ***Slimming World***, *UK's most popular weight management programme, has partnered with **The Royal Society for Public Health (RSPH)**, the world's longest-established public health body. Their common purpose was to set up large-scale research that would eventually release recommendations to supermarkets about their layout, their pricing strategies and general ambience. The report should encourage retailers to create an environment that promotes a healthier diet or at least limits the risk of making unhealthy decisions on impulse. The partnership even resulted in a further collaboration with **The People's Supermarket**, a retailer that is focused on providing the local community with good food – and now healthy choices. The redesign of this London supermarket, with the help of public health experts, met customer expectations by being nearby,*

> *informative, and ambient. But most of all, it emphasises the purpose of all three companies involved.*

The data

Now, I am not a data scientist, nor am I a marketing data architect. And I don't expect that from you either when reading this chapter. But there is one thing we both know. Nowadays, data is critical for an organisation. Whatever that organisation may be, data will simply make it much more customer-centric. In an era where it is no longer just enough to have the product with the best features, customer data has become mandatory for success. It makes health solutions nearby, convenient or simply relevant. It even can make them personal, predictive and (faster than) real-time. Data not only helps you to meet your customers' expectations, it even allows you to keep up with its accelerating pace.

Context – evolving towards true contextual awareness

In the past decades, companies were largely focused on gathering demographical data like age, gender, location, and life situation. Bit by bit, organisations also wanted to know about their customers' personal preferences and interests to create appropriate, yet rather static, segmentation. But people are no longer simply to be categorised based on demographical data and preferences. Earlier in the book I explained how personal "transformations" are much more important today. You can now become who or what you want to become. And that may occur at different times and places for each of us. Therefore, *context* has become the critical data organisations are looking for. It generates a holistic view on the customer at all times and it allows one to really be customer-centric.

> *For example, **Google** already gathers your personal demographical data, your browser history and your personal interests. But the Google home devices, like the Nest Thermostat or the Google smart speakers, will be able to collect so much more contextual data about you. It will know whether you are home, what temperature it is, when you take a bath or watch television, or what items you buy from what store. So don't be surprised some day when you are personally offered a discount on a cosy blanket before you even realised you wanted it. It's winter and it's cold outside. The room temperature is not high enough because you always come home late on Tuesdays. It doesn't make sense to put on the heating for that last half hour of television, before you ask your smart speaker to turn down the lights*

> *and go to bed. Google will be aware of this context. And they will offer you a discount on that cosy, hypo-allergenic, warm blanket. Sounds futuristic? IDC FutureScape (2018) predicts that by 2022, experience-driven organ-isations, like Google, will generate 50% of their revenue through similar contextual discovery experiences.*

Health data is also increasingly about contextual awareness. At least, that is what your customers are expecting (and what scientists are dreaming about). The Electronic Health Record contains our age, gender, geographical informa-tion, personal allergies and medical history. This creates static segmentation that is generally only updated at every doctor's visit. But if we really want to fore-cast epidemics, combat existing diseases more efficiently, prevent our health from deteriorating, or even predict what decisions are best for our health, then more datapoints are needed. We need to gather, evaluate and share contextual data at any given time. Only then will you, with the help of AI-powered plat-forms, be able to have a holistic view of your customer or patient. Only then will you be able to be truly customer-centric and create the solutions that fit your customers. So let's no longer wonder if and why your organisation should 'keep an eye' on the sensor-driven wearables that are swamping the market. Because these devices are gathering the context you should act upon.

---

*Context matters for your customers.
In what area of your business does that context matter
most for your company or brand?*

Marketech – The evolution towards marketing as a science
Creativity has always carried more weight in marketing than number crunch-ing. Today, however, technology is transforming how organisations connect, interact and engage with their customers. Ad Age Datacenter (2018) calculat-ed that in 2017 technology-related activities had already generated 51.3% of the revenue of US marketing agencies. And it is unlikely to decline. Organi-sations really challenge the classic marketing agencies on their digital skills

nowadays. They want them to build new digital solutions, optimise existing marketing technologies and help generate contextual data. That's why digital agencies are moving into the marketing playing field. That is why the marketing services units of consulting-based companies like PwC, Deloitte and Accenture are almost as big as traditional, creative marketing agencies like Publicis and Omnicom. Marketing has evolved into Marketech. Marketing directors are now seconded by directors of marketing data. Numbers crunchers are now called data scientists. Many traditional functions have become data science professions because contextual awareness is paramount in being customer-centric today. Even in healthcare, medical directors in hospitals are now flanked by chief medical information officers (CMIO) to create value out of the patient data. If marketing has turned into science, then treatment surely has turned into management.

Is data the heartbeat of your company yet?
Then how are you keeping a finger on the pulse?

Protection – the evolution of privacy

Ever since social media came along, people have been happy to share their personal lives, preferences and context with others. The previous chapter touched on why people are motivated to do so. But with all of this comes a warning label saying that you should not give people unwelcome surprises. Because the desire to share information did not make privacy obsolete, it simply created a shift in the meaning of "privacy". No longer is privacy about "not publicly sharing information about yourself". It has now become "protecting me from unwelcome surprises when sharing my personal information". People do not expect sharing information to backfire on them. They expect organisations to treat their information ethically and safely.

NUMBER OF DAILY ACTIVE FACEBOOK USERS WORLDWIDE (billions)

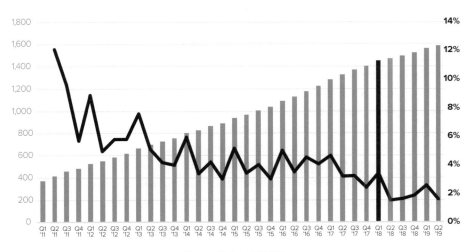

Source: Statista, Q2 2019.

Facebook, the largest social media platform that made sharing a common thing to do, ironically became the poster child of unethical data management. In less than six months during 2018, Facebook inappropriately leaked the data of about 78 million people to political consulting firm Cambridge Analytica and suffered a hack that affected a string of another 30 million users. But even while people now view Facebook somewhat more negatively, the number of daily active Facebook users kept on growing, according to Statista (Q2 2019). The slight decline in growth is a natural decline that is related more to reaching its potential than to unethical data management. There was no real significant drop visible because it did not surprise or impact people's lives individually. Nevertheless, these Facebook scandals sparked a great awakening on privacy, across the globe.

> *CEOs of American companies are more worried about cybersecurity than new competitors or recession, according to The Conference Board (2019). The European Union is very serious about its privacy guidelines as well. Following up on the implementation of the GDPR guidelines very strictly, the EU Information Commissioner's Office (ICO) did not refrain from fining **British Airways** and **Marriott Hotels** over 300 million euros each. But customers are also more occupied with risks involving their personal data. Salesforce (2018) discovered that 63% of customers are convinced that their personal*

> *data is vulnerable to a security breach. Accenture (2019) reported that 75%*
> *are now very concerned about the privacy of their data. When the before-*
> *mentioned PatientsLikeMe was sold to UnitedHealth Group, the largest in-*
> *surer in the United States, patients across the globe feared the privacy of*
> *their data. Numerous Twitter users have flat out said they will delete their*
> *accounts and urge others to do so as well.*

Now, people may think – naïvely – that they do not disclose too much personal information on Facebook. They probably don't even expect to be "surprised" if that information is breached. But personal health information is much more sensitive to them. Today, the medical record is probably a person's most comprehensive record. It contains a wealth of relevant information that attracts hackers like flies to rotten fruit. From demographical information to medical history and diagnoses, your Electronic Health Record contains immutable, invaluable information. Credit cards can be cancelled. Expenses can be refuted. But health information remains related to your own reality. Little wonder that customers have the highest expectations for the protection of their health data. When a health data breach occurs, the Ponemon Institute (2019), a think tank on data protection policy, reported that customers are twice as likely to abandon the company or brand than in any other industry.

In your quest for context, do you protect your customer
from unwelcome surprises at all times?

> *Health-related breaches occur more and more frequently. In 2013, the*
> *Ponemon Institute communicated that 40% of US healthcare institutions*
> *had already reported a criminal cyber-attack. The number of health data*
> *breaches involving more than one million records nearly doubled be-*
> *tween 2013 and 2017. And this is still increasing. Halfway through 2019,*
> *more than 20 million patients' health and financial data had already*
> *been breached from **Opko Health**, **Quest Diagnostics** and **LabCorp***
> *alone. They are coming for your health data. That is certain. So best you*
> *protect yourself and your customers. The average cost of a data breach*

> *of about one million records is nearly USD40 million, according to a new study by IBM security (2018).*

Price

I mentioned in earlier chapters that the healthcare system is no longer financially sustainable in this ageing world. That's why we see a shift from fee-for-service towards value-based pricing that focuses more on the outcome. Authorities and healthcare organisations all over the world are piloting such programmes as we speak. Healthcare providers will increasingly be reimbursed based on the outcome they provide. This system will incentivise them to empower and engage patients with tools, knowledge and skills. The more patients contribute, the more likely the outcome will be improved. Fortunately this makes perfect sense in the light of the Healthusiasm trend.

People do want to impact their own health and happiness. They are also more willing than ever to pay for health solutions. However, due to the social healthcare systems that refund a large part of their medical costs, people in Europe have never really been used to paying for health solutions. But neither have they been able to evaluate the value they have received from healthcare providers. This evaluation requires a comparison between the cost and outcome. And unlike the clearly marked prices on consumer products and services, the cost of healthcare services is generally not transparent. The economics of the healthcare industry are definitely very complex, but for your customers it remains all about the value they receive at a particular price. And it's often very hard to decipher the complex healthcare-specific language on your hospital bill to know what you have actually been charged for. Do you pay for the overhead, for the actual outcome of the health service or for the attempt at a potentially good outcome? In a value-based market, it will be critical for healthcare providers to be able to ensure pricing transparency. Only then will patients be ready to pay for the expected value. If customers can't find or understand the pricing information, it will be assumed that the service is sold too expensively, and they might look to another healthcare provider or even outside the industry. Think about how alternative medicine is now perceived as the more valuable option, how retail clinics in supermarkets are more popular than hospitals and primary care doctors in the States, or how Millennials in Australia increasingly prefer to invest their money in wellness instead of health insurance. The healthcare industry simply needs to provide the patient with a more contemporary and more consumer-like (financial) experience.

*Have you asked yourself on what levels the (financial)
experience with your company or brand differs
from lean-and-mean consumer businesses?*

> *Good customer experience creates value for your patient. The experience and value offered by the previously mentioned **Parsley Health Center** is such that patients are willing to pay an annual subscription fee of at least USD1800 (or USD150 a month). This fee includes five doctor's consultations and five sessions with a health coach per year. That makes the cost of each consultation USD180, while many insurances still do not reimburse this medical centre for its services. Yet the value is such that more and more people are and will be willing to pay for it. It all starts with a good experience. And that's exactly what the **Geisinger Health System** must have thought in 2015 when it launched its ProvenExperience programme. This Pennsylvanian healthcare provider publicly proclaimed the ambition to not only offer the best experience in healthcare but across all industries. To improve customer experience, it implemented a programme that entails a broad range of cultural and process reengineering initiatives like the Talent Plus Hiring Tool (also used by the luxury hotel chain Ritz Carlton) to help recruit only employees with the right service-minded mentality. At the core of the programme lies a "no questions asked" refund policy that permits dissatisfied patients to request refunds of up USD2000. Patients do need to state why and how their experience could have been better, making it beneficial for the healthcare provider in terms of learning, process improvement, and patient experience optimisation. It's beneficial because it allows them to create more value.*

In the past couple of decades, we've seen pricing strategies evolve rapidly in the consumer world, from cost-plus pricing strategies to dynamic pricing on ecommerce websites, and from premium to freemium pricing for digital tools. And as Healthusiasm is making health solutions popular and relevant now, new pricing strategies have entered worlds that previously were rather traditional.

From medical centres applying membership models to hospitals allowing re-funds as an after sales customer service, the healthcare industry is reviewing the pricing strategy of their solutions. And they are forced to do so because people expect to have similar customer-driven pricing options to that of other markets. But these markets are even providing customers with a new variety of health solutions, causing the customer expectation of seeing different pricing models to be even more dominant. Here's a sample of some creative pricing strategies driven by the Healthusiasm trend.

> We discussed how **Nike** is rewarding their Nike+ customers with free per-sonal content, products and services. And they are not the only ones to use "sweat" as a currency. Customers of the sports apparel brand **New Balance** who visit the brand's gym in London can only (!) pay with the miles they've run. Healthcare insurance company **Oscar** allows their subscription members to earn a dollar each day they hit their step goals. It's part of the membership model that is already creating a better expe-rience but also twice as much satisfaction as other insurers. Similarly ap-plying a subscription-based membership model, Canadian athletic brand **RYU** not only offers a wide variety of services that range from fitness to clothing and health tips, but is integrating "sweat as a currency". If one of their members gains a lot of muscle or loses weight so their clothes no longer fit, RYU will offer them a discount for new gear when they turn their clothes in. But discounts for healthy behaviour are also used in res-taurants and hotels now. The room rate at **Hotel Bellora** in Gothenburg is determined by the time spent on social media, while customers at the **Abu Ghosh** restaurant in Jerusalem receive a 50% discount when their phone is turned off.

What pricing strategy is beneficial for your company and for your customer?

In moving away from fee-for-service, companies and brands are looking to create more value for customers. As mentioned in one of the early chapters, that value is created by customising products, services and experiences to something more personal. But the ultimate value is not a health solution, of course. The ultimate value for a customer would be "health" in itself because Healthusiasm is all about making customers healthy and happy. If companies or brands could offer health-as-a-service, then they would really make their customers healthy and happy.

> **BMW** and **Daimler AG** have embraced partnerships across a broader ecosystem to reinvent mobility. No longer are they focusing on creating value by offering "mobility with a comfortable car", they want to offer "mobility" itself. This mobility-as-a-service model offers customers solutions in their urban environment, with or without owning a car. Customers won't just buy one car like they used to. They will engage in an ongoing relationship that offers a seamless transportation experience through an ecosystem of car-share and rental companies, parking aids, charging stations, and location-based mobile lifestyle apps. The purpose of the joint venture is to make moving around feel lighter, cleaner, freer. It aims to be the ultimate value in mobility.

How would you not only deliver a particular solution, but an actual, desired outcome to your customers? What collection of services would you need? Who would you need to partner with?

Healthymania

If strong societal trends like Healthusiasm come along, individuals as well as companies want to jump on that bandwagon. But that fear of missing out could eventually generate a real obsessive desire to participate or even excel in it. "Healthymania" happens when either people or companies pursue the Healthusiasm trend to such an extent that it becomes unhealthy. The balance swings too far. People want to be too healthy and happy. Companies want to present their offerings as being too healthy.

Everybody wants to be (too) healthy

Without a doubt, Healthusiasm is a positive evolution in the way people are conscious of and active in the management of their own health and happiness. What can possibly be wrong with loving and taking care of yourself? However, when that love turns into obsession, then the drive to be(come) better will be infinite, unrealistic and even unhealthy. They will worry sick about their health, even when they aren't sick at all. This obsessive pursuit is no longer about taking care of yourself. It's a disorder that can come from a moral imperative within society that healthy people are good, and the unhealthy are bad. It's partially emphasised by the illusion of the perfection of the average person that is created on social media. People then feel that their lives are inferior to the "highlight reels" of those in their feed that they often aim to be(come). On the other hand, people who feel better than average feed on the dopamine kicks from all the likes and followers, potentially motivating them to push even harder.

> *People mistakenly place too much value on the online world. It generates a false reality to live up to. They want to be as healthy and good looking as the boys and girls in their feed. And they want to be as perfect as their own self-representations. Some even seek surgery to help them appear like the filtered versions of themselves.* **Snapchat** *dysmorphia, for example, is a recent mental condition in which people want to smooth out skin, contour cheekbones, and make eyes and lips bigger, to replicate the filtered perfection.*

The quest for infinite self-care can make us feel worse instead of better. Feelings of guilt and self-loathing can take over if we 'cheat', and of anxiety and unhappiness when we can't cope with all the goals and protocols of our ambition. The UN World Happiness Report (2019) showed that America's "mass-addiction society" is a major driver of the increasing unhappiness there. But beyond the conventional addictions, it's interesting to note that the report mentioned other addictions like excessive exercising and diet-related compulsions for the first time. In fact, almost 5% of the US population overdo exercising beyond the healthy norm. Whether it is the endorphin rush while running, or the reality-dodging mental escape by endless yoga, as soon as it starts interfering with work, school, family life or other relations, that behaviour becomes disordered. Of course, the numbers not exercising enough is a far bigger societal problem than those over-exercising. Nevertheless, Healthymania remains an upcoming trend that should invite companies to help people correctly balance their Healthusiastic decisions.

More and more people are trying too hard to be(come) healthy and happy. What is your role in helping them lead a balanced life?

Everything wants to be (too) healthy

Beyond the fact that everybody wants to be healthy, nowadays everything needs to be healthy too. Companies also often suffer from "Healthymania". That is very present in the food and beverages industry, but just as much in the sleep, furniture, pharmaceutical or fitness market, to name a few. Companies try to keep up with competitors by selling similar health claims. However, the majority of companies that highlight the so-called health attributes of their product or service are actually not that healthy in general. By focusing on one particular attribute, the other elements that lack healthfulness are being ignored. People think they are doing their body good, but the reality is that this "healthwashing" may actually be doing more harm than good.

> *In 2015, **Coca-Cola** launched Coke Life, a new version of its popular drink that contains stevia, a naturally sweet plant. The company tried to target the most health-conscious soft drinkers. But while Coke Life did indeed contain less sugar, a can still had the equivalent of six teaspoons of sugar. And this is the maximum daily sugar intake for an average adult, according to WHO recommendations. Coke Life could hardly be called healthy, of course. Little wonder it has been removed from most markets in the world.*

It has been mentioned previously that people have become very vigilant about anything political or commercial. The recent tsunami of "fake news" makes customers crave authenticity. They dream of purity in a world that is often perceived as toxic – and this definitely applies to health solutions. Yet companies are motivated to label their products and services with trendy wellness-terms because it can be commercially rewarding. However, I believe that most product claims are ignorantly rather than maliciously made. Many companies simply lack doctors or scientists who can help create or approve commercial health claims. This is important because science is characterised by theses and antitheses. Science hardly ever provides a unique, irrefutable synthesis. Putting out health claims requires time, knowledge and dedication in distilling various scientific opinions.

Although Light might implicitly sound healthier, Bud Light never made any health claims. Instead, the company opted to transparently disclose all the ingredients of the beer. It is doubtful that most customers can interpret the nutritional value of these ingredients, but transparency oftens suffice for lifestyle decisions. However, double-blind randomised, and even peer-reviewed, studies are very much a prerequisite for medical decisions.

The new wellness space in between, which takes in well-being and health decisions, is still discovering what level of proof is needed for both customers and authorities. But the more products, services or experiences have a potential impact, the better it would be if claims on efficacy or safety were backed by scientific proof. Products focused on self-care should carefully consider what is needed by balancing the claimed impact with potential (scientific) evidence. Wellness is not a market that a company should enter without at least reflecting on its own knowledge, arguments or even a certain number of proof points. And in the near future, this will become even more important. People have always applied a test-to-fix approach when it comes to well-being and health decisions. They enthusiastically apply one service after another in a vain attempt to optimise their health and well-being. But they are getting tired of jumping from fad to fad without seeing results. And that belief in superficial health claims is starting to crumble. A lack of results will no longer be acceptable. They need some meat to the bone. People expect in-depth, transparent and trustworthy information. It is part of the health solutions they expect to rotate around them.

When you make a claim, there are always people who will go against it. Are you prepared to defend your ground?

Health marketing as a transformation-driven type of marketing should focus on protecting people and companies from this Healthymania. Health claims should be balanced with scientific evidence and complete, transparent information.

> *The consumer brand Benecol may have scientific claims on lowering cholesterol. It's also their responsibility to explain what that means for customers. Neither does it harm to caution people not to stop taking their medication or following other medical recommendations when consuming these cholesterol-lowering spreads and yoghurts, and nor to over-consume them. If it is within the purpose of a company or brand to help people with their Healthusiasm, they should opt to do so with the least possible misunderstanding. And the difficulty of that responsibility is not to be underestimated. Even organisations like the Canadian Heart and Stroke Foundation, a patient organisation with the aim of improving the lives of millions, has the potential to fail miserably. In 2014, they decided to abolish their Health Check programme because their healthy food endorsements were being heavily scrutinised. They naïvely recommended drinks like grape juice, with similar amounts of sugar as Coca-Cola, and approved certain burgers that apparently contained exceptionally high volumes of sodium. Their good intentions were terribly executed. They did not live up to their responsibility. People are enthusiastic about managing their own health and happiness. Let's not extinguish that enthusiasm.*

The Cheat Treat

There is still a final remark to be made. Healthusiasm may be present throughout your life, but it certainly is not an all-or-nothing lifestyle. It might otherwise result in Healthymania. Aspiring to be(come) the best version of yourself would be incorrectly executed if you only wanted to eat the healthiest food, achieve the most extreme sporting ambitions, or have the calmest mind. You can't go all-out at everything all the time. Even when you want to actively impact your health and happiness, there is room for indulgence. In fact, cheating keeps up your spirits. Cheat days are necessary to remain healthy. And as a company or brand, you can play into this cheating game by either helping (yes indeed), or by being there before or after your customers have cheated. Though cheating might be frowned on in relationships or games, it needn't be wrong when it comes to living a healthy life. It's about being mindful. And once in a while, you should allow yourself a Cheat Treat.

What is your role in your customers' Cheating game?

*By combining relaxing yoga asanas with Madonna's "Vogue" poses, the **House of Voga** (Vogue + Yoga) is cheating on the spiritual dimension of yoga. But exercising in clubs or organising yoga retreats that include clubbing nights is exactly what the Cheat Treat is all about: balancing things out to endure over time. Now, some companies specifically offer solutions to balance Cheat Treats out, like helping to overcome the effects of indulgences. **RaveAid** not only educates on the harmful effects of going to a club or music festival every night, but also provides proactive protection and complete restoration. The supplements, which are taken prior to, during and for three days after clubbing, are supposed to prevent or reduce the harmful effects of raving. Based in party cities like Miami Beach, Las Vegas and Ibiza, **Revive Wellness** also helps people to recover from a night out. With specific intravenous therapies, they want to boost people who are suffering from extreme hangovers.*

Healthising canvas

In order to remain relevant to their customers, companies and brands are increasingly looking for ways to help people in the quest to be(come) healthy and happy. They can create value by providing experiences that are based on their Recurring Expectations. And they cannot go against some of the Contemporary Evolutions that mark our world.

Even though this Healthusiasm trend is pretty obvious, it might leave companies pondering what next steps to take. The Healthusiasm Model certainly can help in narrowing down what type of Healthusiastic choice they should be providing. But that still leaves a wide range of opportunities open to "Healthise" your products, services or experiences. To apply the different insightful elements covered in this book, a methodology has been designed to create value that is deeply grounded in the Recurring Expectations of customers and Contemporary Evolutions of this world.

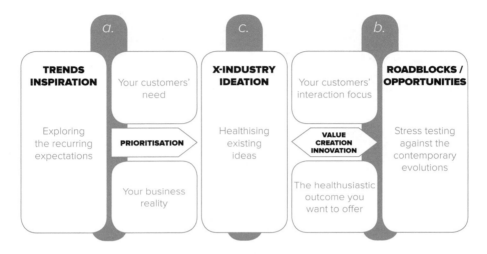

As a starter, you can match the Recurring Expectations with your customers' needs and your own business reality (*a*). But you can also start from a corporate ambition that fits the Contemporary Evolutions (*b*). Perhaps you already have some initial ideas internally that only need to be checked against the elements covered in this book (*c*). Whatever progress you've already made as a company, the Healthising Canvas is an easy-to-follow, one-page tool that provides a structured flow of thought. It divides the process of "healthising" into different parts and invites you to easily combine both internal and external knowledge. But most of all, it is a flexible methodology that will help in "making your customers healthy and happy".

Thank you

Enthusiasm is not enough.
It's the start of things. But it is just not enough.
That's what this book is about.
That's what writing this book was all about as well.

A book grows. It's something that originates from within oneself, from experience one has lived. It has been no different for this book. It grew from all the experiences I've had throughout my professional and personal life. It grew from all the people I've met and the ones I've worked with. I discovered the healthcare sector when working at Pfizer. My colleagues, and most definitely Jörgen Schaffers and Serge Premer, taught me how to navigate in this world. Jeroen Lemaire and Jan Deruyck at In The Pocket, one of Europe's finest digital product studios, strengthened my love for technology and introduced me to entrepreneurship. The founders of InSites Consulting, one of the most innovative market research agencies in the world, showed me how innovation never gets old. My colleagues Magali Geens and Hakim Zemni have continuously taught me about the importance of customer centricity for businesses around the world. All the clients I got to work with along this pathway made the struggles and successes that drive their business real. From Roche to Weight Watchers, from Ageas to L'Oreal, from Merck to Colruyt, from the large hospitals to the small young start-ups. By working with them, they've all fed this book that was growing inside of me.

I've always loved storytelling, and I really embrace being on stage in front of people. But it was Peter Hinssen, back in 2008, who unlocked my desire to inspire people. By crafting this book, I've had the chance to have discussions with many of the greatest keynote speakers. From most creatively entertaining Cyriel Kortleven to best innovation speaker in Europe Ramon Vullings; from world-renowned youth marketing guru Joeri Van den Bergh to health futurists Bart De Witte and Koen Kas. They were all so cooperative and enlightened me with their wisdom and experience. Some even read this book and made valuable amendments. But it was their passion that made me persevere in my belief.

However, stories and talks are nothing without insights from within the business. As this book covers many types of industries, I relied heavily on collaboration with many marketing and business professionals. Dimitri Galle (Pfizer), Nicolas Chalupa (Pfizer, Mylan, Smith&Nephew, Abbott) and Heidi Goossens (Pfizer, Sobi) were the first fans and critics at the same time. Discussions with smart minds like Inge Cnudde (Sandoz, J&J), Danny Evens (Pfizer, Omega Pharma, Janssen, Quick Restaurants), Frank Vanderdonck (Novartis, Ipsen, UCB, Pfizer), Arnoud den Ouden (Pfizer) and Annelies Van Buyten (Roche, Abbvie, MSD) can't be ignored. Picking the brains of consumer marketers like Annelies Lambert (Henkel, VF, Alpro), Ingrid Belmans (Kellog, Electrolux, Inbev, RB), Bert Eeckhoudt (the House of Marketing), Ignace de Nollin (Colruyt Group) and Jan De Lancker (Mars, Nike, Pepsico, Braintower) broadened my view on marketing considerably. Creative souls like the ones of Sarah Latré (De Ambrassade, Shortcut Advertising), Sara Pieters (Redzezel, Luon, Flanders District of Creativity, Voka), Katherina Kitsinis (OnTrend Agency, Dôme Deco) and Koen Wilssens (Runnerslab) brought fresh views to my thinking. If you recognise the challenges your business faces in this book, then chances are that these people might have contributed to achieve that.

During my writing, Niels Janssens and Lotte Demeyer from my publisher LannooCampus have put their experience at my disposal. They've challenged and helped me at the right moments and basically throughout the entire process. But I particularly want to thank Frederik Van Wynsberghe (Infino, Wijs) for challenging, inspiring and motivating me when I needed it the most. You've brought me back on the right track when I lost my direction.

Then there is the huge contribution of all the people who have proofread the manuscript of this book and made it even better in the end: Erik Janssen (UCB, Sanofi-Aventis), Caroline Vervaeke (Braintower, JBC, Alpro), Nico Smets (Merck, MSD), Kristof De Smet (EnergyLab), Peter Geerlings (SJG Weert Hospital), Eugene Borukhovich (Bayer), Laura Fiehm (Novartis, Roche), Carin Louis Van Den Broek (Takeda, Nycomed), Dee O'Sullivan (Patientview), Natalie Bloomfield (Amgen, RB, Unilever), Reinhart Maertens (Antwerp University Hospital), Rik Vera (Nexxworks), Koen Kas (Healthskouts), Isabelle François (Health House), Koen Demyttenaere (Polar, Perrigo, Decathlon), Stijn Coolbrandt (BeHealth, Afga Healthcare), Bart De Witte (Hippo AI Foundation, IBM, SAP) and certainly as well my parents.

Finally, none of this would have been possible without the space and time that my girlfriend Micheline and my son Elouan allowed me to take. Thank you for dealing with my absence during many evenings, weekends and basically the whole summer. Thank you for endorsing this project and keeping my spirits high. If this book radiates enthusiasm, it is largely your enthusiasm it radiates.

Although I've always wanted to write 'a' book in my life, the enthusiasm only grew by talking and working with all of the people above. It made the subject, the storyline, or even some details much more obvious to me. Whether your contributions were big or small, you and many others all supported me in achieving this. After all, my enthusiasm was a start. But it was not enough. I really needed you.

Therefore... I'd wholeheartedly like to thank you for your enthusiasm and support.

Sources

Examples and numbers have been gathered from many different sources across the internet. Below, you can find an inspirational array of references you might want to check out when deep diving into the latest marketing ideas and insights from businesses around the world.

- trendwatching.com
- CB Insights
- Pocket
- JWT Intelligence
- Trend Hunter
- Lidewij Edelkoort
- Contagious
- PSFK
- Harvard Business Review
- Wikitrend
- Cool Business Ideas
- Coolhunting
- Futurism
- Skift
- Pew Research Center
- Deloitte
- Google Trends
- Designboom
- Euromonitor
- Nielsen
- Accenture
- Edelman
- Rock Health
- Well+Good
- Global Wellness Institute
- Monocle
- Gallup

- Sprout Social
- Psychology Today
- VentureBeat
- TechCrunch
- The Verge
- Business Wire
- The Guardian
- Mobile Health News
- The Conversation
- Healthcare Finance
- Cassandra
- And many, many more...